14.95

D0487762

LANCHESTER LIBRARY, Coventry University

Much Park Street   Coventry CVI 2HF   TEL. 0203 838292

This book is due to be returned no later than the date stamped above.
Fines are charged on overdue books

Business forecasting for management

Branko Pecar

Fisher-Rosemount Limited

Advisory Editors

Glyn Davis and Simon Lillystone

Teesside Business School

McGRAW-HILL BOOK COMPANY

London · New York · St Louis · San Francisco · Auckland · Bogotá
Caracas · Lisbon · Madrid · Mexico · Milan · Montreal · New Delhi
Panama · Paris · San Juan · São Paulo · Singapore · Sydney · Tokyo
Toronto

Published by
McGRAW-HILL Book Company Europe
Shoppenhangers Road, Maidenhead, Berkshire, SL6 2QL, England
Telephone 0628 23432
Fax 0628 770224

British Library Cataloguing in Publication Data

Pecar, Branko
  Business Forecasting for Management
  I. Title
  658.40355

  ISBN 0-07-707865-9

Library of Congress Cataloging-in-Publication Data

Pecar, Branko
  Business forecasting for management / Branko Pecar ; advisory
  editors, Glyn Davis and Simon Lillystone.
      p.   cm.
  Includes bibliographical references and index.
  ISBN 0-07-707865-9
  1. Business forecasting – – Statistical methods.   I. Davis, Glyn.
  II. Lillystone, Simon.   III. Title.
  HD30.27.P43   1993
  658.4'0355 – – dc20   93-47175
                                              CIP

12345 PB 97654

Typeset by P&R Typesetters Limited, Salisbury, Wiltshire
and printed and bound in Great Britain by Page Bros, Norwich

Contents

1
Introduction

The whole subject of forecasting only starts to make sense if it is perceived in the context of the growing uncertainty prevalent in the world, and the potential damage that can be caused by making wrong decisions under such circumstances. As the world becomes a global village, the consequences of bad decisions, on whatever front, affect more and more people as the ability to reach and influence others develops. It is obvious that information technology, with all its benefits and side effects, is accelerating this process.

If we take a look at the world of corporations and their role in world affairs, we can see that the methods they are using to signal their existence are becoming more and more sophisticated, demanding more responsible behaviour. This fact has generated awareness on the corporate level that it is not enough to wish to do well—one has to know *how* to do well. Inevitably, large corporations have reached for something that was innovative for their environment, which, in our context, is the presence of science in management. During the last several decades we have witnessed a 'rush' to apply various scientific methods in management, and indeed we have all benefited from this. The result has been more responsible behaviour on the environmental front, more rational utilization of resources, optimization of production techniques, improvement in risk assessment and, consequently, a reduction of uncertainty or, to be more precise, a neutralization of the growing uncertainty.

Despite the benefits that corporations have enjoyed as a result of applying scientific management techniques, their misuse, on the other hand, can cause different problems. It can contribute towards the development of even more chaotic circumstances and inflict serious damage on the corporate environment. The concerns and expectations of such approaches in management were the same as those that accompanied the introduction of computers to the corporate world. Everyone thought that lots of jobs would disappear overnight and that the accuracy and reliability of data would instantly improve. In fact, thousands of new jobs were created as new areas of work were discovered, and data integrity became a bigger problem than ever before, though on a much higher level. Similarly, scientific management methods are not reducing the amount of work to be done, nor are they reducing the risks involved in operating in the ever-increasing uncertainty in the world; on the contrary, they are creating more work as the increasing complexity of possibilities expands, and are merely providing the balance to the higher level of uncertainty.

It is a notorious fact that money creates an avant-garde, and we all know from social sciences theory that, with time, new ideas are passed on, and what was yesterday's latest wonder becomes a practical necessity of today. Consequently, it was a matter of time before new scientific management methods began to be adopted by small to medium-sized companies. Of course, it was not only a matter of time, it was also a matter of means. Fortunately, the popularization of computers made such moves possible. As a consequence, 'the small boys' are emulating 'the big boys', either in hoping to achieve the same results, or because these new ways of working have almost become industry standards.

In our context this creates a small problem. Large companies can afford to employ the élite to provide the basis for scientific management, while it is obvious that smaller companies cannot afford to do so. They are either left in the hands of specialized consultants, again if they can afford it, or forced to try on their own. Many company activities are routinely expected and even legally binding (such as book-keeping, producing annual accounts and so on), while some of them are voluntary or imposed by financial institutions (one of the elementary requests from the bank after asking for an overdraft facility is for a forecast of your turnover and expected profits). There are always different ways of achieving certain aims and producing required results but, as necessary hardware is available, and as experience is teaching small companies that it is wise to emulate larger companies, it is time to make some scientific methods less élitist and more popular.

One of the disciplines of scientific management is forecasting. This discipline, in the wrong hands, could be either irrationally revered or vulgarized. The élite of large corporations tend to over-emphasize it, while a small entrepreneur would inevitably show the tendency to over-simplify it. Our aim is to cast an appropriate light on it and make it available and understandable to everybody. Sometimes this will be not easy and we shall have to reduce some of the theory behind forecasting, but nevertheless our aim is to present a transparency of the methods used in the first place. In this respect we shall observe the discipline of forecasting step by step, primarily elaborating the techniques. As they are very often based on certain statistical and mathematical rules, if we can manage to make them understandable, the rest should be easy. However, we should not equate forecasting with statistics. In fact, this would be one of the biggest mistakes we could make.

Statistics is just a tool we are using, and, as in real life, we can use either sophisticated self-adjustable electrical tools or just a simple hand-saw. The end result should be more or less the same; the question is, what we are more comfortable working with. For this reason the greatest part of this book is devoted to statistical methods, as they are the most difficult to understand. However, the end result should not depend on them alone. There are many other management parameters that should influence our forecasts. In fact we can use a mathematical expression to prove this. The forecasting result should be treated as a product of the multiplication, not addition, of the tools used and other management knowledge acquired. If one of the two is equal to zero, the end result is equal to zero too. As we know, in the case of addition, despite one factor being equal to zero, the end result could still be positive. With our multiplication analogy, this is not possible. That is, sometimes it pays to have a little bit of both, rather than neglecting one of the factors and over-emphasizing the other. This book should present a balance between the factors that, in turn, should guarantee the optimum result.

One can find several computer-forecasting packages on the market and, admittedly, some of them are very good. However, to use them one has to understand the principles and requirements of every method applied. There are also quite a few books available about forecasting, but they fall into one of two categories. Some of them are easily digestible, but only scratch the surface of some of the more complex matters. Some of them are absolutely brilliant, but difficult to understand by anybody who is not engaged full-time and professionally in forecasting. In our attempts to make this area transparent, understandable and usable to as wide a readership as possible—which primarily covers undergraduate and postgraduate students, business people and management in general, and anybody else interested in forecasting—we have had to neglect certain dimensions of forecasting. We have not lost anything or made it incorrect, we have just simplified it in order to make it understandable to almost everybody.

It was apparent that if we were going to do it this way we would have to show as many calculations, graphs and other practical tips and tricks as possible. As everybody today is using computers and probably has access to one or two decent spreadsheet programs, an obvious decision was that all these practicalities could be illustrated in a spreadsheet format. On the other hand, there was a danger that we might start complicating the matter further by using complex spreadsheet commands and functions, which would produce a complete failure. In order to eliminate this, a decision was made that everything has to be very simple and absolutely basic. Therefore, in this book we are using a spreadsheet program called Excel, the basic commands of which are very similar to Lotus 1-2-3 or any other spreadsheet package. We use only basic functions and avoid any complex operations, although there was a temptation to present some of the operations in a more elegant, but somewhat complex way. By doing so and by showing in Appendix 1 the operations that actually took place in the spreadsheets, we are enabling literally everyone to emulate the procedure and insert one's own numbers into the spreadsheet in order to conduct forecasts. However, the text that accompanies every spreadsheet and that constitutes the

main bulk of every chapter is important for understanding the content o
spreadsheets.

We should add that we have attempted to provide the general simplification
of the Box and Jenkins procedure for treating stochastic models. Although the
method was reduced to its basics due to the very simple spreadsheet tools used
its content and complexity have not been affected. We believe that the veil ha
been removed from this method and that everyone who reads this book wil
be encouraged to go back to the source of the method and try to grasp it in it
complexity.

2
The forecasting alphabet

What we are going to elaborate here has existed for quite a few decades, but we can equally say that the theory of relativity is not new and yet we still do not understand it. As opposed to the theory of relativity, which is very fundamental and means almost everything and nothing, depending on your individual view of it, the theory of forecasting is very narrow and certainly, in a global context, is marginal. However, some of its principles and practicalities could help us in solving our daily business, scientific or production problems. In this respect, we can treat forecasting as spice for the meal—we can live without it, but the meal is impoverished.

It is useful to see how interest in forecasting has changed throughout the decades. Although the basic forecasting techniques, in the form of regression methods and classical decompositions, existed for a while and were applied for the purposes of demographic and other studies, the actual boom of forecasting methods started with the beginning of the 1960s. Initially, some basic exponential smoothing techniques were applied for the control and monitoring of military inventory, and later on these were found useful in industry. This was followed by an explosion in econometric methods, which was possibly due to the development of computers, and culminated with stochastic modelling developed and modified for forecasting purposes during the 1970s. The period of technological explosion during the 1960s was also accompanied with developments on the *technological forecasting* front, which combined qualitative and quantitative forecasting.

In one form or another, forecasting methods were attracting attention and it is fair to say that the more uncertain the circumstances and conditions were, the higher the interest in these methods. On the other hand, the more uncertain the conditions, the lower the accuracy of forecasting, so we have a phenomenon where the more interest you show in one activity, the less satisfying are the results being produced. People tried to compensate for this disadvantage by integrating forecasting more closely with other decision-making techniques, by educating management, or by interacting it with other information systems, but it remains a fact that forecasting was never properly understood. People tended to get into a trap where they either overestimated the past, thus creating a stumbling block for understanding the future, or they mystified the significance of the future, refusing to see that it was nothing other than an extension of the past. It is important to stress that whoever deals with the future should have the courage to anticipate what seems impossible in the present, but also enough wisdom to accept the past trends as an important guide. An ideal mix of the two makes our forecasts accurate and reliable.

Let us examine what forecasting is and why we should bother to make forecasts at all. The most important point when answering this question is realizing the purpose of forecasting. Why should we bother to forecast? Why do we want to know the future? Obviously, the answer is because we want to make some decisions today that could help us to cope with tomorrow when it comes. So, it seems that the decision-making process is the main reason for producing forecasts. If we make decisions based on our intuition, or just allow things to happen, we are ignoring a scientific approach to decision making. Production techniques have evolved, process control methods have become very sophisticated, we are using numerical methods in all sorts of analyses and at the same time, we are leaving the most important management activity, the decision making, completely undeveloped. Can we really afford to allow things to happen by chance, and make wrong decisions affecting capital, jobs and other valuable resources? Obviously not. A decision-making process should become a science as exact as possible. One of the most important links in this process is the forecasting method.

Before we deal with details about forecasting methods, let us learn the forecasting alphabet. Forecasting deals with phenomena whose future shape we want to predict by using their past values or the matters related to them. This is done by applying specific methods, the purpose being to make relevant decisions. So, we have to understand what the phenomenon is, what the past values are and how they could affect our forecast, which methods are available and what decisions we want to make on the basis of our forecasts. If we know these answers our forecast should be very accurate, reliable and will represent a sound basis for anticipating the future.

Every event that we can present in the form of a series of numbers, we can call a forecasting phenomenon. When we say a series of numbers it is implied that we have measured or recorded a phenomenon. Examples are all around us: unemployment figures, sales figures, inventory levels, patients' temperatures, process pressures, percentages of inadequate products in a lot, etc. Obviously, in every aspect of our activity, and not only in business, we have phenomena that we could analyse and forecast. There is only one requirement we have to fulfil when gathering or measuring these series of numbers that represent phenomena. The data have to be equidistant, i.e. every point in the series has to be, in terms of time, equally apart from the one before and the one ahead.

If we measure the sales figures then we can compile the series of monthly data, quarterly data, annual data or any other units of time. If we want to forecast such a series, it has to be consistent and contain the data measured in same time-units at all times. Another requirement is that no data should be missing in our series, as continuity is very important.

Once we have a series of numbers, this series represents past values of our phenomenon and is called a *time series*. If we make a graph of this time series we shall see that it has a certain shape. Our intention is to guess, i.e. forecast the future shape of this time series. As we have agreed that the past will, to a certain extent, determine the future, we had better try to understand this past shape as best we can. It will tell us a lot about the future. We can see that the shape resembles one of the theoretical curves, although it is never exactly the same. Very often our time series will be like a straight line, although not exactly straight. Sometimes it will be like a parabola, sometimes it will pulse at almost exact frequencies. But, whatever the resemblance, it is never exactly the same as those curves we remember from our A-level maths—the reason being that our times series is full of disturbance factors. In reality, something is always happening that slightly modifies the theory. Therefore, it is right to say that our time series consists of two basic components. Using jargon again we can call them:

$$\text{Time series} = \text{Pattern} + \text{Residual}$$

This means that if the time series looks like that shown in Fig. 2.1, then it consists of the pattern and residual component shown in Fig. 2.2. The art of forecasting is to tell the one from another and forecast the pattern, as this is the key to the future. Various methods will help us to distinguish one pattern from another, but in order to apply an appropriate method we have to know what patterns exist.

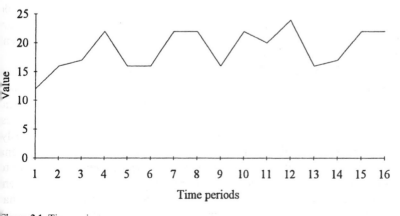

Figure 2.1 Time series

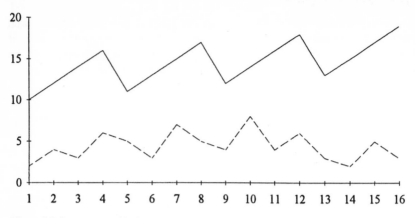

Figure 2.2 Pattern + residual

There are several basic types of pattern; let us call them:

- Stationary
- Non-stationary
- Seasonal

A *stationary* pattern is a horizontal pattern in which the curve oscillates around one central value, usually the mean (Fig. 2.3). A *non-stationary* pattern is an upward or downward trend that oscillates around a changing value, which usually represents a straight line or one of the theoretical curves (Fig. 2.4).

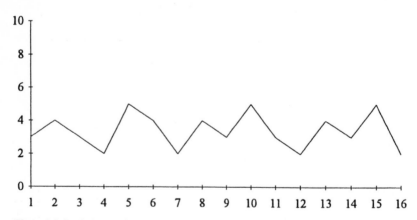

Figure 2.3 Stationary series

This non-stationary pattern could have some cyclical or seasonal variations which are repeated at fixed intervals, and, as such, is treated as a separate pattern called the *seasonal* (Fig. 2.5). In fact, seasonal variations occur also in cases where we have a horizontal flow of the series, but for notation reasons

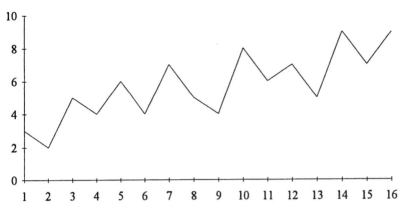

Figure 2.4 Non-stationary series

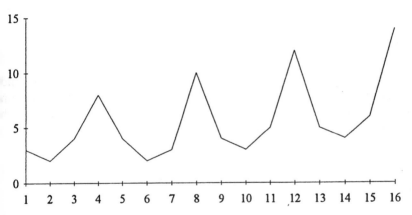

Figure 2.5 Seasonal series

we do not call them stationary. So, seasonal patterns are classified as a separate group of patterns, regardless of whether the series shows upwards, downwards or horizontal trend.

The nature of the pattern incorporated in our time series will determine which method we are going to use. Another factor that will determine the method to be used is the horizon of our forecast. It is natural to divide all the forecasts into short term, medium term and long term. It would be wrong to identify this classification with the actual time units that we are using in our time series. This classification reflects the length of the time horizon we are going to use as a boundary for our forecast. If we are interested just in the next month's sales figures, i.e. forecasting one period ahead, then we should use short-term methods. Equally, just one year ahead represents one period if we are using annual figures and, as such, is treated as a short-term forecast. For one to three periods ahead, again regardless of the time unit of our time series, we could consider that we are using medium-term methods. If we want to forecast more than five periods ahead, then we had better use long-term methods.

One consideration we have to bear in mind is the length of our historical time series that will represent the basis for our forecast. It is logical to say that we cannot forecast five periods ahead if our historical time series is only three periods long. A very interesting dilemma is whether we can use the ratio 1:1, i.e. forecast 10 periods ahead on the basis of 10 periods of historical data. Practice teaches us that we would make an error that is not acceptable. In fact, we can make two mistakes. By using the wrong method we can reduce the accuracy of our forecast, and by using the wrong horizon we can reduce the reliability of our forecast. There is more than a subtle difference between the two, but we shall address that in later chapters.

Let us introduce a few more technicalities and jargon terms. We have said that time series consist of data. These data are often called *observations*. Every observation is placed in a particular period of time, so sometimes the length of time series or the length of time horizon is defined in a number of periods. Another term often used in forecasting is *ex-post forecasting* or *fitting*. When we are applying a forecasting method our intention is to make sure that it is suitable for our data, i.e. to fit them as best as possible. This fitting is achieved by calculating the so-called *ex-post forecasts*, i.e. fitting the original series with our modelled data or, as some would say, forecasting backwards. Sometimes you can hear the term *ex-ante forecasting* which is the opposite of ex-post and, in fact, represents a real forecast.

Now, let us mention very briefly the various methods. Depending on the data available to us, and on the required results to be achieved, we can use different methods. The most common distinction in forecasting is between qualitative and quantitative methods. Qualitative methods do not necessarily use time series as the basis for forecasting, and, although the procedures for applying them are rather rigid sometimes, the results could vary depending on who represents the forecasting panel. In the case of quantitative methods, we should mention that the results could also vary, but, provided that the same method is used, no matter who is doing the forecasting, the result will always be the same. As we are going to concentrate on quantitative methods, let us elaborate various types.

Quantitative methods can be divided into:

- Causal methods or regression methods
- Decomposition methods
- Smoothing methods
- Stochastic methods
- Econometric methods

Regression methods are classical statistical methods in which we are using one variable or phenomenon, and relating this variable to another that is correlated with the first one or with the time, i.e. following the past in order to tell the future on the basis of some statistical laws.

Decomposition methods are based on the previous group of methods, i.e. certain statistical techniques are used to split the pattern into basic components, which could be recomposed later in order to make a forecast.

Smoothing methods use their own logic, that the previous values of the historical time series have an absolute influence on the future values of the series, but that this influence decreases with time, i.e. the older the data we use. The trick is to determine this influence by using various techniques.

Stochastic methods assume that our historical time series, which represents the phenomenon, is a random series of numbers generated by chance and put through a filter, after which it takes a shape. By identifying the filter we identify the laws that are turning our stochastic series into a predictable one, and therefore we can forecast its future values.

Econometric methods involve various matrix principles or other algebra principles, in order to get future values of complex phenomena, which are either interrelated or restricted with a series of conditions.

An additional division that we have to keep in mind is that in forecasting we can forecast future values of a series by extrapolating this method in time, using any of the above methods, or, alternatively, by using several related time series (called independent series) in order to forecast our 'dependent' time series. The first case is called a *univariate case* while the latter is called *multivariate forecasting*.

Which method we are going to use will depend on various things. Reiterating the main factors let us say that it depends, predominantly, on: the character of our data; a time horizon; aims that we want to achieve; desired accuracy; skills and experience that we have; and last, but not least, the money available. If we have to produce dozens of forecasts on a regular basis, we cannot afford to devote a personal touch to every phenomenon that we are dealing with. Such an approach would be time consuming and expensive.

3
Inspecting and preparing data

Having examined different types of time series and methods available, let us discuss, still on the principle and descriptive level, how to approach the work of forecasting.

We mentioned that we have to know what we want to forecast, and that we have to find or create a series of numbers (statistical data) that represent our phenomenon. After we have done this, the first step, regardless of what our intentions are, is to present this time series in graphic form. Only by doing so can we draw certain conclusions about the time series, without getting into complicated mathematical analysis.

A time series could be presented in several graphic formats, the most common and clear way being to plot it in the form of a line graph. As we have measured our time series in equidistant time periods, a horizontal line, axis x, will represent the time. The vertical line, axis y, will represent the values we have. When we draw the graph our phenomenon will assume a shape of one of the theoretical curves, which are defined with some mathematical equation. It is a part of the forecasting procedure in some of the methods to 'guess' which theoretical curve our time series resembles, and then to approximate this series to the theoretical curve. Sometimes this is very easy, as the time series is clean cut and the curve shape obvious; however, at other times it is not easy to see any resemblance. In this case we have to apply more complicated mathematical formulas.

Let us say that our original series looks like that shown in Fig. 3.1. If we change or vary the values of our y axis we can modify the scale and see the things that are not instantly recognizable. If our series has values that are fluctuating from 20 to 80, then it is natural that our axis y will start with 10 and go up to 100. But, if the values in our time series vary a lot and they fluctuate significantly, then very often we are going to see just a series of dramatic ups and downs, fluctuating like a cardiograph, and we are not going to be able to see the pattern. In situations like this we can use little graphic 'tricks' to determine the pattern, and make it more obvious. Figure 3.2 demonstrates, using

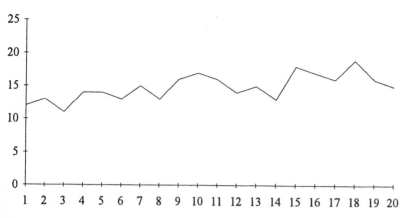

Figure 3.1 Original series

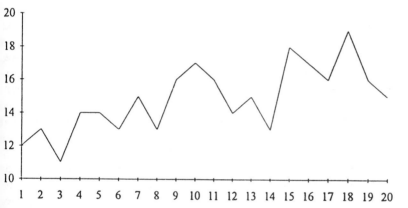

Figure 3.2 Original time series: small scale

an extreme case and by increasing the scale, how our time series takes a dramatic shape if we start the scale with 10 and finish with 20.

One of the simplest tricks to eliminate this dramatic appearance of the time series is to reduce the scale of our y axis. If we now start the values on our axis y with 10 and make it grow at the rate of 10 up to, say, 100, then it is obvious that our time series will be almost a straight line, taking a specific shape and having a certain trend (Fig. 3.3). This will help us to see if our time series has a horizontal trend (stationary) and whether it is really a straight line or, more likely, a slightly bent, modified exponential curve. The trick uses the same principle as taking photographs from different altitudes; the higher we go the fewer details we can see, but the better idea of the shape of the object we have.

What is important to emphasize here is that this preliminary graphical analysis should, in fact, be called just a visual inspection. It cannot be a substitute

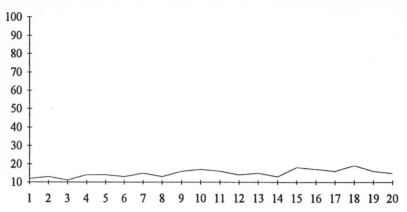

Figure 3.3 Original time series: large scale

for more accurate methods; however, it is a valuable tool for gaining a first impression and an idea about which direction to go in and which more sophisticated methods to apply. In fact, this simple visual procedure is compensation for the human inability to visualize numbers, but at the same time is taking advantage of the great human ability to make approximations and draw conclusions on the basis of visual impressions.

Sometimes the series is so dynamic that, no matter how we present it, we cannot see certain logic or regularity. In this case, we can transform the original series into a derivative of itself in order to eliminate some of the disturbances that are disabling us from seeing what should be seen. If we transform it into, say, its logarithmic values and then present it in a graphic form, these regularities might become obvious. For example, we could have a series of the shape shown in Fig. 3.4. As we can see, the series is growing exponentially, but is also showing some fluctuations in its growth and we do not know how regular and significant they are. At this moment, we are deliberately not interested in guessing whether this time series has a shape of a parabola, exponential curve or any other theoretical curve, although we are going to deal with this issue very soon. We are simply interested in the nature of variations as they seem significant, although we cannot see any logic in them.

If we show the graph of log values of this series we might be able to tell more (Fig. 3.5). We can now see that the fluctuations are very regular but, at the same time, are slowly losing their dynamics as the series becomes more stable, despite what the original graph was suggesting. A valuable conclusion is very easy to make, thanks to a simple graph.

There is one problem related to empirical time series that we have to mention as it might happen in practice. For some reason, sometimes we end up with our time series with one or two items of data missing from it. We have stressed the importance of observations being equidistant, which means we have to fill in these gaps. If our series is of stationary nature (horizontal), then we are making

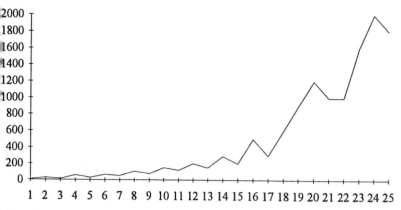

Figure 3.4 Series with fluctuations and significant growth

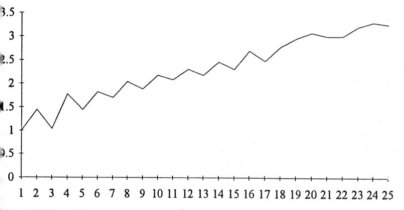

Figure 3.5 Logarithmic version of Fig. 3.4

the smallest error by substituting the missing data with the mean value. If we are dealing with a non-stationary series then we shall be much safer if we use the two neighbouring observations (the period before and the period after the missing observation) and insert their average (the first one plus the second one divided by two) for the missing observation.

Once again, let us repeat what we have to bear in mind: that graphics have an enormous impact on our understanding of the series, as our perception is dependent on visual impressions. Presenting the series and its derivatives in various forms of graphs can only help us in understanding it better. Still, this is just the first job that we have to do, and the purpose of it is to draw some preliminary conclusions. One of the basic conclusions we are also expected to draw on the basis of visual inspection, is to find the similarity of our time series to some theoretical curves. Chapter 4 will deal with this issue.

4
Recognizing different curves

If we say that we are interested in discovering which theoretical curve our time series resembles, then before we proceed we have to know which curves to look for. Generally speaking, curves can be divided into two basic groups:

1. Algebraic curves
2. Transcendent curves

Algebraic curves are often divided further into rational ones and irrational ones, but for forecasting purposes we should take interest in rational ones only. The rational ones could be of various degrees, so we are talking about linear curves of the first degree, the second degree (parabola), etc.

A parabola (Fig. 4.1) is just one of the curves from the set of curves of the second degree. In fact, it resembles greatly the exponential curve (Fig. 4.2) which is in fact a transcended curve; to be more precise, the time series that we might be using in practice very often resembles either a parabola or exponential curve.

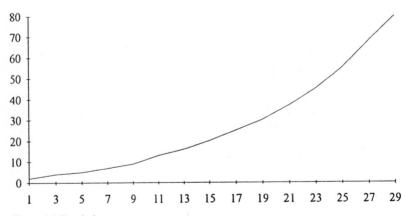

Figure 4.1 Parabola

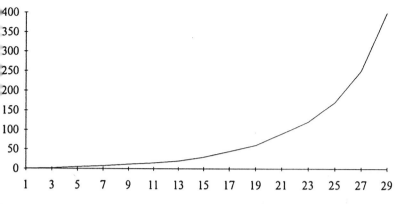

Figure 4.2 Exponential curve

and we have to find out which is correct. As curves are grouped in 'families' we might think that all the curves in one family look similar. Unfortunately, the 'family' connection comes from the common mathematical equation that they share, which, in graphical terms, could mean that curves in one family assume a completely different shape (Fig. 4.3), while some curves from different families could have a similar appearance.

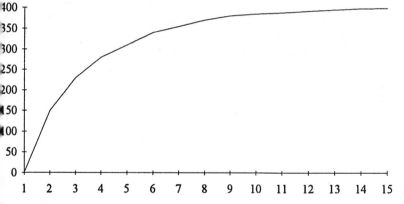

Figure 4.3 Modified exponential curve

Transcendent curves are also symmetric or asymmetric to various degrees, the most common ones being the *Gompertz curve* (Fig. 4.4) and *logistic curve* (or *Pearl–Reed curve*).

So, we have said that in order to gain some useful information about the phenomenon, our job is to guess which theoretical curve our time series resembles. It is fair to say that sometimes we cannot see a certain logic, no matter how much we reduce the scale, and visual inspection does not lead us

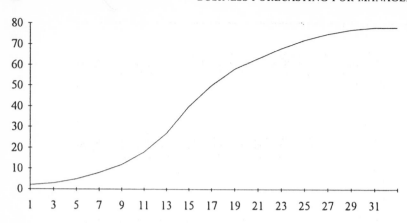

Figure 4.4 Gompertz curve

to any conclusions. In fact, often it is not even necessary to reduce the scale or use any of the tricks previously mentioned. Sometimes we are better off making certain mathematical transformations to our time series, and graphically examining these transformations to draw some conclusions.

These transformations could involve various things such as: calculating logs of the values in our time series (do not confuse this with graph presentation of logs that we made in the previous chapter); taking reciprocal values of the series; subtracting the values one from another or subtracting them from their mean value, etc. All these simple calculations, and their graphic presentations will help us further in determining the nature of our time series. Let us examine some of these examples in practice.

Every theoretical curve follows certain laws and regularities. So, behind every graph presentation we look at and conclude 'this is a straight line', there is strong logic supporting it. The transformations that we mentioned above contain this logic. Which transformations are we advised to make? Usually they are:

- Differencing (subtracting the first value in the series from the second, the third from the second, the fourth from the third, etc.)
- Second differencing (the same as above, but we subtract the values from the previously differenced series, not from the original one)
- Third differencing (the same logic as above)
- Logs
- Log differences (as in the first three cases, but using the series of logs not the original series)
- Reciprocal values (dividing number 1 by each value in the series)
- Reciprocal values differences (as previously mentioned but for the series of reciprocal values)

Now, let us take some of the most commonly used theoretical curves and see which laws they obey (Table 4.1). What transformations should we use? By

The table below uses spreadsheet row numbers (1–26) down the left side and column letters (A–H) across the top.

	A	B	C	D	E	F	G	H
4	PERIOD	SERIES	FIRST DIFFERENCES	SECOND DIFFERENCES	LOGARITHMS	LOG DIFFERENCES	RECIPROCAL VALUES	REC. VALUES DIFFERENCES
6	A	B	C	D	E	F	G	H
7	1	12			1.08		0.08	
8	2	13	1		1.11	0.03	0.08	−0.01
9	3	11	−2	−3	1.04	−0.07	0.09	0.01
10	4	14	3	5	1.15	0.10	0.07	−0.02
11	5	14	0	−3	1.15	0.00	0.07	0.00
12	6	13	−1	−1	1.11	−0.03	0.08	0.01
13	7	15	2	3	1.18	0.06	0.07	−0.01
14	8	13	−2	−4	1.11	−0.06	0.08	0.01
15	9	16	3	5	1.20	0.09	0.06	−0.01
16	10	17	1	−2	1.23	0.03	0.06	0.00
17	11	16	−1	−2	1.20	−0.03	0.06	0.00
18	12	14	−2	−1	1.15	−0.06	0.07	0.01
19	13	15	1	3	1.18	0.03	0.07	0.00
20	14	13	−2	−3	1.11	−0.06	0.08	0.01
21	15	18	5	7	1.26	0.14	0.06	−0.02
22	16	17	−1	−6	1.23	−0.02	0.06	0.00
23	17	16	−1	0	1.20	−0.03	0.06	0.00
24	18	19	3	4	1.28	0.07	0.05	−0.01
25	19	16	−3	−6	1.20	−0.07	0.06	0.01
26	20	15	−1	2	1.18	−0.03	0.07	0.00

Figure 4.5 Input series transformations

Table 4.1

Curve	Formula	Transformation
1. Straight line (linear)	$Y = a + bx$	First differences constant
2. Parabola	$Y = a + bx + cx^2$	Second differences constant
3. Third degree parabola	$Y = a + bx + cx^2 + dx^3$	Third differences constant
4. Hyperbola	$Y = \frac{a}{x}$	First differences of reciprocal logs are constant
5. Exponential curve	$Y = ab^x$	First differences of logs are constant
6. Modified exponential curve	$Y = k + ab^x$	First differences are declining at a constant percentage
7. Gompertz curve	$Y = ka^{b^x}$	Growth of first differences logs is declining at a constant percentage
8. Logistic curve	$\frac{1}{Y} = k + ab^x$	First differences of reciprocal values are declining at a constant percentage

looking at our initial three graphs of our time series (Figs 3.1 to 3.3) where w₁ presented our phenomenon at three different scales, it is obvious that our series has an upward trend in a certain linear pattern. To prove this we need to do only one transformation, which is to calculate the first differences of the time series (although in Fig. 4.5 we made more transformations simply to demonstrate what was mentioned earlier).

Example 4.1   Recognizing different curves

Suppose that you have collected the information shown in Table 4.2 on the number of cheques processed by a local bank during the previous 12 years.

(a) Graph $x(t)$ versus t.
(b) It is expected from the equation that a parabolic curve of the form $y = a + bt + ct^2$ will result. Verify that the relationship between the number of cheques processed and time is indeed parabolic by showing that the second differences are stationary.

Table 4.2

Year	Number of cheques	Year	Number of cheques
1982	5 000	1988	71 005
1983	11 001	1989	89 008
1984	19 001	1990	109 000
1985	29 003	1991	131 010
1986	41 003	1992	155 006
1987	55 003	1993	181 008

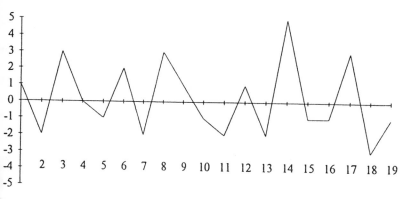

Figure 4.6 First differences

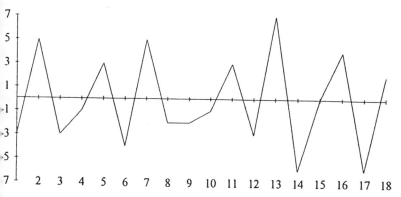

Figure 4.7 Second differences

According to the principles by which linear curves of the first degree move, in Fig. 4.5 the series of first differences should consist of more or less the same number. As we can see, this is unfortunately not true, the reason being the fluctuations of our time series. Still, if we look at the values (Fig. 4.6), they do not show any growth or decline, but vary between −3 and 3 (and, on only one occasion, 5). This should be a sufficient clue to indicate that our time series is varying around a straight line, showing a tendency (or trend) of growth. Fig. 4.7, although not relevant to this chapter, illustrates second differences. What if we had some doubts, and the pattern in the original time series was not so obvious?

From the above example it is clear that the variations happening in the real-life time series are, in a way, a disturbance factor in relation to the theoretical and underlying shape of the real-life time series. As already mentioned, every real-life time series consists of a pattern and residuals, thus our first job is to eliminate the residuals in order to recognize the pattern. This should not be

confused with certain forecasting methods (decomposition), as we are dealin;
with preliminary analysis terms only.

By looking at our time series (Fig. 3.1) we can see that all these residuals ar
creating peaks, which digress from some imaginary straight line that could b
considered a theoretical curve fitting our time series. The most natural way o
eliminating these peaks would be to simply 'iron' them out or smooth them
One of the simple techniques of smoothing a series is called *moving average*
(Fig. 4.8).

	A	B	C	D	E	F
1						
2						
3						
4	PERIOD	SERIES	Moving averages – 3	Moving averages – 5	Moving averages – 10	Moving averages – 20
5						
6	A	B	C	D	E	F
7	1	12				
8	2	13	12.00			
9	3	11	12.67	12.80		
10	4	14	13.00	13.00		
11	5	14	13.67	13.40	13.80	
12	6	13	14.00	13.80		
13	7	15	ˋ 13.67	14.20		
14	8	13	14.67	14.80		
15	9	16	15.33	15.40		
16	10	17	16.33	15.20		14.85
17	11	16	15.67	15.60		
18	12	14	15.00	15.00		
19	13	15	14.00	15.20		
20	14	13	15.33	15.40		
21	15	18	16.00	15.80	15.90	
22	16	17	17.00	16.60		
23	17	16	17.33	17.20		
24	18	19	17.00	16.60		
25	19	16	16.67			
26	20	15				

Figure 4.8 Simple forecasting techniques

We know that calculating the mean involves dividing the sum of all the valu
in the series with the number of them, i.e.:

$$x' = \frac{\sum_{i=1}^{n} x_i}{n}$$

If we draw this value in the graph it will be a straight line, which could we
represent a series with a horizontal (or stationary) pattern, but not a no

tationary series. Obviously, we need a dynamic value that will grow or decline
s the series changes. If we divided the series into two equal parts, and for each
art calculate its mean, we are going to get a straight line, not a horizontal
ne. As we can visualize it, this one more realistically approximates our series,
nd gives a straight line around which our time series quite religiously fluctuates.

But let us try to make this line more dynamic, again to represent our series
ut without all the big fluctuations. If we divide the series into four sections
nd calculate the mean for each section, we get an abstract of our curve, i.e.
ne new curve around which our time series fluctuates. Or, in other words, we
ave reduced many of the fluctuations by smoothing them and reducing our
me series to its abstract. Let us jump several steps and say that we want to
ake three consecutive values of our series, and calculate their mean. For example,
e take the first, second and third values and calculate their mean, then the
econd, third and the fourth values and calculate their mean, etc. The values
nat we would be calculating are, in fact, moving averages of our series. If we
hoose to calculate moving averages of the groups of five, we shall see that
nese values are smoother than moving averages of the groups of three (Fig.
.9). Of course, by increasing the number of elements in the group, we are going
o reach the values mentioned at the beginning of this section, i.e. we are going
o reach the actual mean of the series.

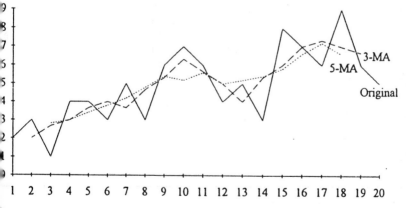

igure 4.9 Different types of moving averages

So, moving averages are a method, or rather a technique, for eliminating
uctuations and disclosing the underlying pattern of the time series. If we take
ne first differences of moving averages, we can see that these values are more
onstant than differences taken from the original time series. We are now closer
o our theoretical curve, and we are certain that our time series is a linear curve.
owever, in real life the doubts do not necessarily end here, and there is a
ossibility that we are still not certain if our time series is stationary or

non-stationary, let alone what theoretical curve it resembles. In this cas
we have some powerful techniques available, which involve calculating th
autocorrelations.

Exercises

4.1 A company invests £5000 in a simple interest account for 25 years at
rate of 18 per cent per annum.
   (a) Use the simple interest formula:

$$x(t) = P(1 + Rt/100)$$

   where $x(t)$ = the return at the end of year t
   P = initial sum invested
   R = interest rate per annum
   t = time period in years
   to set up a spreadsheet model to find $x(t)$ given t.
   (b) Graph $x(t)$ versus t.
   (c) It is expected from the equation that a linear relationship of the for
   $y = a + bx$ will result.
      (i)   What is a equivalent to in the simple interest formula?
      (ii) What is b equivalent to in the simple interest formula?
      (iii) What is x equivalent to in the simple interest formula?
   (d) Show that the relationship between financial return and the duratio
   of the investment t is linear by showing that the first differences of th
   returns are constant.

4.2 A company invests £5000 in a compound interest account for 25 years
a rate of 18 per cent per annum.
   (a) Use the compound interest formula:

$$x(t) = P(1 + R/100)^t$$

   where $x(t)$ = the return at the end of year t
   P = initial sum invested
   R = interest rate per annum
   t = time period in years
   to set up a spreadsheet model to find $x(t)$ given t.
   (b) Graph $x(t)$ versus t.
   (c) It is expected from the equation that a simple exponential curve of th
   form $y = ab^x$ will result.
      (i)   What is a equivalent to in the compound interest formula?
      (ii) What is b equivalent to in the compound interest formula?
      (iii) What is x equivalent to in the compound interest formula?

(d) By taking the first differences of the logarithm returns show that the relationship between financial return and the duration of the investment, t, is simple exponential.

3   A toy company has monitored its monthly production of its flagship product called 'Quasar' for the previous 24 months. Having graphed the monthly production levels the management suspects that the production may be modelled by the modified exponential equation:

$$x(t) = a + bc^t$$

The monthly production figures (in hundreds) are given in Table 4.3.

Table 4.3

Month	Production	Month	Production	Month	Production
1	20.00	9	86.58	17	97.75
2	36.00	10	89.26	18	98.20
3	48.80	11	91.41	19	98.56
4	59.04	12	93.13	20	98.85
5	67.23	13	94.50	21	99.08
6	73.79	14	95.60	22	99.26
7	79.03	15	96.48	23	99.41
8	83.22	16	97.19	24	99.53

(a) Reproduce the graph of $x(t)$ against t and comment on the suitability of applying the modified exponential curve.
(b) What is the monthly saturation level of the product 'Quasar'?
(c) Verify that the above model gives an appropriate description of the production curve by using the transformation suggested on page 20.

4   A national company which produces light bulbs has entered a new long life light bulb onto the market. The monthly sales (in £1000s) of the light bulb following a vigorous initial six-month advertising campaign is as shown in Table 4.4.

Table 4.4

Month	Sales	Month	Sales	Month	Sales
1	26.32	9	318.80	17	333.27
2	48.78	10	325.91	18	333.30
3	85.11	11	329.58	19	333.32
4	135.59	12	331.45	20	333.33
5	192.77	13	332.39	21	333.33
6	244.27	14	332.89	22	333.33
7	281.94	15	333.10	23	333.33
8	305.49	16	333.21	24	333.33

(a) Produce the graph of $x(t)$ against t and comment on the suitability $\lessdot$ applying the logistic curve.

(b) Considering the graph would you suggest that a further advertisin campaign is in order?

(c) Verify that the above model gives an appropriate description of tl sales curve by using the transformation suggested on page 20.

4.5 A construction company has part of its accounting function calculate tl total monthly construction costs (labour and materials) of each of i construction projects. One of the projects involves the construction of supermarket for 'Cheepo Products' and it is envisaged that the proje will take four years to complete. The total monthly construction costs (i £1000s) for the first two years are given in Table 4.5.

Table 4.5

Month	Costs	Month	Costs	Month	Costs
1	6.93	9	310.56	17	1596.06
2	13.51	10	430.97	18	1806.26
3	24.64	11	536.18	19	2019.01
4	42.32	12	676.73	20	2231.83
5	68.85	13	834.47	21	2442.48
6	106.69	14	1007.64	22	2649.01
7	158.26	15	1194.02	23	2849.79
8	225.66	16	1391.07	24	3043.46

(a) Produce the graph of $x(t)$ against t and comment on the suitability $\lessdot$ applying the Gompertz curve.

(b) Comment on the suitability of applying the Gompertz curve to the li span of the full project (four years).

(c) Verify that the above model gives an appropriate description of th sales curve by using the transformation suggested on page 20.

5
Recognizing different models

et us start this chapter with a little theory and jargon. We have said that our me series is, in fact, based on a theoretical curve, and one of the skills of recasting is, by using some of the available methods, to recognize this eoretical curve. If we change the philosophy and say that our time series has ecome similar to a theoretical curve, because it has been through a so-called *ack box* which turned it into a curve-like graph, then we present ourselves ith a question: what was this time series before and what is the content of the ack box?

Some theories, and we call them stochastic, say that every empirical time ries we are handling is, in fact, *white noise* which goes through a linear filter lack box) and becomes a time series. What does this mean? A white noise is linear combination (a series) of random and independent observations. It has me very strong statistical properties, the most important being that it contains pattern whatsoever. This makes the process unpredictable as each value has rtain probability of being the next one in the series. The linear filter is a set weights with which the white noise process is multiplied, and after which it ecomes our empirical time series that we have measured or recorded. What re the practical implications of these theories?

It is very simple. In real life we can visualize the black box as a set of various ctors and variables that are influencing our time series. If, for example, we re forecasting the sales of bread in one town and, for the sake of simplicity, e assume that we are the only bakery in the town, then it would appear that othing could be easier than this forecast. We just multiply the number of habitants with the average consumption of bread per capita and we have a sult! However, we all know that in real life this is not the case. One day it ight be raining heavily and quite a few people could decide to eat yesterday's read rather than go out. Another factor could be that quite a few people decide buy rolls, rather than bread. By using just these two examples (let alone olidays), our sales could significantly go down. On some other occasion we could have an event in the town which would attract a lot of people, and th might cause our sales to increase. These factors are weights from the black bc which will affect something that could and should have a shape of a *random walk*

So, it appears that our job is to convert our time series into a random wa series, and guess the weights that influence this random walk. To convert ti time series into a random walk should not be difficult and, in fact, we ha done it already. Look at our differencing values. The first differences, if we shc them on the graph, go up and down, and the second differences make ev more and obvious random jumps. So, differencing is a simple technique converting the series. In fact, we can never make it completely and really rando but at least we are trying to make it horizontal. While the original time seri has an obvious upwards trend, our differenced series are no longer movi upward. They are becoming horizontal or, as we call it, stationary. Now th is the buzz word: we want to make our series stationary and the way to do is to difference it. What about all the weights that we have called the black box?

There is no problem! Every series can be simulated by applying a set of weigh to a theoretical curve that approximates this series. The only problem is th we would have to have as many weights as observations, and would still ha a problem in guessing which are the weights to apply to future values. So, o job is to develop the *parsimonious model*, i.e. a model (or a formula) that w describe our time series with the minimum possible number of parametei Naturally, we are going to have to compromise, the consequences being th we are not going to approximate our time series perfectly, and, as a result that, our forecasting model will produce certain errors. The combination of th expected error and a number of parameters is the guideline we are going follow in order to use the optimum model. However, this is the subject of later chapter, so let us return to the subject of stationarity.

The stochastic theory has developed several models and, basically, they a say that every time series consists of either autoregressive components, movi average components, or a mixture of the two. A moving average (MA) compone is a component in the model which will determine how much each observatic is dependent on the residuals. If the series could be described in this mann only then could we call it an MA model. An autoregressive (AR) compone will determine how much each observation is dependent on the previo observations in the series. If we have this case, then we say that our seri belongs to the group of AR models. There is a good example in real life. Let pretend that the Christmas sales are a residual component (although in real l it is a strong seasonal component), and that our sales figures have been stead growing from month to month. We are now in November and we have forecast the sales for December. Which figure will have greater significance f use: the previous month's figures or the last Christmas sales figures? The answ is obviously both, and we have to figure out how much each of them shou influence us. So, this is an example of the so-called ARIMA model. Now, ARM is obviously a combination of AR and MA models, so what is ARIMA?

Well, we have said that random walk is a stationary series. In reality a lot
f series are non-stationary and, according to our theory, we have to put a
near stationary series through a black box in order to get an approximation
f our time series. So, we have to make our series stationary (by differencing it)
 we want to use certain methods. If we make it stationary, and if it happens
 be a combination of AR and MA components, then it is called an
utoregressive integrated moving average (ARIMA) model. To cut a long story
hort, ARIMA models are used for non-stationary series where both AR and
1A factors are relevant, and we have to difference the series to make it stationary.

If it is so important to make the series stationary, why do we not do it
utomatically by differencing every series before we start doing anything else?
*irst of all, it is not good to overtransform the series, as we then lose some of
ts properties and we would be guessing a slightly different model, which would
esult in an increased forecasting error. On the other hand, we do not want to
ndertransform the series as we would again have a distorted picture. So, it is a
eal art to guess when our series is 'stationary enough'. Obviously, with every
lifferencing we make it more and more stationary, and we have to stop
omewhere. Equally, sometimes we are not even sure whether to start the
lifferencing, as our time series already looks stationary. As mentioned at the
*eginning of this chapter, a mechanism that can help us is autocorrelations
nalysis.

If we lag our series by one observation, and then measure the correlation
etween the original series and the lagged series, we have, in fact, measured the
rst correlation factor between the series and its previous values. We can go
n lagging the series for more and more observations, and finally end up with
series of *autocorrelation coefficients*. These autocorrelations, when lined one
fter another, represent an autocorrelations function that should tell us:

Whether the data in our series are random
Whether the data are stationary
After how many differencing they will be stationary
Whether the data are seasonal
What the length of the seasonality is

o, if our series is really random, the autocorrelation coefficients will show that
here is no relationship between the original series and its lagged series. If there
 a pattern, then it has to affect the autocorrelations function and we are going
 notice it. Autocorrelation coefficients are like the mean (after all, this is
tatistics!), which means that a certain number of them have to be within certain
orders before we call the series random. If 95 per cent of all autocorrelation
oefficients are within

$$\pm \frac{2}{\sqrt{n}} \quad \text{where } n \text{ is a number of autocorrelations in the series}$$

*en the series is random. In theory, autocorrelation coefficients will drop

A	B	C	D	E	F	G	H
	PERIOD	SERIES	D=C-X'	E=D^2	F=D1*D2	G=D1*D3	H=D1*D4
A	B	C	D	E	F	G	H
	1	12	-2.85	8.12	5.27	10.97	2.42
	2	13	-1.85	3.42	7.12	1.57	1.57
	3	11	-3.85	14.82	3.27	3.27	7.12
	4	14	-0.85	0.72	0.72	1.57	-0.13
	5	14	-0.85	0.72	1.57	-0.13	1.57
	6	13	-1.85	3.42	-0.28	3.42	-2.13
	7	15	0.15	0.02	-0.28	0.17	0.32
	8	13	-1.85	3.42	-2.13	-3.98	-2.13
	9	16	1.15	1.32	2.47	1.32	-0.98
	10	17	2.15	4.62	2.47	-1.83	0.32
	11	16	1.15	1.32	-0.98	0.17	-2.13
	12	14	-0.85	0.72	-0.13	1.57	-2.68
	13	15	0.15	0.02	-0.28	0.47	0.32
	14	13	-1.85	3.42	-5.83	-3.98	-2.13
	15	18	3.15	9.92	6.77	3.62	13.07
	16	17	2.15	4.62	2.47	8.92	2.47
	17	16	1.15	1.32	4.77	1.32	0.17
	18	19	4.15	17.22	4.77	0.62	
	19	16	1.15	1.32	0.17		
	20	15	0.15	0.02			
SUM		297.00		80.55	31.98	29.11	17.08

30

	I	J	K	L	M
1					
2					
3	I=D1*D5	J=D1*D6	K=D1*D7	L=D1*D8	AUTOCOR-
4					RELATIONS
5	I	J	K	L	M
6	2.42	5.27	-0.43	5.27	0.40
7	3.42	-0.28	3.42	-2.13	0.36
8	-0.58	7.12	-4.43	-8.28	0.21
9	1.57	-0.98	-1.83	-0.98	-0.02
10	-0.98	-1.83	-0.98	0.72	0.15
11	-3.98	-2.13	1.57	-0.28	0.08
12	0.17	-0.13	0.02	-0.28	-0.04
13	1.57	-0.28	3.42	-5.83	
14	0.17	-2.13	3.62	2.47	
15	-3.98	6.77	4.62	2.47	
16	3.62	2.47	1.32	4.77	
17	-1.83	-0.98	-3.53	-0.98	
18	0.17	0.62	0.17	0.02	
19	-7.68	-2.13	-0.28		
20	3.62	0.47			
21	0.32				
22					
23					
24					
25					
26	-1.94	11.89	6.72	-3.01	
27					

gure 5.1 *Continued*

wards zero after the first, second or third lag, and will not go out of the
ove-mentioned borders. In practice, we need some tolerance and imagination
see the same, but in the end the results are obvious (Fig. 5.1).

Let us look at our time series (Fig. 4.5). We know that it is not stationary, as
obvious from its graph (Fig. 3.1). Still, for the sake of an exercise, let us calculate
e autocorrelations. After we have put them on the graph we can see that they
e mainly above zero, which confirms a strong pattern in the series (an upward
end in our case), and indicates that the series is not stationary (Fig. 5.2).

After the first differencing (Fig. 5.4) we measure autocorrelations of this
fferenced series, and can see more of a random walk (Fig. 5.3). However, the
aph indicates a seasonality, as after every two positive factors the third one
a negative.

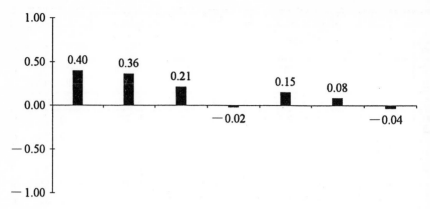

Figure 5.2 Original series autocorrelations

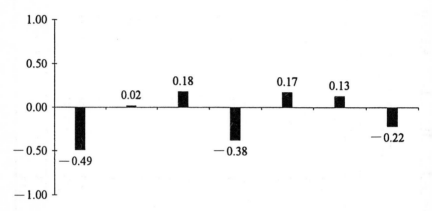

Figure 5.3 Autocorrelation analysis of first differences

As we are not sure whether the series is stationary enough, we difference t
series for a second time and measure its autocorrelations (Fig. 5.5). The gra
confirms our assumptions, and we are now sure that we cannot gain anythi
by differencing the series further, so we stop at the level of the first differences.

How are the autocorrelations calculated? The formula is not as complicat
as it looks:

$$r_k = \frac{\sum_{t=1}^{n-k} (x_t - x')(x_{t+k} - x')}{\sum_{t=1}^{n} (x_t - x')^2}$$

Let us explain what this means. The number of all observations is n, while
is the number of autocorrelations. A piece of advice: never calculate autocorrelatio

	A	B	C	D	E	F	G	H
1								
2								
3		PERIOD	SERIES	D=C-X'	E=D^2	F=D1*D2	G=D1*D3	H=D1*D4
4								
5		B	C	D	E	F	G	H
6		1	1	0.85	0.72	-1.83	2.42	-0.13
7		2	-2	-2.15	4.62	-6.13	0.32	2.47
8		3	3	2.85	8.12	-0.43	-3.28	5.27
9		4	0	-0.15	0.02	0.17	-0.28	0.32
10		5	-1	-1.15	1.32	-2.13	2.47	-3.28
11		6	2	1.85	3.42	-3.98	5.27	1.57
12		7	-2	-2.15	4.62	-6.13	-1.83	2.47
13		8	3	2.85	8.12	2.42	-3.28	-6.13
14		9	1	0.85	0.72	-0.98	-1.83	0.72
15		10	-1	-1.15	1.32	2.47	-0.98	2.47
16		11	-2	-2.15	4.62	-1.83	4.62	-10.43
17		12	1	0.85	0.72	-1.83	4.12	-0.98
18		13	-2	-2.15	4.62	-10.43	2.47	2.47
19		14	5	4.85	23.52	-5.58	-5.58	13.82
20		15	-1	-1.15	1.32	1.32	-3.28	3.62
21		16	-1	-1.15	1.32	-3.28	3.62	1.32
22		17	3	2.85	8.12	-8.98	-3.28	
23		18	-3	-3.15	9.92	3.62		
24		19	-1	-1.15	1.32			
25		20						
26	SUM		3		88.5275			
27	X'=sum(C)/n		0.15					

Figure 5.4 First differences autocorrelations

	I	J	K	L	M
1					
2					
3	I = D1*D5	J = D1*D6	K = D1*D7	L = D1*D8	AUTOCOR-
4					RELATIONS
5	I	J	K	L	M
6	-0.98	1.57	-1.83	2.42	-0.49
7	-3.98	4.62	-6.13	-1.83	0.02
8	-6.13	8.12	2.42	-3.28	0.18
9	-0.43	-0.13	0.17	0.32	-0.38
10	-0.98	1.32	2.47	-0.98	0.17
11	-2.13	-3.98	1.57	-3.98	0.13
12	4.62	-1.83	4.62	-10.43	-0.22
13	2.42	-6.13	13.82	-3.28	
14	-1.83	4.12	-0.98	-0.98	
15	-5.58	1.32	1.32	-3.28	
16	2.47	2.47	-6.13	6.77	
17	-0.98	2.42	-2.68	-0.98	
18	-6.13	6.77	2.47		
19	-15.28	-5.58			
20	1.32				
21					
22					
23					
24					
25					
26					
27					

Figure 5.4 *Continued*

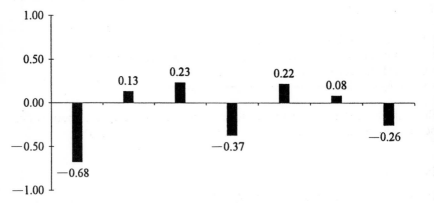

Figure 5.5 Second differences autocorrelations

more than one third of the length of the series, as it is pointless. Make sure that $k_{max} = n/3$. For the mean we have used symbol x'.

If we use the original series (Fig. 4.5) then the autocorrelation coefficients are calculated as:

$$r_1 = \frac{(12 - 14.85)(13 - 14.85) + (13 - 14.85)(11 - 14.85) + (11 - 14.85)(14 - 14.85) + \ldots}{(12 - 14.85)^2 + (13 - 14.85)^2 + \ldots}$$

$$\frac{+ \ldots (19 - 14.85)(16 - 14.85) + (16 - 14.85)(15 - 14.85)}{\ldots + (15 - 14.85)^2}$$

$$r_2 = \frac{(12 - 14.85)(11 - 14.85) + (13 - 14.85)(14 - 14.85) + (11 - 14.85)(14 - 14.85) + \ldots}{(12 - 14.85)^2 + (13 - 14.85)^2 + \ldots}$$

$$\frac{+ \ldots (16 - 14.85)(16 - 14.85) + (19 - 14.85)(15 - 14.85)}{\ldots + (15 - 14.85)^2}$$

.
.
.

$$r_4 = \frac{(12 - 14.85)(14 - 14.85) + (13 - 14.85)(14 - 14.85) + (11 - 14.85)(13 - 14.85) + \ldots}{(12 - 14.85)^2 + (13 - 14.85)^2 + \ldots}$$

$$\frac{+ \ldots (17 - 14.85)(16 - 14.85) + (16 - 14.85)(15 - 14.85)}{\ldots + (15 - 14.85)^2}$$

As we have said that it is worth calculating only $n/3$ autocorrelation coefficients, we stopped after the seventh one. The graph of these has been discussed above.

Now, when we have discovered how to determine the character of our time series, this will help us to determine which method to use. Let us not forget that, beside the character of the time series, i.e. the pattern, there are other elements that have to be taken into consideration. The time horizon could be very important, as:

• Various methods show different reliability
• Different methods have different sensitivity on data variations
• Some of them require more data, some less
• Some could give forecasts with higher accuracy, etc.

These are all factors which should help us in making a decision about which method to use. Let us now examine some of the methods available.

Exercises

5.1 Consider the time series in Table 5.1.

(a) Construct a suitable graph containing the time series in Table 5.1.

Table 5.1

Time point	Series
1	5
2	11
3	19
4	29
5	41
6	55
7	71
8	89
9	109
10	131
11	155

(b) Determine whether a parabola or simple exponential curve would provide the better model to describe the series. (Hint: use the transformations on page 20.)

5.2 Consider the time series in Table 5.2.

Table 5.2

Time point	Series
1	132.00
2	145.20
3	159.72
4	175.69
5	193.26
6	212.59
7	233.85
8	257.23
9	282.95

(a) Construct a suitable graph containing the above time series.
(b) Determine whether a parabola or simple exponential curve would provide the better model to describe the series.

5.3 Consider the time series in Table 5.3.

(a) Construct a suitable graph containing the time series shown in Table 5.3.
(b) Determine whether a modified exponential or logistic curve would provide the better model to describe the series.

Table 5.3

Time point	Series
1	50.00
2	71.00
3	85.70
4	95.99
5	103.19
6	108.24
7	111.76
8	114.24
9	115.96
10	117.18
11	118.02
12	118.62
13	119.03
14	119.32
15	119.53
16	119.67

.4 Consider the time series in Table 5.4.

Table 5.4

Time point	Series
1	26.32
2	48.78
3	85.11
4	135.59
5	192.77
6	244.27
7	281.94
8	305.49
9	318.80
10	325.91
11	329.58
12	331.45
13	332.39
14	332.86
15	333.10
16	333.21

(a) Construct a suitable graph containing the above time series.
(b) Determine whether a modified exponential or logistic curve would provide the better model to describe the series.

5.5 Consider the time series in Table 5.5.

Table 5.5

Time point	Series
1	7.24
2	13.92
3	25.06
4	42.56
5	68.55
6	105.28
7	154.88
8	219.22
9	299.71
10	397.12
11	511.60
12	642.59
13	788.93
14	948.92
15	1120.48
16	1301.25

(a) Construct a suitable graph containing the above time series.
(b) Determine whether a Gompertz or logistic curve would provide th better model to describe the series.

6
Curve fitting

Before we introduce the first forecasting method, let us recall some of the things mentioned at the very beginning of this book. We noted that with casual methods, by knowing the values of one variable that is related to another unknown variable, we can forecast the future values of this unknown variable. There is a special type of casual method, which is called *simple regression* and which is, in most cases (at least in the forecasting context), related to just one variable, the time.

So, we have a phenomenon that we want to forecast which is called a 'time series', and this time series represents a dependent variable that depends on time only. We know that, in reality, time just allows other factors to influence our phenomenon, but for the sake of simplicity let us assume that the time is a 'carrier' of influence. Let us introduce another assumption: that the relationship between our time series and the time is linear, i.e. the changes that are taking place in our time series are behaving in accordance with a linear pattern. This does not necessarily mean that our time series is a straight line, but that it varies round an imaginary straight line. This, in fact, is a repeat of our assertion in chapter 2, where we stated that a time series is a pattern plus residual.

As we have already mentioned, a part of forecasting is to guess which curve our time series resembles and then to calculate this curve so that it approximates our time series. Our job now is to do some calculations. We are going to concentrate on the simplest and very useful example, the straight line.

One of the methods used in statistics to estimate parameters of an equation is called a method of *least squares*. This method helps us to calculate the curve that approximates the time series, so that the total value of all the distances of each observation of the time series from this curve, when raised to the second power and summed, is minimal. This principle guarantees us minimum error, and gives us a certainty and reliability that the same rules will continue in the future. If we are using the linear method of least squares and trying to fit a straight line, then this line is called a *linear trend*. Every linear trend line could be expressed by the following equation:

$$Y = a + bx$$

The parameter a represents an intercept at the axis y, i.e. the value at whic
our line starts, and parameter b is basically a coefficient at which our line i
growing (or declining if negative) with each time unit. So if, for example, w
monitor a monthly level of inventory and say that it could be represented b
a trend equation of $y = 3250 + 250x$, this means that the initial value of ou
inventory when we started to measure it was 3250 and it has been growing s
far at the pace of 250 units a month. It is very easy to make a forecast nov
because, if we have been monitoring this inventory level for the last five month
we can expect to have a level of inventory in the next month of:

$$y = 3250 + 250\,(6) = 4750$$

Of course this trend just approximates the actual value of the inventory, so i
is not necessarily true that the level has been growing at exactly 250 units
month. The good news about trend fitting with this method is that we ca
measure errors and the confidence level of our forecast so that, in the end, w
can even say that it is 95 per cent certain that the next month's level will b
between, say, 4500 and 5000. Anyway, let us see how to calculate our parameter
a and b.

We have mentioned that statistics knows one handy method for calculatin
parameters of equations, which is called the method of least squares, and w
should use this. Without explaining how the parameters were developed,
parameter b is calculated as:

$$b = \frac{n\sum_{i=1}^{n} yx - \sum_{i=1}^{n} y \sum_{i=1}^{n} x}{n\sum_{i=1}^{n} y^2 - \left(\sum_{i=1}^{n} y^2\right)}$$

and parameter a is calculated as:

$$a = \frac{\sum_{i=1}^{n} x}{n} - b\frac{\sum_{i=1}^{n} y}{n}$$

As we can assume n is the number of data in our time series, y starts with th
value of 1 with the first data in our series and goes to n, and x are the value
of our data, i.e. observations in the time series.

Figure 6.1 shows the calculations, and graphically we can quite clearly se
what we have done (Fig. 6.2). It is obvious that our calculated trend onl
approximates the actual time series, and we are aware that it is far from
perfect fit. However, we have said that what we are doing here is merel
calculating the underlying pattern. Everything else we can treat as residual

	A	B	C	D	E	F	G
							LINEAR
3		PERIOD	SERIES	D=B*C	E=B^2	FUTURE PERIOD	FORECAST
4	A	B	C	D	E	F	G
6		1	12	12	1		12.56
7		2	13	26	4		12.80
8		3	11	33	9		13.04
9		4	14	56	16		13.28
10		5	14	70	25		13.52
11		6	13	78	36		13.76
12		7	15	105	49		14.01
13		8	13	104	64		14.25
14		9	16	144	81		14.49
15		10	17	170	100		14.73
16		11	16	176	121		14.97
17		12	14	168	144		15.21
18		13	15	195	169		15.45
19		14	13	182	196		15.69
20		15	18	270	225		15.94
21		16	17	272	256		16.18
22		17	16	272	289		16.42
23		18	19	342	324		16.66
24		19	16	304	361		16.90
25		20	15	300	400		17.14
26	SUM	210	297	3279	2870	21	17.38
27	X'=sum(B)/n		14.85			22	17.63
28	b=(n*sum(D))-	0.24				23	17.87
29	sum(B)*sum					24	18.11
30	(C))/(n*sum					25	18.35
31	(E)-sum(B)^2)					26	18.59
32	a=sum(C)/n-	12.32				27	18.83
33	b*sum(B)/n					28	19.07

Figure 6.1 Linear trend method forecasting

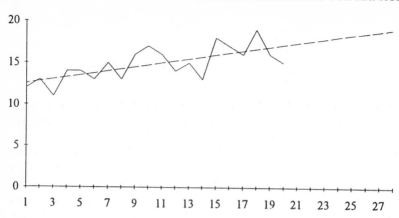

Figure 6.2 Linear trend forecast

and we will find other methods to forecast these residuals. Still, in many cases, we are going to be satisfied just by calculating the trend, as we are not necessarily going to be interested in variations and therefore can sometimes afford to call these variations 'an error' around our linear trend.

Let us stay for a while with this idea of just calculating the trend, as we are going to learn other methods later on. We might face a problem if our time series does not have an underlying pattern that can be approximated with a linear trend. Obviously, there are formulas for covering this event too. Let us use an example of a trend having a shape of a parabola.

If we stick to the method of least squares, and if the basic formula of the parabola is:

$$Y = a + bx + cx^2$$

and if we transform the x values to x'' using the transformation:

$$x'' = x - x'$$

where x' represents the mean value, as used before, then the parameters are calculated as:

$$a = \frac{\sum_{i=1}^{n} y \sum_{i=1}^{n} x''^4 - \sum_{i=1}^{n} x''^2 \sum_{i=1}^{n} yx''^2}{n \sum_{i=1}^{n} x''^4 - \sum_{i=1}^{n} x''^2 \sum_{i=1}^{n} x''^2}$$

$$b = \frac{\sum_{i=1}^{n} x''y}{\sum_{i=1}^{n} x''^2}$$

$$c = \frac{n \sum\limits_{i=1}^{n} yx''^2 - \sum\limits_{i=1}^{n} x''^2 \sum\limits_{i=1}^{n} y}{n \sum\limits_{i=1}^{n} x''^4 - \sum\limits_{i=1}^{n} x''^2 \sum\limits_{i=1}^{n} x''^2}$$

If it happens that we have a model, i.e. a time series, that is showing a tendency to reach a certain asymptotic value and it has an 'S' shape, then we are probably dealing with the so-called Gompertz curve, or a logistic curve. The method of least squares would be too complicated to adopt for the way we are using calculations, so we might use more simple methods for calculating parameters. One particularly easy and attractive method is that of *three selected points*. It is really very easy and fairly accurate. We basically use three selected points, i.e. data values from our times series, and using them we calculate the parameters.

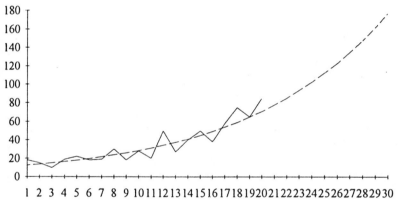

Figure 6.3 Parabola trend forecast

Here is a simple example.

A Gompertz curve has a formula:

$$y = ka^{b^x}$$

which could alternatively be expressed as:

$$\log y = \log k + b^x \log a$$

If our time series has nineteen points then $n = 19$. We are going to have to define a parameter r and it is going to be $r = (n - 1)/2$. So, $r = 9$. We select the three points by defining:

$$T_1(0, y_1) \qquad T_2(r, y_2) \qquad T_3(2r, y_3)$$

This means that the first point will be equal to the first value in the time series, the second point will be equal to the ninth data point and the third point will be equal to the last data point in the time series. The parameters are calculated as:

$$b = \sqrt{\frac{\log y_3 - \log y_2}{\log y_2 - \log y_1}}$$

$$a = \frac{\log y_2 - \log y_1}{br - 1}$$

$$k = \log y_1 - \log a$$

If our time series approaches a certain value as an asymptotic value, but does not have an 'S' shape, rather a shape of inverse parabola or exponential curve, then this is probably a modified exponential curve. The formula is:

$$Y = k + ab^x$$

Using the same principle, this trend is calculated as:

$$b = \sqrt{\frac{y_3 - y_2}{y_2 - y_1}}$$

$$a = \frac{y_2 - y_1}{br - 1}$$

$$c = y_1 - a$$

A much more accurate method for calculating the modified exponential curve is by using the following equations:

$$a = \frac{\sum_{i=1}^{n} x_i - b \sum_{i=1}^{n} cY_i}{n}$$

$$b = \frac{n \sum_{i=1}^{n} cY_i x_i - \sum_{i=1}^{n} cY_i \sum_{i=1}^{n} x_i}{n \sum_{i=1}^{n} c^2 Y_i - \left(\sum_{i=1}^{n} cY_i\right)^2}$$

$$c = \frac{(n-1) \sum_{i=1}^{n-1} x_i x_{i+1} - \sum_{i=1}^{n-1} x_i \sum_{i=1}^{n-1} x_{i+1}}{(n-1) \sum_{i=1}^{n-1} x_i^2 - \left(\sum_{i=1}^{n-1} x_i\right)^2}$$

All these curves were mentioned and graphically presented in Chapter 4.

Example 6.1   Curves fitting

Consider again the cheque processing example in Chapter 4. It was shown that a parabolic curve of the form:

$$x(t) = a + bt + ct^2$$

provides a suitable fit.

(a) Calculate the least squares regression coefficients a, b and c.
(b) Write down the resulting trend equation.

Table 6.1

Year	Number of cheques	Year	Number of cheques
1982	5 000	1988	71 005
1983	11 001	1989	89 008
1984	19 001	1990	109 000
1985	29 003	1991	131 010
1986	41 003	1992	155 006
1987	55 003	1993	181 008

So, now that we have learned how to calculate different types of trends, we might be interested in handling the 'residuals'—the inverted commas signify that they can be called residuals only in the context of trend calculations. Other methods give proper attention to everything that is outside the trend line and, indeed these residuals are important. If we use the analogy of small and large scales again, as we did in Chapter 3, we can say that the smaller the scale the larger the importance of residuals. Or, alternatively, if we are interested in the short-term developments of the time series, then the residuals are certainly of great importance to us. Basically, trend extrapolation methods are suitable for long-term forecasting and, as such, are of great value.

Exercises

6.1 Returning to Exercise 5.1, we find that a parabolic curve would provide a suitable fit to the given data (Table 6.2). (The data has been reproduced in this and the following exercises for easy reference.)

(a) Determine the coefficient values a, b and c using the equations found on page 42.
(b) Write down the least squares approximating equation for the above data shown in Table 6.2.
(c) Construct a suitable graph containing the above data series shown in Table 6.2 and the parabolic curve fit.

Table 6.2

Time point	Series
1	5
2	11
3	19
4	29
5	41
6	55
7	71
8	89
9	109
10	131
11	155

6.2 Returning to Exercise 5.2, we find that a simple exponential curve woul provide a suitable fit to the given data (Table 6.3).

Table 6.3

Time point	Series
1	132.00
2	145.20
3	159.72
4	175.69
5	193.26
6	212.59
7	233.85
8	257.23
9	282.95

(a) Determine the coefficient values a and b using the equations foun on page 44.

(b) Write down the least squares approximating equation for the abov data.

(c) Construct a suitable graph containing the above data series and th simple exponential curve fit.

6.3 Returning to Exercise 5.3, we find that a modified exponential curve wou provide a suitable fit to the given data (Table 6.4).

(a) Determine the coefficient values a, b and c using the equatio found on page 44.

Table 6.4

Time point	Series
1	50.00
2	71.00
3	85.70
4	95.99
5	103.19
6	108.24
7	111.76
8	114.24
9	115.96
10	117.18
11	118.02
12	118.62
13	119.03
14	119.32
15	119.53
16	119.67

(b) Write down the least squares approximating equation for the above data.

(c) Construct a suitable graph containing the above data series and the modified exponential curve fit.

Returning to Exercise 5.4, we find that a logistic curve would provide a suitable fit to the given data (Table 6.5).

Table 6.5

Time point	Series
1	26.32
2	48.78
3	85.11
4	135.59
5	192.77
6	244.27
7	281.94
8	305.49
9	318.80
10	325.91
11	329.58
12	331.45
13	332.39
14	332.86
15	333.10
16	333.21

(a) Determine the coefficient values *a*, *b* and *c* using the equatio found on page 20.
(b) Write down the least squares approximating equation for the abo data.
(c) Construct a suitable graph containing the above data series and t logistic curve fit.

6.5 Returning to Exercise 5.5, we find that a Gompertz curve would provi a suitable fit to the given data (Table 6.6).

Table 6.6

Time point	Series
1	7.24
2	13.92
3	25.06
4	42.06
5	68.55
6	105.28
7	154.88
8	219.22
9	299.71
10	397.12
11	511.60
12	642.59
13	788.93
14	948.92
15	1120.48
16	1301.25

(a) Determine the coefficient values *a*, *b* and *c* using the equatic found on page 20.
(b) Write down the least squares approximating equation for the abc data.
(c) Construct a suitable graph containing the above data series and Gompertz curve fit.

7

Classical time series decomposition

We mentioned in Chapter 6 that after we calculated the trend, everything else that remained (according to that calculation approach) was called the residuals. We also stated that there are other methods that give particular importance to these 'residuals'. These methods treat this remainder as a valuable component of the time series, and the basis for using these methods is to find the components that make up the series.

Let us develop further our initial formula according to which:

$$\text{Time series} = \text{Pattern} + \text{Residuals}$$

If we give a name to the pattern and call it a trend, then the residuals could be called variations around the trend. The variations could be of a different nature and we can differentiate the following variations:

Cyclical variations
Seasonal variations
Irregular variations

In the past, when this method was developed for census purposes, trend was called a 'secular variation' or a 'secular tendency'. Almost a hundred years ago, statisticians developed a method that we call today a *classical decomposition method*, and the basic assumption of this method was that each time series consisted of the following components:

$T =$ trend
$C =$ cyclical component
$S =$ seasonal component
$I =$ irregular variations

There is no need to explain each component, except to clarify the difference between the cyclical and seasonal variations. As one would assume, cyclical variations happen over a period of several years, while the seasonal have effect within the period of one year. Therefore, if we have annual data in our time series, we are not going to worry about the seasonal component. At the same time, if we have monthly data and our time series is several years long, then it will consist of the seasonal as well as the cyclical component. Of course the cyclical component need not be so obvious and, indeed, it will not be obvious if the cycle is longer than our time series. We could, for example, forecast the demand of certain petrochemicals and have a time series consisting of monthly data, which is three years long. Providing the cycle is also three years long and our data cover one full cycle, our forecast might overestimate or underestimate the future values as it will implicitly incorporate the wrong phase of the cycle.

We have mentioned that every time series consists of certain components but we have not described the way they are interrelated. Let us use just two examples:

1. $Y = T + C + S + I$
2. $Y = T \times C \times S \times I$

As we can see, the component could be in an additive relationship or they could be in a multiplicative relationship. The difference is not only of a theoretical nature, as you can see in this example. If our present sales volume is 100 units and if we expect a regular increase of 20, the question is, what are our new expected sales figures going to be? If we have assumed that our time series has an additive shape, then the forecast is 120 and after that linearly 140, 160, 180 etc. If we have accepted a multiplicative model, then we are talking of a multiplicative factor of 1.20, and the figures are 120, 144, 172.8, 207.4, etc. As we can see, after only four periods our two forecasts differ more than 20 units which is an error of 20 per cent in terms of the present value. So, we cannot talk just about theoretical differences in relationship between the components.

An additional complication to this is that the components could have a mixed relationship, so, for example, it is not unusual to say that the basic components take the shape of a multiplicative model with an irregular component added to them:

$$Y = (T \times C \times S) + I$$

In fact, it is not a bad idea to accept this model as the most realistic one. If we do not put the irregular component in the additive relation to the other components, and if it is fairly large during some periods, it could affect the model unrealistically when we multiply other components with it. It will soon be obvious what we mean by this.

So, it is evident that our job is to find the components contained in our time series, then to separate them (i.e. decompose the series), then after that, to define what the regularities are and, finally, to recompose the series using the future time units to forecast the future values of the time series. Let us use a more appropriate model, a multiplicative model, and use some basic mathematical

	A	B	C	D	E	F	G
1							
2							
3	PERIOD	SERIES	TREND	Eliminating	Eliminating	Typical	Recomposi-
4				trend	irregulars	cycles	tion
5	A	B	C	D	E	F	G
6	1	12	12.56	0.96		1.02	12.81
7	2	13	12.80	1.02	0.94	1.06	13.57
8	3	11	13.04	0.84	0.97	1.08	14.08
9	4	14	13.28	1.05	0.98	1.04	13.81
10	5	14	13.52	1.04	1.01	1.00	13.52
11	6	13	13.76	0.94	1.02	0.96	13.21
12	7	15	14.00	1.07	0.98	0.98	13.72
13	8	13	14.24	0.91	1.03	1.02	14.52
14	9	16	14.48	1.10	1.06	1.06	15.35
15	10	17	14.72	1.15	1.11	1.08	15.90
16	11	16	14.96	1.07	1.05	1.04	15.56
17	12	14	15.20	0.92	0.99	1.00	15.20
18	13	15	15.44	0.97	0.91	0.96	14.82
19	14	13	15.68	0.83	0.98	0.98	15.37
20	15	18	15.92	1.13	1.00	1.02	16.19
21	16	17	16.16	1.05	1.05	1.06	17.05
22	17	16	16.40	0.98	1.06	1.08	17.76
23	18	19	16.64	1.14	1.02	1.04	17.22
24	19	16	16.88	0.95	0.99	1.00	16.81
25	20	15	17.12	0.88		0.96	16.47
26	21		17.36			0.98	16.96
27	a =	12.32					
28	b =	0.24					

Figure 7.1 Classical decomposition method forecasting

skills to perform some operations. For the sake of simplicity, in our first example we shall ignore the seasonal component.

If we divide the time series with the calculated trend values of this time series we obtain some interesting results:

$$Y = \frac{T \times C \times I}{T} = C \times I$$

By looking at Fig. 7.1 we can see in column D that this is exactly what we have done, i.e. divided column B (original series) with the column C (trend values as calculated in Chapter 6). What is left over is a cyclical component containing irregular variations, which we can visualize as both of them jumping up and down around the trend (Fig. 7.2). We should remember from Chapter 4 that moving averages, as such, smooth the curve and therefore eliminate irregular variations. So, if we calculate the moving averages of this '$C \times I$' series we can assume that we are going to get a pure cyclical component (see column E):

Moving averages of $C \times I = C$

Although we have smoothed the cyclical + irregular component, extracting in this way a pure cyclical component (Fig. 7.3), we can see from the graph that this component still fluctuates with a very irregular pattern.

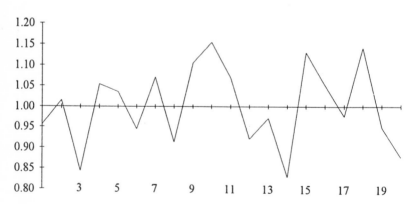

Figure 7.2 Influence of cyclical and irregular components

The next important step is to change this unpredictable variation into a regular and typical variation. There are several acceptably accurate methods that we could use. We have decided to use the simplest and, unfortunately, most arbitrary method. By looking at the graph we decide that the cycles consist of two depression periods and five prosperity periods. By taking all the first values from each depression period and calculating their average values, we find a typical first value in the depression period. We then do the same for all the other values and obtain a graph as shown in Fig. 7.4.

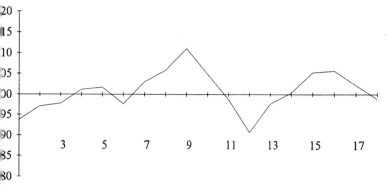

gure 7.3 Graph of cyclical component only

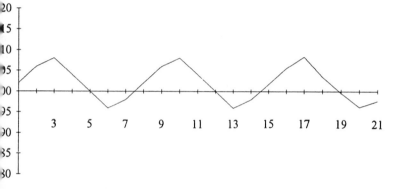

gure 7.4 Typical cycles

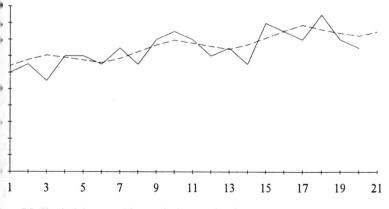

gure 7.5 Classical decomposition method approximation

It is easy now to recompose the series by multiplying the trend values wit the typical cyclical components, as we did in column G of Fig. 7.1. As in th case of trend fitting in Chapter 6, our fitted curve (Fig. 7.5) will again diff somewhat from the original time series, and the difference will be almost equa to the value of irregulars (not completely, as we have used average values fo calculating the typical cyclical component). However, this time the difference should be smaller, which means that our forecast may be more accurate.

Example 7.1 Classical time series analysis

Consider the time series data in Table 7.1 and resulting graph (Fig. 7.6).

Table 7.1 Sales of Doogie Co. Ltd, 1976–1979 (tons)

Year	Quarter 1	Quarter 2	Quarter 3	Quarter 4
1976	672	636	680	704
1977	744	700	756	784
1978	828	800	840	880
1979	936	860	944	972

Sales of Doogie Co. Ltd
1976–1979 (tons)

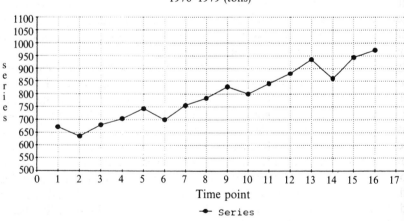

Figure 7.6 Sales of Doogie Co. Ltd, 1976–1979 (tons)

(a) Fit a least squares regression line to the above data and use the tren line to provide a simple forecast.

(b) Produce a forecast for the first quarter of 1980 using:
   (i) the proportional model ($A = T \times S$), and

(ii) the additive model $(A = T + S)$.
Fit both forecasts onto the original graph and comment on the accuracy
of the forecast.

So far we have failed to mention the seasonal component, although we can
-obably guess that the principles of decomposition and recomposition are the
ime. The seasonal component can be calculated in several different ways and
e shall mention a few. If we say that the influence of the cyclical factor is not
ovious for the period that we are investigating, and at the same time seasonal
ictuations within a year are very strong, then we should be using a somewhat
fferent technique. Dividing the original series with the trend values gives us,
this case, just seasonal and irregular variations (components):

$$Y = \frac{T \times S \times I}{T} = S \times I$$

we look at Fig. 7.7, which deals with seasonal decomposition, we can see
hat we mean by this.
We have used a time series that has monthly values, and that is four years
ng. As in the previous example with the cyclical component, we have found
e trend value of the time series. If we make a graphic presentation of what
e have done so far, then it will appear as shown in Fig. 7.8.
Column E of Fig. 7.7 contains what is shown in the formula above, the series
ith eliminated trend component. However, this time we are going to call this
·lumn an index column, as it is actually telling us how much, in terms of index
imbers, every month is above or below the trend line. From these indices
ig. 7.9) we are supposed to eliminate the irregular component and there is a
ry elegant and easy way of doing this. If we take the same months in every
ar of our time series (see Fig. 7.10), and find the average value of them, we
ll have got rid of irregulars. It is important to stress that we should not use
e mean as an average value but rather as the median. The mean is very
nsitive to extremes, and this might affect our average for the month. The
edian is a simple value that we can calculate if we list all January values,
om the smallest to the largest (regardless of the chronological order although,
our example, it just so happens that the values are chronologically increasing),
d then take the two middle ones and calculate their mean by adding them
d dividing by two. If we had an odd number of months then the median
ould simply be equal to the middle value of this mini-series.
Unfortunately, median values do not eliminate irregulars completely. If there
no influence of a seasonal component then, in theory, the value of each month
ould be equal to 100 (and we can call it a monthly index). Of course, then
· total value of all indices for the year should be equal to 1200. If we add
r monthly indices the value could be somewhat above or below 1200 (in our
ie, in Fig. 7.10 it was 1183). Dividing 1200 with our annual value, we get a

	A	B	C	D	E	F	G
	DESCRIPTION	PERIOD	SERIES	TREND	INDEX E = C/D	DESEASONALISED VALUES	RESIDUAL INDICES
	A	B	C	D	E	F	G
Jan 1986.		1	55	83	66	137	165
Feb		2	53	91	58	137	151
Mar		3	61	99	62	117	118
Apr		4	95	106	89	114	107
May		5	118	114	103	118	103
Jun		6	153	122	126	110	90
Jul		7	253	130	195	134	103
Aug		8	289	137	210	140	102
Sep		9	240	145	165	144	99
Oct		10	136	153	89	149	98
Nov		11	92	161	57	178	111
Dec		12	92	168	55	224	133
Jan 1987.		13	59	176	34	147	84
Feb		14	65	184	35	169	92
Mar		15	94	191	49	180	94
Apr		16	147	199	74	176	88
May		17	194	207	94	194	94
Jun		18	315	215	147	226	105
Jul		19	422	222	190	224	101
Aug		20	469	230	204	227	99
Sep		21	428	238	180	256	108
Oct		22	222	246	90	243	99
Nov		23	145	253	57	280	111

	A	B	C	D	E	F	G
30	Jan 1988.	25	97	269	36	242	90
31	Feb	26	112	276	41	291	105
32	Mar	27	123	284	43	235	83
33	Apr	28	247	292	85	295	1C1
34	May	29	327	300	109	327	109
35	Jun	30	414	307	135	297	97
36	Jul	31	572	315	182	303	96
37	Aug	32	624	323	193	302	94
38	Sep	33	542	331	164	325	98
39	Oct	34	304	338	90	333	98
40	Nov	35	154	346	45	298	86
41	Dec	36	127	354	36	309	87
42	Jan 1989.	37	157	361	43	392	108
43	Feb	38	102	369	28	265	72
44	Mar	39	202	377	54	387	103
45	Apr	40	309	385	80	369	96
46	May	41	353	392	90	353	90
47	Jun	42	560	400	140	402	100
48	Jul	43	741	408	182	393	96
49	Aug	44	842	416	203	408	98
50	Sep	45	689	423	163	413	98
51	Oct	46	445	431	103	487	113
52	Nov	47	182	439	41	352	80
53	Dec	48	187	447	42	455	102
54			a = 75.47				
55			b = 7.73				

Figure 7.7 Seasonal decomposition

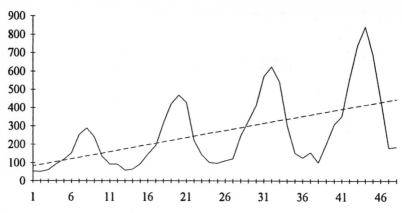

Figure 7.8 Original seasonal series and trend

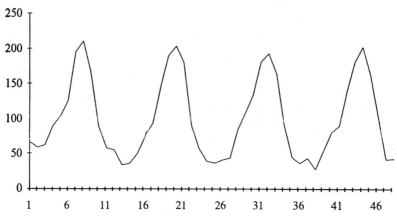

Figure 7.9 Indices

correction factor (1.01) with which we have to multiply our seasonal indices i.e. median values. Now we have typical seasonal indices for our time series (Fig. 7.11).

For the sake of this exercise, if we now divide each actual value with a corresponding typical seasonal index value (see column F in Fig. 7.7), we can see how the time series would look if there were no seasonal influences at all. This is now just a deseasonalized value with some irregular components present in it (Fig. 7.12). If we eliminate the irregular component by dividing the deseasonalized values of the series with the trend, what we are left with is a measure of other influences or an index of irregular fluctuations (see column G in Fig. 7.7). Each value is telling us how much a particular month is affected by other influences, and not only seasonal fluctuations. Graphically it appears as shown in Fig. 7.13.

	A	B	C	D	E	F	G
1				YEAR			
2							Seasonal
3	Month	86	87	88	89	Average	Indices
4	Jan	34	36	43	66	40	40
5	Feb	28	35	41	58	38	39
6	Mar	43	49	54	62	52	52
7	Apr	74	80	85	89	83	84
8	May	90	94	103	109	99	100
9	Jun	126	135	140	147	138	139
10	Jul	182	182	190	195	186	189
11	Aug	193	203	204	211	204	206
12	Sep	163	164	165	180	165	167
13	Oct	89	90	90	103	90	91
14	Nov	41	45	57	57	51	52
15	Dec	36	39	42	55	41	41
16	SUM					1183	1200

Figure 7.10 Typical monthly indices

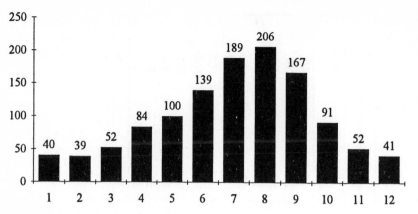

Figure 7.11 Typical monthly indices (graph)

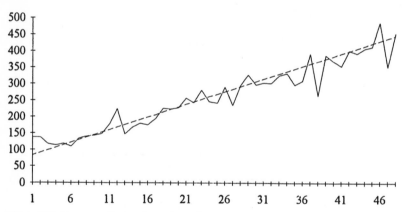

Figure 7.12 Deseasonalized series and trend

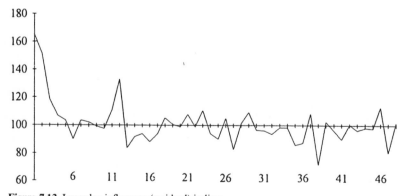

Figure 7.13 Irregular influences (residual) indices

pical monthly indices, we get a future forecast. Of course, by using a
readsheet function we could have easily found the values of parameters a and
of the trend, by applying a spreadsheet formula '= linest(C1:C48)', but this is
t the purpose of this exercise.
Anyway, the values of the parameters, in our case, are:

$$a = 7.73$$
$$b = 75.46$$

e can see in Fig. 7.14 the final results of multiplying typical indices from

	A	B	C	D	E
8	DESCRIPTION	FUTURE	TREND	TYPICAL	RECOMPOSITION
9		PERIODS	FORECAST	INDICES	I.E. FORECAST
0	Jan 1990.	49	454	40	182
1	Feb	50	462	39	180
2	Mar	51	470	52	244
3	Apr	52	477	84	401
4	May	53	485	100	485
5	Jun	54	493	139	685
6	Jul	55	501	189	946
7	Aug	56	508	206	1047
8	Sep	57	516	167	862
9	Oct	58	524	91	477
0	Nov	59	532	52	276
1	Dec	60	539	41	221
2	a=	75.47			
3	b=	7.73			

gure 7.14 Classical decomposition forecast

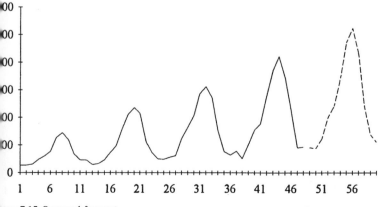

ure 7.15 Seasonal forecast

Fig. 7.10 with the future linear trend values. This recomposed series, which represents our forecast, is presented in the form of a graph (Fig. 7.15).

Obviously, there are several ways of doing what we have just described. Thi might automatically imply that the method of classical decomposition is no particularly accurate. Fortunately, this is not true. It is a fairly accurate method but the problem with it is that it is very arbitrary, as the results can var depending on who is doing the forecasting.

From the classical decomposition method were developed several new modifications during the 1960s and 1970s; if you discover the Census II or X-1 methods anywhere, note that they are just modernized and computerize versions of the good old classical decomposition method.

Exercises

7.1 Table 7.2 shows the number of cans (in 100 000s) of lager sold by manufacturer in each quarter of three successive years.

Table 7.2

Year	Q1	Q2	Q3	Q4
1985	9.8	11.5	13.0	10.9
1986	11.0	12.1	12.9	11.9
1987	11.1	13.6	14.4	12.6

(a) Draw a graph of $x(t)$ against t.
(b) Compute the trend equation using linear regression analysis.
(c) What are the differences between an 'additive' and 'proportional' effec model when calculating the seasonal components?
(d) Estimate the number of cans sold in each quarter of 1988 using bot the 'proportional' $(A = T \times S)$ and 'additive' $(A = T \times S)$ models.

7.2 The figures in Table 7.3 relate to the sales of heating oil.

Table 7.3

Year	Q1	Q2	Q3	Q4
1	320	185	215	395
2	345	200	230	420
3	365	210	240	440

(a) Draw a graph of $x(t)$ against t.
(b) Compute the trend equation using linear regression analysis.
(c) Use the 'proportional' model, $A = T \times S$, to provide a forecast for th first quarter of year 4.

Table 7.4 below gives the index of average earnings (GB) of insurance, banking and finance employees (base: 1976 = 100).

Table 7.4

Year	March	June	Sept.	Dec.
1979	141.8	138.3	150.8	169.8
1980	183.9	199.3	182.9	204.1
1981	212.9	213.3	206.4	230.5
1982	242.8			

(a) Draw a graph of $x(t)$ against t.
(b) Compute the trend equation using linear regression analysis.
(c) Provide an index forecast for June, September and December in 1982. Give reasons for your model choice.

Table 7.5 shows the historical sales demand for a recently released pharmaceutical product.

Table 7.5

Year	Month	Sales demand
1987	1	28.02
	2	48.08
	3	83.73
	4	138.56
1988	5	206.04
	6	260.62
	7	309.95
	8	349.20
1989	9	364.73
	10	318.05
	11	356.13
	12	358.83
1990	13	410.09
	14	346.78
	15	348.49
	16	354.94
1991	17	363.39
	18	362.64
	19	340.90
	20	348.59
1992	21	366.56
	22	362.64
	23	360.19
	24	382.60

(a) Plot the sales demand against time.

(b) Compute the trend equation using a logistic curve fit.

(c) The pharmaceutical company would like to use the above informati to provide a forecast for the first quarter of 1993. Provide this forec using the proportional time series model ($A = T \times S$).

8

Moving averages forecasting

e have seen in previous chapters that moving averages, as a statistical chnique, are used in various methods. We shall now move on and describe e way to apply this useful technique as a forecasting method.

We are familiar by now with the concept of a time series containing a set of mponents. As opposed to the classical decomposition method, which is trying separate 'pure' components, the method of moving averages forecasting has somewhat simpler approach. The underlying assumption of this method is at, regardless of what has influenced the time series in the past, and regardless which components the time series consists of, the method simply attempts eliminate the irregular influences and extrapolate the whole pattern as it is, the future.

This is the concept that is used in many other time series analysis and recasting methods, the only difference being the tools used to achieve it. In e example described here, only moving averages are used, and, in the examples at follow, some other techniques such as smoothing constants, learning nstants, moving average and autoregression parameters, etc. will be adopted.

As we emphasized in Chapter 7, moving averages 'iron' the time series and erefore eliminate or, at least, neutralize the irregular component. Assuming at we have a stationary time series, we can, with reasonable certainty, say at a moving average of the three data in the time series could represent a recast for the fourth data point in the series. If we then eliminate the first ta point from this interval and add the fourth one, their moving average is ain a forecast for the fifth period. As the mathematicians would say:

$$M'_t = \frac{x_t + x_{t-1} + \ldots + x_{t-N+1}}{N}$$

ere M_t is a moving average at the point t, x_t is a data point in the time ries, and N is the number of data in the period for which the moving average

66 BUSINESS FORECASTING FOR MANAGEMENT

is calculated. Therefore, the forecast for the future period could be expressed as:

$$F_{t+1} = \frac{x_t + x_{t-1} + \ldots + x_{t-N+1}}{N}$$

Sometimes the mathematicians prefer to express themselves in the format:

$$F_{t+1} = \frac{1}{N} \sum_{i=t-N+1}^{t} x_i$$

If we agree that this is a very easy and elegant way of forecasting the future we have to say also that there are quite a few limitations to this forecasting method. In the first place this method cannot forecast the non-stationary series well enough. Imagine that we have constantly increasing numbers in the series. A moving average of the first three data points would undoubtedly be below the fourth data point, and so would the fifth and every other moving average/forecast. This would make our forecasts constantly fall behind the actual events. Another problem arises when the time series is 'heavily polluted' with irregulars. In order to eliminate this heavy pollution, we would have to increase the number of periods for which the moving averages are calculated. By doing so we are smoothing the series more deeply, but at the same time we have to remember that the larger the number of moving averages in the period, the more stationary, or horizontal, our values are going to be. It is obvious that this simple method has some serious limitations.

It is time to introduce a new concept that will help us to overcome the above-mentioned limitations. If we calculate the moving averages of moving averages, what we obtain is *double moving averages*. In this case we can say that every moving average lags behind the original data point for a fraction and, at the same time, each double moving average lags behind the single moving average for a fraction. In fact, we can say that every data point is equal to double the value of its single moving average, minus the double moving average. Unfortunately, if the series is non-stationary, we still have to think of the increasing or decreasing tendency, and add something to this value to make sure we follow the trend.

Now, having described the trend, we can use moving averages to construct an equation that will simulate our upwards or downwards series. This could be, of course, a simple straight line equation that would handle the non-stationary time series. What has been mentioned above about every data point consisting of single and double moving averages, could be converted into an intercept (or parameter *a*) of our projected straight line. Therefore:

$$a_t = 2M'_t - M''_t$$

where M'_t is a single moving average and M''_t is a double moving average.

	A	B	C	D	E	F	G	H
4	PERIOD	SERIES	Single moving averages	Double moving averages	Parameter "a"	Parameter "b"	Forecast by single moving averages	Forecast by double moving averages
7	A	B	C	D	E	F	G	H
8	1	12						
9	2	13						
10	3	11	12.00					
11	4	14	12.67				12.00	
12	5	14	13.00	12.56	13.44	0.44	12.67	
13	6	13	13.67	13.11	14.22	0.56	13.00	13.89
14	7	15	14.00	13.56	14.44	0.44	13.67	14.78
15	8	13	13.67	13.78	13.56	-0.11	14.00	14.89
16	9	16	14.67	14.11	15.22	0.56	13.67	13.44
17	10	17	15.33	14.56	16.11	0.78	14.67	15.78
18	11	16	16.33	15.44	17.22	0.89	15.33	16.89
19	12	14	15.67	15.78	15.56	-0.11	16.33	18.11
20	13	15	15.00	15.67	14.33	-0.67	15.67	15.44
21	14	13	14.00	14.89	13.11	-0.89	15.00	13.67
22	15	18	15.33	14.78	15.89	0.56	14.00	12.22
23	16	17	16.00	15.11	16.89	0.89	15.33	16.44
24	17	16	17.00	16.11	17.89	0.89	16.00	17.78
25	18	19	17.33	16.78	17.89	0.56	17.00	18.78
26	19	16	17.00	17.11	16.89	-0.11	17.33	18.44
27	20	15	16.67	17.00	16.33	-0.33	17.00	16.78
28							16.67	16.00

Figure 8.1 Single and double moving averages method of forecasting

67

To find the parameter b we have to use the following formula:

$$b_t = \frac{2}{N-1}(M'_t - M''_t)$$

We can now say that every data on our time series could be approximated by:

$$F_{t+1} = a_t + b_t$$

It is very simple to calculate the forecasts of our time series by saying that:

$$F_{t+m} = a_t + b_t m$$

where m is a number of periods ahead which we are forecasting.

By using the example from Fig. 8.1, we can see the mechanics of calculating forecasts. If we compare single and doubly moving average forecasts, then graphically they appear as shown in Fig. 8.2. We can see that double moving average forecasts are following the pattern of the original time series in a more lively fashion, which is exactly what we wanted to achieve in the case of the non-stationary series.

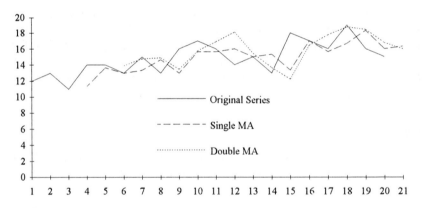

Figure 8.2 Single and double moving average forecasts

Example 8.1   Moving averages forecasting

Consider the time series data in Table 8.1.

Table 8.1 Sales of Doogie Co. Ltd, 1976–1979 (tons)

Year	Quarter 1	Quarter 2	Quarter 3	Quarter 4
1976	672	636	680	704
1977	744	700	756	784
1978	828	800	840	880
1979	936	860	944	972

(a) Draw a graph of $x(t)$ against t and comment upon whether or not the data appears stationary.
(b) Calculate a single and double moving average forecast of length 3 and superimpose both forecasts onto your graph.
(c) Calculate the forecast for quarter 1, 1980 using the double moving average and compare this result with your result from Chapter 7.

Unfortunately, there are some further limitations even in the case of double moving averages forecasting. As we can see from the formula above, in order o forecast at the end of the series, all we can do is to use the last values of the parameters a and b. This means that only a forecast of the next value, i.e. data point, can be reliable. Every following forecast is based on the same values of a and b, and we only change the value of m, which is the number of periods ve forecast ahead. This naturally produces a linear forecast that will probably o longer follow the actual future values of the series (when they happen) as losely. This leads us to the conclusion that our double moving averages orecasting method is only good for very short-term forecasts, as well as only or the linear time series. Another limitation of this method is that it gives qual importance to the data that are at the beginning of the time series, as vell as to those at the very end of it. We know, in real life, that although the lata from the beginning of the series are useful for indicating the trend of the eries, their actual values do not have too much influence on the current, or ndeed, the possible future values of the time series. Let us see how we are going o overcome these limitations.

Exercises

.1   Table 8.2 shows the number of cans (in 100 000s) of lager sold by a manufacturer in each quarter of three successive years.

Table 8.2

Year	Q1	Q2	Q3	Q4
1985	9.8	11.5	13.0	10.9
1986	11.0	12.1	12.9	11.9
1987	11.1	13.6	14.4	12.6

(a) Draw a graph of $x(t)$ against t and comment upon whether or not the data is stationary.
(b) Superimpose onto the above graph a moving average forecast of suitable length. Give reasons for your model choice.
(c) Use this moving average to provide a forecast for the first quarter of 1988.

8.2   The figures in Table 8.3 relate to the sales of heating oil.

Table 8.3

Year	Q1	Q2	Q3	Q4
1	320	185	215	395
2	345	200	230	420
3	365	210	240	440

(a) Draw a graph of $x(t)$ against t and comment upon whether or not the data is stationary.
(b) Superimpose onto the above graph a moving average forecast of suitable length. Give reasons for your model choice.
(c) Use this moving average to provide a forecast for the first quarter of year 4.

8.3   Table 8.4 gives the index of average earnings (GB) of insurance, banking and finance employees (base: 1976 = 100).

Table 8.4

Year	March	June	Sept	Dec
1979	134	142	154	170
1980	190	214	242	274
1981	310	350	394	442
1982	494	550	610	674
1983	742	814	890	970
1983	1054	1142	1234	1330

(a) Draw a graph of $x(t)$ against t and superimpose on the graph moving averages of length 3 in order to show the general trend.
(b) Provide an index forecast for the four quarters of 1984.

9

Exponential smoothing forecasting

To eliminate some of the disadvantages mentioned in Chapter 8, we shall introduce a concept of exponential smoothing. We can treat exponential smoothing as a special type of moving averages which decreases exponentially the older the data in the series are. Basically, we start doing the so-called ex-post forecasts (fitting the time series), from the very beginning of the series. After each new item of data happens, we measure the difference between the actual value and the forecast, and correct our next forecast for a fraction of this error. So, we can say that:

New forecast = Old forecast + Error fraction

Obviously, an error fraction is only a part of the actual error, and we get it by multiplying this actual error with a constant number between 0 and 1. This constant number is called a 'smoothing constant' (α) and is a very relevant statistic, in the same way as was the number of periods in moving averages.

If we use mathematical notation to express what is said in the descriptive formula above, then it would be as follows:

$$F_{t+1} = F_t + \alpha(x_t - F_t)$$

where F_{t+1} is a forecast for the next period, F_t is a forecast for this period, and x_t is the actual value in this period.

If we rearrange this formula, as mathematics allows us to, then we have:

$$F_{t+1} = \alpha x_t + (1 - \alpha)F_t$$

and we can rearrange it further into:

$$F_t = \alpha x_{t-1} + (1 - \alpha)F_{t-1}$$

which means that every data point in the series is equal to all the previous data points weighted with the decreasing error fractions. Or, in other words, the influence of the smoothing constant is decreasing exponentially with the time

in the past and, when all the weights are summed, their total cannot be highe
than one.

To illustrate this, let us say that we are going to use a smoothing constar
of 0.5. This means that for the present value we are going to use 0.5, for th
previous one 0.25, etc. The order looks like this:

$$\alpha = 0.5$$
$$\alpha(1 - \alpha) = 0.25$$
$$\alpha(1 - \alpha)^2 = 0.125$$
$$\alpha(1 - \alpha)^3 = 0.0625$$
$$\alpha(1 - \alpha)^4 = 0.031\,25, \text{ etc.}$$

It is quite clear that by multiplying the newer data with higher values we ar
giving them higher importance, and this is exactly what we have tried to de
as moving averages were not selective enough. There is, however, a clos
relationship between moving averages and the smoothing constant. In the sam
way as the larger the number of data we had in the moving average perioc
the more the moving averages smoothed the series, so too the smaller th
smoothing constant the smoother the series. To convert moving averages int
a smoothing constant we can use a relation where:

$$\alpha = \frac{2}{M + 1}$$

if M is a number of data in the moving average period. Say that we are usin
moving averages of three data points, then this is equivalent to a smoothin
constant of $\alpha = 0.5$. Equally, a smoothing constant of 0.2 is equal to movin
averages of nine data in a period. So, the smaller the value of the smoothin
constant, the more horizontal the series will be and, vice versa, the larger th
value of the smoothing constant, the more dynamic the series of estimates.

How do we decide which value to assign to the smoothing constant, followin
the above rule? The answer is, in the same way we decided about movin
averages. Many books advise us to use values between 0.1 and 0.3, which :
logical, and we are going to explain why a little later on. So, the smoothin
constant controls the number of past data from the series which are going t
influence our forecast. A small constant gives weights to older data, and resul
in the very slow response of our forecasts to any changes. A larger constar
follows more closely any changes, but could be over-sensitive to some irregula
components that might occur at any data point. In this case, it would over-rea
and forecast a sudden growth, although there is no reason for such reaction.

We have resolved the problem of equal treatment of older and more recer
data in the series, but we have not resolved the problem of the dynamic patterr
that could occur. Or, in other words, exponential smoothing is a valuabl
method if we are dealing with a stationary series, and this is the reason why w
have accepted the suggestion that the constant should be between 0.1 and 0.
As we now know, these constants will smooth the series more than the bigge

ones, and, if we are dealing with a stationary series, this is a desirable characteristic. In the event of dealing with a non-stationary series we should use a similar trick as with double moving averages. We should introduce double or even triple exponential smoothing.

Let us change the notation and call the whole matter presented so far a single exponential smoothing. If $F_{t+1} = S'_t$ and, therefore, $F_t = S'_{t-1}$, then

$$S'_t = \alpha x_t + (1 - \alpha)S'_{t-1}$$

A double exponential smoothing is then equal to:

$$S''_t = \alpha S'_t + (1 - \alpha)S''_{t-1}$$

According to the analogy with double moving averages, parameters a and b are:

$$a_t = 2S'_t - S''_t$$

$$b_t = \frac{\alpha}{1 - \alpha}(S'_t - S''_t)$$

and therefore our forecast for m periods ahead could be calculated as:

$$F_{t+m} = a_t + b_t m$$

Let us repeat that, as with moving averages, with this method we can only cover non-stationary series that are linear. So, besides the problem of non-stationarity, and the problem of equal importance of various data that we have just resolved, we have to resolve the problem of linearity.

Let us introduce triple exponential smoothing which, according to the known pattern, is equal to:

$$S'''_t = \alpha S''_t + (1 - \alpha)S'''_{t-1}$$

As we are now assuming to be dealing with a non-linear series, we should have more than two parameters, and therefore parameters a, b and c are:

$$a_t = 3S'_t - 3S''_t + S'''_t$$

$$b_t = \frac{\alpha}{2(1 - \alpha)^2}[(6 - 5\alpha)S'_t - 2(5 - 4\alpha)S''_t + (4 - 3\alpha)S'''_t]$$

$$c_t = \frac{\alpha^2}{2(1 - \alpha)^2}(S'_t - 2S''_t + S'''_t)$$

And therefore we have a non-linear forecast:

$$F_{t+m} = a_t + b_t m + c_t m^2$$

This method is often called Brown's one parameter quadratic exponential smoothing, and it shows very good results in the practice (Fig. 9.1). The only problem that this method could cause is in the case of a short time series. If

PERIOD	SERIES	Single exponential smoothing values	Double exponential smoothing values	Triple exponential smoothing values	Double smoothing "a"	Exponential parameters "b"
				(al = .3)		
A	B	C	D	E	F	G
1	12	12.00	12.00	12.00	12.00	
2	13	12.30	12.09	12.03	12.51	0.09
3	11	11.91	12.04	12.03	11.78	−0.05
4	14	12.54	12.19	12.08	12.89	0.15
5	14	12.98	12.42	12.18	13.53	0.24
6	13	12.98	12.59	12.30	13.38	0.17
7	15	13.59	12.89	12.48	14.29	0.30
8	13	13.41	13.05	12.65	13.78	0.16
9	16	14.19	13.39	12.87	14.99	0.34
10	17	15.03	13.88	13.17	16.18	0.49
11	16	15.32	14.31	13.52	16.33	0.43
12	14	14.93	14.50	13.81	15.35	0.18
13	15	14.95	14.63	14.06	15.26	0.14
14	13	14.36	14.55	14.21	14.18	−0.08
15	18	15.45	14.82	14.39	16.09	0.27
16	17	15.92	15.15	14.62	16.68	0.33
17	16	15.94	15.39	14.85	16.50	0.24
18	19	16.86	15.83	15.14	17.89	0.44
19	16	16.60	16.06	15.42	17.14	0.23
20	15	16.12	16.08	15.62	16.16	0.02
21						
22						
23						
24						
25						

Figure 9.1 Single, double and triple exponential smoothing forecasting method

	H	I	J	K	L	M
1						
2						
3	Triple	Exponential	Smoothing	Single exponential	Double exponential	Triple exponential
4	parameters	"b"	"c"	smoothing	smoothing	smoothing
5	"a"			forecast	forecast	forecast
6	H	I	J	K	L	M
7						
8	12.66	0.23	0.01	12.00	12.60	12.90
9	11.65	−0.18	−0.01	12.30	11.73	11.46
10	13.13	0.38	0.02	11.91	13.04	13.53
11	13.84	0.53	0.03	12.54	13.77	14.40
12	13.48	0.27	0.01	12.98	13.54	13.76
13	14.57	0.57	0.03	12.98	14.59	15.17
14	13.74	0.13	0.00	13.59	13.93	13.87
15	15.27	0.61	0.03	13.41	15.33	15.90
16	16.62	0.91	0.04	14.19	16.67	17.58
17	16.54	0.63	0.02	15.03	16.76	17.19
18	15.10	−0.06	−0.02	15.32	15.54	15.01
19	15.00	−0.11	−0.02	14.93	15.40	14.87
20	13.64	−0.59	−0.05	14.95	14.09	13.00
21	16.29	0.46	0.02	14.36	16.36	16.77
22	16.92	0.55	0.02	15.45	17.01	17.49
23	16.51	0.25	0.00	15.92	16.73	16.76
24	18.23	0.77	0.03	15.94	18.33	19.03
25	17.04	0.13	−0.01	16.86	17.37	17.17
26	15.74	−0.38	−0.04	16.60	16.18	15.32
27				16.12	16.20	14.83
28					16.22	14.25
29					16.23	13.60
30					16.25	12.87
31						

Figure 9.1 *Continued*

75

we are dealing with a short time series then it is logical that the parameters o
our model should be fairly reliable and accurate, as otherwise our fitted mode
would have difficulties in catching up with the actual series. The values o
parameters are critical and, as such, should be carefully estimated.

As we can see in our example, the initial values we are using for calculating
the single, double and triple exponential smoothing values, are the actual value
of our series. In turn, these initial exponential smoothings are used for calculating
the parameters of the model. To be brief, one mistake could lead to anothe.
and our parameters would not be too accurate. In cases like this, although we
have not included it in our practical example, we would recommend the following
procedure.

First we find the *initial parameters* of the series by using, say, the least square:
method. These parameters we can call a_0, b_0, and c_0. We can use the values o
these parameters to find the so-called initial values of smoothings. Let us cal
them S'_0, S''_0, and S'''_0:

$$S'_0 = a_0 - \frac{(1 - \alpha)}{\alpha} b_0 + \frac{(1 - \alpha)(2 - \alpha)}{a^2} c_0$$

$$S''_0 = a_0 - \frac{2(1 - \alpha)}{\alpha} b_0 + \frac{2(1 - \alpha)(3 - 2\alpha)}{a^2} c_0$$

$$S'''_0 = a_0 - \frac{3(1 - \alpha)}{\alpha} b_0 + \frac{3(1 - \alpha)(4 - 3\alpha)}{a^2} c_0$$

On the basis of these initial smoothings, we calculate S'_1, S''_1, S'''_1, S'_2, S''_2, S'''_2
S'_3, S''_3, S'''_3, etc. Then we find, as mentioned above, parameters a_t, b_t, and c_t
which could be treated as fairly reliable and accurate parameters for forecasting.

Let us use an example that will cover all the forms of smoothing we have
explained so far. Do not be confused by Fig. 9.1 as it does not include the
technique for calculating initial smoothing values, as just explained. If we
compare the single, double and triple smoothed series, the graph looks as shown
in Fig. 9.2. As we can see, the single smoothed series assumes almost the same
shape as the original one, but it is a little more smoothed (no prizes for this
discovery!) and it seems to have shifted to the right of the original series.

We used the double and triple exponential smoothed method to forecast the
next five periods, while we forecasted just one period ahead with the single
method. It is obvious that the single exponentially smoothing could be used for
only one period ahead forecasts. Comparing the double and triple forecasts, we
can see that the triple values are more dynamic than the double, and will
produce more realistic forecasts the further we go in the future, as explained
previously. However, our example teaches us that we should be very careful
with the triple exponentially smoothed forecasts as everything, including the
possible errors, is growing, or declining, at the rate of a parabola. The double
exponentially smoothed method is somewhat more conservative, and the rea

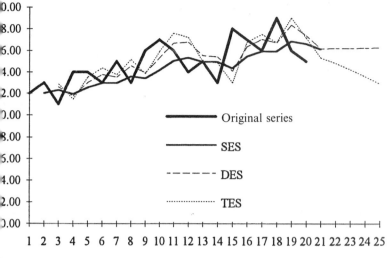

gure 9.2 Single, double and triple exponential smoothing forecasts

recasts are a line, like a linear trend. How to decide which method and which arameter are the best to use, we will learn later on. For the moment, just dmire the variety of possibilities!

Example 9.1 Brown's exponential smoothing

Consider the time series in Table 9.1.

Table 9.1 Sales of Doogie Co. Ltd, 1976–1979 (tons)

Year	Quarter 1	Quarter 2	Quarter 3	Quarter 4
1976	672	636	680	704
1977	744	700	756	784
1978	828	800	840	880
1979	936	860	944	972

(a) Draw a graph of $x(t)$ against t and comment upon whether or not the data appears stationary.
(b) Calculate a single, double and triple smoothing average forecast and superimpose both forecasts onto your graph.
(c) Calculate the forecast for quarter 1, 1980. Compare this result with your results from Chapters 7 and 8.

recapitulate some of the advantages of the method of exponential smoothing, can say that it is an ideal method due to its simplicity, acceptable accuracy,

efficiency and adaptability. On top of everything it is cheap to develop a
very cheap to run. However, we have to stress that it is not capable of handli
any turning points in the pattern of data, its application is restricted to mc
or less short to medium term horizons, it can be too sensitive to random
irregular components and the choice of the constant is very arbitrary.

Exercises

9.1   The figures in Table 9.2 are the numbers of driving tests conducted in t
United Kingdom (in 100 000s) for the years 1974–1991.

Table 9.2

Time	Series	Time	Series
1	3169	10	2502
2	3682	11	5006
3	2655	12	6885
4	4500	13	4196
5	3682	14	2728
6	3568	15	5262
7	5045	16	3719
8	4733	17	5707
9	5164	18	4580

(a) Plot the graph of the number of driving tests against time.
(b) Can the variation in driving tests over time be described as stationary?
(c) Use double exponential smoothing ($\alpha = 0.1$) to provide a forecast f
the number of driving tests for 1992.

9.2   In order to control production a forecast is made at the end of each we
for the following week's sales. The data in Table 9.3 represents the week
sales of an item over the last 20 weeks.

Table 9.3

Week	Sales	Week	Sales
1	177	11	263
2	182	12	236
3	123	13	208
4	216	14	269
5	212	15	298
6	240	16	300
7	203	17	278
8	204	18	285
9	220	19	277
10	180	20	298

In the past, forecasts have been based on a simple moving average taken over just two weeks, even though there are severe weekly fluctuations in sales. It has been proposed that forecasting accuracy could be improved by using some form of exponential smoothing.

(a) Plot a graph of sales against time.
(b) Can the variation in sales over time be described as stationary or non-stationary?
(c) Describe whether single, double or triple exponential smoothing is appropriate to provide a forecast for week 21.
(d) Provide a suitable forecast for week 21 (suitable starting value $\alpha = 0.1$).

.3 Consider the rainfall data in Table 9.4, collected by a team of engineers over a period of 30 weeks.

Table 9.4

Time	Series	Time	Series
1	10.07	16	8.03
2	9.85	17	8.79
3	8.89	18	9.60
4	8.50	19	10.30
5	6.70	20	10.70
6	7.40	21	15.78
7	6.50	22	18.00
8	8.40	23	23.00
9	8.30	24	27.00
10	7.40	25	35.67
11	6.30	26	48.00
12	5.95	27	52.79
13	6.67	28	65.04
14	6.89	29	73.02
15	7.05	30	84.00

(a) Plot the rainfall level (mm) against time.
(b) Can the variation in rainfall be described as stationary or non-stationary?
(c) Determine whether single, double or triple exponential smoothing is appropriate to provide a forecast of the rainfall.
(d) Provide a rainfall forecast for week 31.

10
Winters' seasonal forecasting

So far we have dealt with several problems and possible situations that we ca[n] expect to encounter when handling time series. Every problem we hav[e] mentioned has its own way of being resolved. We have found methods f[o] dealing with stationary and non-stationary series, methods to give more weigh[t] to more recent data, methods of handling dynamic series, and ways of handlin[g] seasonality, etc. Each time we found a solution to something, the metho[d] introduced had some shortfalls so we had to look for another metho[d] Unfortunately, this is the nature of forecasting in business. The method we ar[e] going to describe now is equally incapable of handling every situation and ca[n] therefore only be viewed as a platform for jumping one step higher to a mo[re] superior method.

Imagine a situation where we have a dynamic non-stationary series, reasonabl[y] long and, at the same time, pulsating in some seasonal pattern. We want t[o] integrate several properties from the methods we have already mentioned, an[d] we want to have a new method that will be relatively simple to use. In fact, th[is] will mean mixing some properties from the classical decomposition method, suc[h] as indexes for handling seasonality, together with a smoothing constant tha[t] would be capable of handling a dynamic pattern of the time series. It seems tha[t] we have a solution, but only with several smoothing constants! The solution [is] called the *Winters' method*.

Let us use an example and work our way through it. We shall assume that w[e] have the series as shown in Figs 10.1 and 10.2 and that we can approximate [a] linear trend to it. We can see that our series is showing a stable growth wit[h] some fluctuations, which, in fact, look very regular. Using a trick from th[e] classical decomposition, where we calculated the trend and divided the origin[al] series with the trend values, we can get a confirmation for our observation tha[t] the fluctuations are regular. Indeed, if we do this and present the values [as] indices fluctuating around the value of 1, the graph appears as shown in Fig. 10.3

At the beginning of the series, the actual values obviously deviated from th[e]

PERIOD	SERIES	TREND	INDEX	a	b	I'	FORECAST
A	B	C	D	E	F	G	H
1	12	7	1.81			1.07	
2	13	10	1.30			1.03	
3	14	13	1.05			1.02	
4	7	17	0.42			0.92	
5	22	20	1.10	20.00	3.30	1.08	
6	24	23	1.03	23.30	3.30	1.03	24.00
7	27	27	1.01	26.59	3.30	1.02	27.08
8	24	30	0.80	29.51	3.26	0.89	27.50
9	35	33	1.05	32.74	3.26	1.08	35.36
10	37	37	1.01	35.99	3.26	1.03	37.08
11	41	40	1.02	39.35	3.27	1.02	39.92
12	40	43	0.92	42.86	3.29	0.90	37.85
13	50	47	1.07	46.19	3.30	1.08	49.66
14	52	50	1.04	49.58	3.31	1.04	50.94
15	52	53	0.97	52.68	3.28	1.01	54.19
16	52	57	0.92	56.13	3.30	0.91	50.45
17	61	60	1.02	59.15	3.27	1.06	64.07
18	65	63	1.02	62.46	3.28	1.04	64.62
19	69	67	1.03	65.97	3.30	1.02	66.62
20	71	70	1.01	70.15	3.39	0.94	62.97
21		73					78.25
22		77					79.77
23		80					82.18
24		83					78.68
25		87					92.67
26		90					93.82
27		93					96.05

a = 3.30
b = 3.34

0.1	0.1	0.3
Alpha	Gamma	Beta

Figure 10.1 Forecast by Winters' method

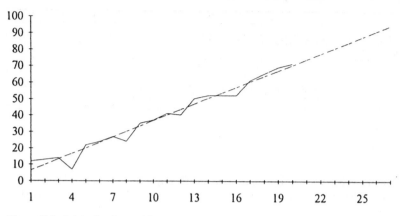

Figure 10.2 Original series and linear trend

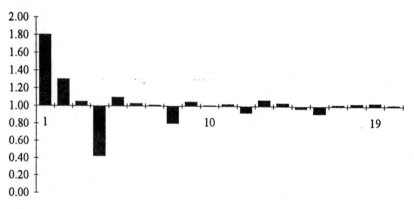

Figure 10.3 Indices

trend more significantly, and our indices are, therefore, showing larger deviation
the further we go into the past. In a way this shows us that the trend line fits th
more recent happenings in our time series well, which could be quite relevant fo
forecasting. The purpose of this analysis is to show that the fluctuations ar
regular, so let us reconsider this.

By analysing the graph in Fig. 10.3 we can easily see that observations 4,
12 and 16 are negative, and that, therefore, they deviate in the minus directio
from the trend line. Observation 20 is somewhat positive, but is lower than th
other three in the last sub-period of four observations, so we can quite confidentl
draw a conclusion that an average seasonal period repeats itself every fou
observations. If this is the case, then we should list all the comparabl
observations in the corresponding stage of the season, and find an average on
for this seasonal moment (Fig. 10.4). A typical seasonal period will consist c
four seasonal moments, which may correspond to quarters. As we have alread

	A	B	C	D	E	F	G
1							
2	SEASONAL	INTERVAL 1	INTERVAL 2	INTERVAL 3	INTERVAL 4	INTERVAL 5	AVERAGE
3	MOMENT						
4	1	1.81	1.10	1.05	1.07	1.01	1.07
5	2	1.30	1.03	1.01	1.04	1.02	1.03
6	3	1.05	1.01	1.02	0.97	1.03	1.02
7	4	0.42	0.80	0.92	0.92	1.01	0.92

Figure 10.4 Seasonal indices

mentioned, a seasonal component can be of any length, although in the majority of cases it corresponds with either number 12 (number of months) or 4 (number of quarters in the year).

Now, we have said that the beginning of the series is not so well fitted to our trend line and as a consequence the initial index values are much bigger than the ones occurring later on. If we attempt to find typical seasonal indices by just adding all the corresponding ones and then calculating the mean for each seasonal moment, the initially high values of our indices will artifically increase these typical indices. As we have mentioned once before, a solution to this problem is to find the median value.

We have stated that in our series we have five intervals which consist of similar seasonal moments. Each interval has four moments, and the middle value (median) for the first seasonal moment is equal to the one from period 4. The second seasonal moment is equivalent to period 2, the third to period 3 and the fourth to either period 3 or 4, because they are both the same (0.92). So, our typical seasonal indices are as shown in Fig. 10.5. We are going to use these typical seasonal indices to calculate some other parameters that are used in the Winters' method.

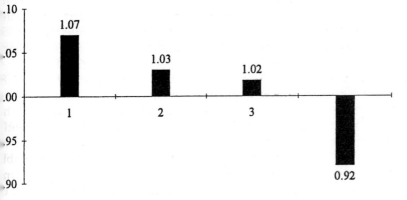

Figure 10.5 Typical seasonal indices

Because the Winters' method is linear it uses, as any other linear method, jus two parameters to calculate the estimates. These are parameter *a*, or an intercep and a parameter *b*, or the slope. Seasonal variations are estimated by usin another factor, *S*, or the seasonal factor. The formula looks like this:

$$F_{t+m} = (a_t + b_t m)S^*$$

The values of the seasonal factor are the last ones calculated for the seasona interval, i.e. the optimal values, and we are consequently using notation S^*.

As we can see, this is an ordinary linear equation in which we hav incorporated a seasonal factor to enable us to achieve the fluctuations. Howeve index letters attached to parameters a_t and b_t tell us that this is not an ordinar straight line equation, as the values of the parameters are changing with ever observation. In fact, in order to enable the changes to take place while the tim series is changing, we have to have a smoothing constant to ensure that prope weight is given to different parts of the time series. In this respect, Winters ha introduced not just one, but three smoothing constants. One for the paramete estimating intercept, one for the parameter estimating the slope and one fo the seasonal factor. Because the seasonality component has not been treate as such in previously described methods, let us just say that the seasonalit could be marked with the letter *L*, which in our case, is equal to four.

So, the parameters are calculated as:

$$a_t = \alpha \frac{x_t}{S_{t-L}} + (1 - \alpha)(a_{t-1} + b_{t-1})$$

$$b_t = \gamma(a_t - a_{t-1}) + (1 - \gamma)b_{t-1}$$

$$S_t = \beta \frac{x_t}{a_t} + (1 - \beta)S_{t-L}$$

Before we explain any of these formulas we have to understand the meanin of the seasonal factor S_t. When we described earlier the way that we have t extract typical seasonal indices for each moment within a seasonal interval, w basically extracted an optimal estimate of all typical seasonal indices. Th formula for S_t is telling us that every current value is calculated on the basis of th corresponding previous value of the seasonal index, shifted for *L* periods in th past and corrected for the proportion of the new observation x_t, which i decreased or increased by the value of the current intercept a_t. In fact, if th intercept is larger than the actual observation, then an overall result is less tha one, and the previous seasonal factor is relatively reduced.

The intercept a_t depends also on the current observation, seasonal facto shifted *L* periods, its previous values and, at the same time, the previous value of the slope. This parameter is actually deseasonalizing the model so that w can apply an appropriate seasonal factor for ex-post forecasting.

The slope b_t smooths the model, eliminating any irregularities, and thu enabling it to grow at the correct rate.

In fact, it all sounds rather complicated, while the actual mechanics are relatively simple. We are really only using the same formula for calculating the ex-post forecast as well as for calculating the real forecast, although with somewhat different variables. For calculating the ex-post forecasts, m is always equal to one and the values of the parameters are changing. Once we have reached the end of the series, and are ready to make a real forecast, the values of parameters a_t and b_t are going to freeze, but we are going to add (in fact, multiply with) the appropriate optimal value of the typical seasonal index, as well as the appropriate m (which is equal to the number of periods ahead we are forecasting).

So, if everything is all right our forecast could look something like that shown in Fig. 10.6. Before we go through a detailed workshop procedure, in order to understand the mechanics better, we shall give a practical example of some of the parameters.

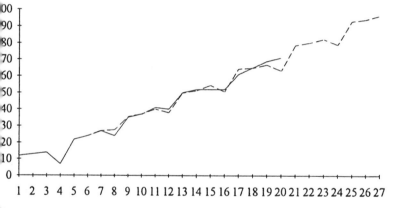

Figure 10.6 Winters' method forecast

As the analysis of indices shows that the seasonal interval consists of four moments, the first possible period in the time series for which we can calculate the parameters and ex-post forecast is period 5. For initial values of typical indices we can use median values calculated previously. As we have calculated the trend earlier, we have the values of linear trend parameters a and b. We can use these values as initial values of parameters a and b in the Winters' method. In other words, $a_{20} = 3.30$ and $b_{20} = 3.34$. In fact, to speed up the convergence to an optimum solution, for the initial value of a_{20} we can use the current trend value for period 5, which is 20. The reason for this is a_{20}, which was calculated with origin at period 20, and we are now using it for period 5. It is obvious that the same parameter should have different values at these two origins, as our series is non-stationary, and it would take too much time (or the errors would be too great), if we started the estimate with unrealistic values.

So, if the current period is period 20, the parameters for this period are calculated as:

$$a_{20} = \alpha \frac{x_{20}}{S_{16}} + (1 - \alpha)(a_{19} + b_{19})$$

$$b_{20} = \gamma(a_{20} - a_{19}) + (1 - \gamma)b_{19}$$

$$S_{20} = \beta \frac{x_{20}}{a_{20}} + (1 - \beta)S_{16}$$

and some of the forecasts are:

$$Y_{21} = (a_{20} + b_{20} \times 1)S_{17}$$

$$Y_{22} = (a_{20} + b_{20} \times 2)S_{18}$$

$$Y_{24} = (a_{20} + b_{20} \times 4)S_{19}$$

$$Y_{25} = (a_{20} + b_{20} \times 5)S_{20}$$

Notice that, for the real forecasts, we are using the last set of typical indices and we are treating it as an optimal set.

Example 10.1   Winters' seasonal forecast

Consider the time series data in Table 10.1.

Table 10.1 Sales of Doogie Co. Ltd, 1976–1979 (tons)

Year	Quarter 1	Quarter 2	Quarter 3	Quarter 4
1976	672	636	680	704
1977	744	700	756	784
1978	828	800	840	880
1979	936	860	944	972

(a) Draw a graph of $x(t)$ against t and comment upon whether or not the data appears stationary.
(b) Use Winters' forecast method to provide a forecast fit to the above data and superimpose this forecast onto your graph.
(c) Calculate the forecast for quarter 1 of 1980 and compare this result with your results from Chapters 7, 8 and 9.

Basically, that is the Winters' method. It is very useful when dealing with seasonal, non-stationary and linear patterns; relatively easy to use, and simple to understand. Naturally, several smoothing constants do not make our lives particularly easy, but with a little bit of experimenting we can overcome this difficulty too. It is useful to put each constant in its cell underneath the column or which it is used, and declare in other formulas these three cells as the absolute ones. We can then change the values of each constant, and see how the graph and forecasting errors change accordingly. A cocktail of the three different values for each constant, which produces the smallest error and the most credible graph, is the best to use for a particular case.

As in previous chapters, we have found some good reasons to explore and introduce a new method, and, as before, we have eliminated some drawbacks of the methods previously discussed and have opened up some new possibilities. Yet the new method, as well as all those previously mentioned, has limited capabilities. Maybe it is time to introduce methods that start to show some signs of intelligence.

Exercises

10.1 Table 10.2 shows the number of cans (in 100 000s) of lager sold by a manufacturer in each quarter of three successive years.

Table 10.2

Year	Q1	Q2	Q3	Q4
1985	9.8	11.5	13.0	10.9
1986	11.0	12.1	12.9	11.9
1987	11.1	13.6	14.4	12.6

(a) Draw a graph of $x(t)$ against t and comment upon whether or not the data is stationary.

(b) Superimpose onto the above graph Winters' forecast fit.

(c) Use Winters' method to provide a forecast for the first quarter of 1988.

10.2 The figures in Table 10.3 relate to the sales of heating oil.

Table 10.3

Year	Q1	Q2	Q3	Q4
1	320	185	215	395
2	345	200	230	420
3	365	210	240	440

(a) Draw a graph of $x(t)$ against t and comment upon whether or not the data is stationary.

(b) Superimpose onto the above graph Winters' forecast fit.

(c) Use Winters' method to provide a forecast for the first quarter of year 4.

10.3   Table 10.4 gives the index of average earnings (GB) of insurance, banking and finance employees (base: 1976 = 100).

Table 10.4

Year	March	June	Sept	Dec
1979	205	234	324	245
1980	190	265	350	298
1981	320	350	540	442
1982	494	550	720	650
1983	720	875	923	870
1983	901	1013	1300	1056

(a) Draw a graph of $x(t)$ against t and superimpose onto the graph Winters' forecast fit.

(b) Provide a forecast for the four quarters of 1984.

11
Adaptive filtering

The following method represents not only a modification and improvement over the previously mentioned methods, but also a further development into a brand-new forecasting concept. The method has built-in principles of exponential smoothing, as well as the principles of various models from the stochastic theory (remember the AR, MA, ARMA and ARIMA models from Chapter 5). In fact, when the method was developed it was suitable mainly for autoregressive models, but later on many other properties were elaborated; it became very versatile and applicable to all types of time series. For the purposes of this chapter we will stick to the basics of the method. Due to the iterative procedure required, it is not possible to apply the method through a normal spreadsheet routine, so we have to give some additional explanations. It is possible to apply the method elegantly and in one run, but we would have to use macro programming. As this would be beyond the intended scope of this book, we are just going to elaborate the principles and practicalities for a two-weight model.

In previous chapters we have explained the meaning of the smoothing constant α. No matter what modifications were made to a basic exponential smoothing model (double or triple smoothing), it always required only one constant (i.e. weight). There are, of course some exceptions and we have already mentioned one of them, i.e. the Winters' method with three constants. However, the method we are going to elaborate now, the *adaptive filtering method*, also uses several weights, but of a different nature. It also requires one constant but a rather unique one.

In very simple terms, the adaptive filtering method starts with a small interval, or a sub-period of the series that we are forecasting, and assigns a weight to each value (data point) of this interval. This short interval is used to forecast the next data point in the series, which comes immediately after the interval, and any error that occurs is used to correct the forecast for the interval after that. The first value from the interval is then deleted, and the next one taken in order to forecast the following period. This is the same principle as in moving averages and exponential smoothing, but the difference is that once we have reached the en of the series, we start the whole procedure again with improved values of th weights, thereby improving the ex-post forecasts. Through iterations we ar seeking optimum weights which will provide a perfect ex-post forecast anc therefore, we can expect an optimum forecast ahead. This iterative procedure including some other elements that we shall mention, is a very useful techniqu as it enables us to use this method for all types of time series, including th ones that have significant turning points in their history.

The first trick is to define how long our interval is going to be and, therefor how many weights we are going to have. At the time the method was inventer it was not specified that the number of weights should correspond with th autocorrelation and partial autocorrelation functions, as is the case with th method today. Nevertheless, let us adopt the principle that intervals should nc contain more than three data points, and, therefore, not more than three weight (remember what was said about the level of differencing and a degree of model in ARIMA models, i.e. that it is not practical for the model order to be highe than (3,3,3)).

If the total number of data in the series is equal to N, then we can assign a initial value to every weight of:

$$w_i = \frac{1}{N}$$

This is not necessarily the best start, but is the easiest one. After initial weight have been defined we have to adjust them through iterations, and we can do th by using a constant, the learning constant k. This enables the model to improv on the basis of errors made and, as such, is a unique concept that we have no covered as yet. So, the adjustment of the weights is done by the formula:

$$w_i' = w_i + 2ke_{t+1}x_{t-i+1}$$

where:

$\quad w_i' = $ revised weight
$\quad w_i = $ old weight
$\quad k = $ learning constant
$\quad e_{t+1} = $ error in the period
$x_{t-i+1} = $ observation, i.e. data point
$\quad i = 1, 2, \ldots, p$ ($p = $ number of weights)
$\quad t = p + 1, p + 2, \ldots, N$ ($N = $ number of observations)

The learning constant enables the weights to be changed automatically as th time series changes its pattern. The value of this constant, as in the case of α i exponential smoothing, determines the speed at which the approximated serie ex-post forecasts, will fit the actual time series.

This is the first method we have so far discussed that is not only capable c handling all types of series, but also has the ability to generate the knowledge c ast inaccuracy and correct itself. These signs of primitive intelligence are chieved through the iterative procedure and the learning constant. The actual recasts are calculated as weighted sums of previous observations:

$$F_{t+1} = \sum_{i=1}^{N} w_i x_{t-i+1}$$

et us go through some of the technicalities. In order for the system to converge o an optimal solution, a learning constant has to be either equal or smaller than . So, if we have a dynamic series and $p = 2$, then the value of the learning onstant should be at maximum $k = 0.5$. According to some sources, the value f the learning constant should never be higher than 0.25 and, in fact, the ecommended value is 0.1. In any case, if one is using a computer for forecasting, pays off sometimes to experiment a bit with different values of k. If we are ealing with a seasonal series then $p = L$ ($L =$ seasonality period), and we can ow extract the value of k from this.

In some books one can even find that it is desirable to use a smaller learning onstant (otherwise the system is too 'absorbing' and overreacts to every change the pattern), but it is also necessary to transform the data. We have mentioned everal types of transformations, such as differencing, and one of the types used this context is *standardizing*. Very often it means deducting each value of the eries from the mean, and thus creating a new standardized series. If we do this, he sources say, we can achieve a more uniform convergence of results, regardless the fluctuations in the pattern.

The convergence mentioned above is not only related to how closely we are oing to get to the optimal solution of the model, but also to how quickly we re going to achieve this. Our aim is that the weights stop changing, which means he forecasting model is very close to the actual series, and that we achieve this the smallest possible number of iterations. We mentioned that the smaller the earning constant, the longer it takes for the model to adjust. So, it is to be xpected that, in this case, it will take more iterations before we reach an optimal olution. Sometimes the number of iterations could be so large or, indeed, it could e that the model does not converge to optimum, that it is inconvenient to wait hile the computer is calculating it. It is therefore advisable to monitor the rate t which the mean square error is decreasing. Once the reduction becomes too ow, the model has reached its convergence level, and any improvement would e insignificant in comparison with the time used to achieve it. At this moment e have to stop and say that it is not 'economical' to iterate the model further. Jsually the loop has two criteria, and they are either the number of iterations rough which the model is going to run, or the rate of error reduction. Vhichever value is reached first, the calculation is stopped and the model exits e loop.

Needless to say, if the number of weights is correctly chosen, and their initial alues are close to their optimum values, then we are significantly shortening the rocedure of optimization. Autocorrelation analysis can give us quite useful

answers as to how to determine the optimal number of weights. A general rul
without going into details, is that the number of weights should correspond t
the time lag of the largest positive autocorrelation after a time lag three. Th
reason for choosing coefficients after time lag three is the autocorrelatio
function which usually has the first two coefficients much higher than the other
and choosing the first two could be misleading. However, this is a very genera
rule, as many time series can be well simulated with only one or two weights, so
competent decision regarding the number of weights used can be made only o
the basis of proper autocorrelation analysis.

As far as the initial values of weights are concerned, there is also a very accurat
way of starting them through autocorrelation analysis. We can use the values
these autocorrelation coefficients to calculate the inverse square matrix, which
developed from the array of these coefficients. This is known as *Yule–Walke
equations* and the result is very near optimal values of initial weights.

Let us bring some of the material discussed in the paragraphs above closer t
practical understanding. Say that we have a series which is 20 periods long, an
that we have decided to use a model with two weights only. If this is the cas
the learning constant will be $k = \frac{1}{2} = 0.5$. According to the previously mentione
'easy start', we can assign to both weights an initial value of:

$$w_{1,2} = \frac{1}{20} = 0.05$$

The forecast for period 3 on this basis is:

$$F_3 = w_1 x_2 + w_2 x_1$$

Error for this period is:

$$e_3 = x_3 - F_3$$

The first two adjusted (or optimized) weights are calculated as:

$$w'_1 = 0.05 + 2 \times 0.5 \times e_3 x_2$$
$$w'_2 = 0.05 + 2 \times 0.5 \times e_3 x_1$$

The forecast for period 4 is:

$$F_4 = w_1 x_3 + w_2 x_2$$

Error for this period is:

$$e_4 = x_4 - F_4$$

To repeat the whole procedure we have:

$$w'_1 = 0.05 + 2 \times 0.5 \times e_4 x_3$$
$$w'_2 = 0.05 + 2 \times 0.5 \times e_4 x_2$$
$$F_5 = w_1 x_4 + w_2 x_3$$

$$e_5 = x_5 - F_5, \text{ etc.}$$

When we reach the end of all our iterations and find the optimal set of weights, the real forecast is conducted somewhat differently. For all the future periods we keep the same values of weights, but we change the values of actual observations, i.e. we have to make the assumption that our forecasts become actual values. The forecast for some future periods is calculated as:

$$F_{21} = w_1 x_{20} + w_2 x_{19}$$

$$F_{22} = w_1 F_{21} + w_2 x_{20}$$

$$F_{23} = w_1 F_{22} + w_2 F_{21}$$

$$F_{24} = w_1 F_{23} + w_2 F_{22}, \text{ etc.}$$

Let us learn some practical 'tricks'. First of all the spreadsheet (Fig. 11.1) contains the value of $k = 0.1$, as for this case this will speed up the result convergence. Secondly, in the Excel spreadsheet pop-down menu called 'Options' there is an option called 'Calculations...'. Under this option we have a selection box in which we should mark 'X' at 'Calculation Automatic'. This enables automatic iterations for calculating circular references in the spreadsheet. Underneath this one, at the 'Iteration' line, we should enter a maximum number of iterations to one.

After we have changed the number of iterations to one we can start entering initial values of weights, and we should start with $w_1 = 0.05$ and $w_2 = 0.05$. We assign these values into a cell 2 of the two columns into which we are going to calculate the weights values. After that, we use a normal copy routine to copy the third cell which contains, in one column the formula $w'_1 = w_1 + 2ke_3x_2$, and in another column $w'_2 = w_2 + 2ke_3x_1$.

In fact, in order to speed up the computation we can use another trick, which is to standardize the values of errors and actual observations. Our formula for weights is, therefore, slightly modified and looks like this:

$$w'_i = w_i + 2k \frac{e_{t+1}}{h_{t+1}} \frac{x_{t-i+1}}{h_{t+1}}$$

where h is:

$$h_t = \sqrt{\sum_{i=1}^{p} x_{t-i}^2}$$

we started with, say 0.05 for both values of the weights, some of the values of adjusted weights during the first iteration will be as in Table 11.1

So, after the first iteration the optimal values become $w_1 = 0.54$ and $w_2 = 0.66$. Now we have to change a number of iterations in the spreadsheet program.

In the iteration line in the 'Options' pop-down menu of the spreadsheet we should put a maximum number of 'Iterations' of 100 as well as 'Maximum

	A	B	C	D	E	F	G	H	I
2	PERIOD	SERIES	FORECAST	FORECAST ERROR	WEIGHT 1	WEIGHT 2	SQUARED SERIES	SUMMED SQUARE VALUES	SQUARE ROOTS
3			k = 0.1		w = 0.05	w = 0.05	B^2		ROOTS SQRT H
4	A	B	C	D	E	F	G	H	I
6	1	12					144		
7	2	13					169		
8	3	14	15.27	-1.27	0.23	1.02	196	313	18
9	4	7	16.25	-9.25	0.22	1.01	49	365	19
10	5	22	14.28	7.72	0.15	0.94	484	245	16
11	6	15	11.53	3.47	0.20	1.03	225	533	23
12	7	18	26.28	-8.28	0.22	1.04	324	709	27
13	8	28	18.26	9.74	0.19	0.99	784	549	23
14	9	16	25.87	-9.87	0.25	1.04	256	1108	33
15	10	28	31.57	-3.57	0.20	1.01	784	1040	32
16	11	20	21.26	-1.26	0.19	0.99	400	1040	32
17	12	48	31.38	16.62	0.19	0.99	2304	1184	34
18	13	28	32.94	-4.94	0.24	1.07	784	2704	52
19	14	40	57.13	-17.13	0.22	1.06	1600	3088	56
20	15	55	35.90	19.10	0.19	1.01	3025	2384	49
21	16	38	56.19	-18.19	0.26	1.05	1444	4625	68
22	17	60	64.21	-4.21	0.21	1.02	3600	4469	67
23	18	75	50.76	24.24	0.21	1.01	5625	5044	71
24	19	65	82.58	-17.58	0.26	1.05	4225	9225	96
25	20	90	92.05	-2.05	0.24	1.02	810)	9850	99
26	21		87.27		0.23	1.02			
27	22		112.13						
28	23		115.15						
29	24		141.20						
30	25		150.35						
31	26		179.05						
32	27		195.07						
33	28		228.08						

Table 11.1

Period	Weight w_1	Weight w_2
1	0.16	0.15
2	0.18	0.17
3	0.28	0.38
4	0.33	0.39
.		
.		
19	0.53	0.65
20	0.54	0.66

'hange' to 0.001. This second criterion of 0.001 ensures that iterations may be :opped before 100 circles, if all cells in the spreadsheet circular reference change y less than the amount in the 'Maximum Change' box. This is a useful tool, reventing divergence of calculations, and shortening iterations if convergence reached sooner.

After we have changed the number of iterations to 100, we go back to the :cond cell for both weights and, instead of having an absolute value of 0.05 s we entered initially in both cells, we now enter that each cell is equal to the st cell in the column. By doing this a computer will start iterating 100 mes on every occasion, using as a starting value the last and, therefore, an ptimal value of weights from the previous iteration. If we do this we are going ⊃ reach the optimal values of $w_1 = 0.23$ and $w_2 = 1.02$. This is the final and ptimal set of weights, with which we are starting a real forecast. The forecasting done as explained before, which means that our forecasts are going to be ʾeated as actual observations in the forecasting equation.

If we have done everything correctly, our graph should appear as shown in ig. 11.2. Notice that our original series has the rather dynamic shape of a ırabola and that our forecast, at least visually, simulates this pattern quite ıccessfully. This proves the point made at the beginning of this chapter that ıis method can treat various patterns, and that it is not limited to only stationary ıodels. This is achieved through an ability of primitive learning that is built ıto the method, via iterations.

Example 11.1   Adaptive filtering

Consider the time series data in Table 11.2.

(a) Draw a graph of $x(t)$ against t and comment upon whether or not the data appears stationary.

(b) Apply the adaptive filtering forecast method to provide a forecast fit to the above data and superimpose this forecast onto your graph.

(c) Calculate the forecast for quarter 1, 1980 and compare this result with your result from Chapters 7, 8, 9 and 10.

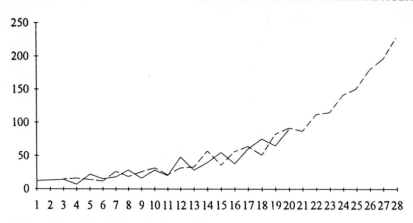

Figure 11.2 Adaptive filtering method forecast

Table 11.2 Sales of Doogie Co. Ltd, 1976–1979 (tons)

Year	Quarter 1	Quarter 2	Quarter 3	Quarter 4
1976	672	636	680	704
1977	744	700	756	784
1978	828	800	840	880
1979	936	860	944	972

So, as we can see, this is a relatively simple method, which is very economic and has a self-adapting mechanism, indicating traces of primitive numeric intelligence. Once the initial parameters are set, it does not require an intervention, as do some more complicated methods we have not yet discusse This makes it quite a superior method, as it eliminates the subjective inervention of forecasters or, at least, reduces them down to a minimum. However, it lack some statistical properties, in particular with regard to the confidence interva which makes it somewhat unquantifiable—at least from the mathematical poi of view. If we intend to eliminate this drawback, as we are going to with th method discussed next, we will encounter some other problems, which will l explained in Chapter 12.

Exercises

11.1 The figures in Table 11.3 are the numbers of driving tests conducted the United Kingdom (in 100 000s) for the years 1974–1991.

(a) Plot the graph of the number of driving tests against time.
(b) Apply the adaptive filtering method to provide a forecast for t number of driving tests for 1992.

Table 11.3

Time	Series	Time	Series
1	3169	10	2502
2	3682	11	5006
3	2655	12	6885
4	4500	13	4196
5	3682	14	2728
6	3568	15	5262
7	5045	16	3719
8	4733	17	5707
9	5164	18	4580

.2 In order to control production a forecast is made at the end of each week for the following weeks sales. The data in Table 11.4 represents the weekly sales of an item over the last 20 weeks.

Table 11.4

Week	Sales	Week	Sales
1	177	11	263
2	182	12	236
3	123	13	208
4	216	14	269
5	212	15	298
6	240	16	300
7	203	17	278
8	204	18	285
9	220	19	277
10	180	20	298

In the past forecasts have been based on a simple moving average taken over just two weeks, even though there are severe weekly fluctuations in sales. It has been proposed that forecasting accuracy could be improved by using some form of exponential smoothing.

(a) Plot a graph of sales against time.
(b) Apply the adaptive filtering method to provide a forecast for week 21.

.3 Consider the rainfall data in Table 11.5, collected by a team of engineers over a period of 30 weeks.

(a) Plot the rainfall level (mm) against time.
(b) Apply the adaptive filtering method to provide a rainfall forecast for the next four weeks.

Table 11.5

Time	Series	Time	Series
1	10.07	16	8.03
2	9.85	17	8.79
3	8.89	18	9.60
4	8.50	19	10.30
5	6.70	20	10.70
6	7.40	21	15.78
7	6.50	22	18.00
8	8.40	23	23.00
9	8.30	24	27.00
10	7.40	25	35.67
11	6.30	26	48.00
12	5.95	27	52.79
13	6.67	28	65.04
14	6.89	29	73.02
15	7.05	30	84.00

11.4 Table 11.6 gives an index of average earnings (GB) of insurance, bankin
and finance employees (base: 1976 = 100).

Table 11.6

Year	March	June	Sept	Dec
1979	205	234	324	245
1980	190	265	350	298
1981	320	350	540	442
1982	494	550	720	650
1983	720	875	923	870
1983	901	1013	1300	1056

(a) Draw a graph of $x(t)$ against t and superimpose onto the graph a
    adaptive filtering forecast fit.
(b) Provide forecast for the four quarters of 1984.

12
Box–Jenkins model fitting

ne method that is certainly worth attention is the Box–Jenkins method. It is
unique approach to forecasting in many ways, especially because it is based
very solid theoretical foundations. It is unfortunate that to many people it
not comprehensible and thus remains more or less a property of a 'forecasting
te'. The problems started with the original publication by Box and Jenkins
)76), which is one of the best of its kind. For a layman, unfortunately, it is
t too clear which aspects of the method are theoretical and which are of
actical value, so many have given up deciphering it. An additional difficulty
the complicated mathematical notation using Greek letters that is used
roughout the book to describe various models. Furthermore, when Box and
nkins mention various stochastic models, they constantly switch from a
eoretical one to a concrete model, changing at the same time, naturally, the
thematical notation, as one is representing the total population of models
ile the other is just a sample. One way or other the text can be quite confusing
your gaps in knowledge of statistics are significant.
A book that tried to make the whole matter much more practical was written
Nelson (1973). Indeed, it helped to a great degree, but still looked quite
sterious to anyone frightened by mathematical formulas. Admittedly, during
last several years quite a few good books simplifying this method have been
blished, but they still rely on the third party software packages. We are going
attempt to make it even more simple. Unfortunately, in attempting to make
mething more transparent, one inevitably risks over-simplification, and the
estion is where to stop to achieve the balance. We are going to try to make
method usable and understandable, even to those wary of maths, and we
deliberately going to sacrifice some of the variety and subtleties of the
thod for the sake of simplicity. Our main aim, besides understanding the
hnique, is going to be to present the method in a format suitable for
eadsheet applications, which is not always easy using just the simplest
eadsheet functions.

Let us start with clarifications of some of the points very briefly mentione in Chapter 5. If we have a phenomenon that is time dependent and whose futu events could be exactly calculated, such as a satellite travelling in orbit, the we say that the behaviour of this phenomenon could be described by mathematical model called *deterministic*. However, there are very few entire deterministic phenomena, and it is more appropriate to say that almost eve phenomenon has a certain probability of happening. If future events of phenomenon depend on some probability distribution, then we call it *stochast* Stochastic process, in its theoretical capacity, consists of infinite numbers observations. Each observation has its probability of happening, and our origin series is just one possible sample that happened from the infinite number possible realizations. If every observation has equal probability distribution happen, then it implies that stochastic process has to vary around one consta value, or as we should say, it has to stay in equilibrium about a constant mea level. We know this is not always true, as many series show upward or downwa trends and, in fact, have a moving mean level. We have already mentioned th difference between stationary and non-stationary series, and it is the mean lev that is differentiating them.

Stationary and non-stationary models could take several forms, and we ha already referred to AR, MA and ARMA models. Each of these models could b of a certain degree providing it was a stationary one. If we are dealing with non-stationary series, we have to make it stationary, which we did b differencing the series. So, for autoregressive models we say that they are order p or AR(p); for moving average models we say that they are of order or MA(q); and, if we have to difference them, then we say that they have ord d. If we have an integrated autoregressive moving average model, then it cou be described with notation ARIMA (p,d,q) where d is greater than 0, whic means we had to difference the model d times to make it stationary. In practi we are going to deal with a maximum degree of ARIMA(2,2,2) and even th very seldomly.

Autoregressive model AR(p) is telling us that the current value in our seri is a finite and linear aggregate of previous values in the series, and a rando element called *shock* (a_t). The formula for this model or order p is:

$$z_t = f_1 z_{t-1} + f_2 z_{t-2} + \ldots + f_p z_{t-p} + a_t$$

We can see that each observation is a result of the weighted sum of the previo observations in the series, weighted with parameters f, plus an error variable a.

Moving average model MA(q) shows that every observation depends on number of shocks a, which are weighted with q number of parameters t.

$$z_t = a_t - t_1 a_{t-1} - t_2 a_{t-2} - \ldots - t_q a_{t-q}$$

Mixed autoregressive-moving average model ARMA(p,q) is, as we can gue saying that every observation in the series is a mixture of the previou mentioned two terms, and could be formulated as:

$$z_t = f_1 z_{t-1} + \ldots + f_p z_{t-p} + a_t - t_1 a_{t-1} - \ldots - t_q a_{t-q}$$

If we have to difference the model d times to achieve the stationarity then it is called an autoregressive integrated moving average model ARIMA(p,d,q), and it looks exactly as ARMA, the only difference being that z is a differenced, not an original, observation.

It is all very clear, but we can quite rightly ask ourselves how we are going to know to which group of theoretical stochastic processes our empirical series belongs. The answer is relatively easy (although not necessarily the calculation). Every process, i.e. model, is described with certain properties, and if we can detect the same properties in our original series then our search has come to an end. Without going into too many details, there are two major functions that differentiate every model: the autocorrelation function and the partial autocorrelation function. To recapitulate, if we shift our original series k times and measure the correlation between these shifted series, we have, in fact, measured the correlation of the series and its previous values shifted k times. The series of these correlation coefficients is called the autocorrelation function. If, on the other hand, we try to measure the correlation of the series and its previous values shifted k times (but this time one at a time), by keeping the influence of every shifted series out of the equation, we get partial correlation coefficients. Again, the series of these coefficients is called the partial autocorrelation function.

So, let us look at some practicalities. The way to tell which theoretical model we should use in order to fit our series, is to calculate the autocorrelations and partial autocorrelations and present them in a graphical form. We have previously explained how to calculate autocorrelations, so it only remains to describe how to extract partial autocorrelation.

Partial autocorrelations are calculated for the same number of lags k as autocorrelations. For the first lag it is easy to calculate the first partial autocorrelation as it is equal to the first autocorrelation, i.e. for $k = 1$:

$$p_{1.1} = r_1$$

For a number of lags greater than one, i.e.: for $k = 2, 3, \ldots, L$:

$$p_{k.k} = \frac{r_k - \sum_{j=1}^{k-1} p_{k-1.j} r_{k-j}}{1 - \sum_{j=1}^{k-1} p_{k-1.j} r_j}$$

where for $j = 1, 2, \ldots, k - 1$:

$$p_{k.j} = p_{k-1.j} - p_{k.k} p_{k-1.k-j}$$

In other words, to calculate $p_{2.2}$, the second partial autocorrelation, we have to use the formula:

$$p_{2.2} = \frac{r_2 - p_{1.1}r_1}{1 - p_{1.1}r_1}$$

However, in order to calculate $p_{3.3}$, one has first to calculate $p_{2.1}$, which is done by using the above-mentioned formula:

$$p_{2.1} = p_{1.1} - p_{2.2}p_{1.1}$$

To summarize, to calculate partial autocorrelations, for example for periods 3 to 6, we use the following formulas:

$$p_{3.3} = \frac{r_3 - (p_{2.1}r_2 + p_{2.2}r_1)}{1 - (p_{2.1}r_1 + p_{2.2}r_2)}$$

$$p_{4.4} = \frac{r_4 - (p_{3.1}r_3 + p_{3.2}r_2 + p_{3.3}r_1)}{1 - (p_{3.1}r_1 + p_{3.2}r_2 + p_{3.3}r_3)}$$

$$p_{5.5} = \frac{r_5 - (p_{4.1}r_4 + p_{4.2}r_3 + p_{4.3}r_2 + p_{4.4}r_1)}{1 - (p_{4.1}r_1 + p_{4.2}r_2 + p_{4.3}r_3 + p_{4.4}r_4)}$$

$$p_{6.6} = \frac{r_6 - (p_{5.1}r_5 + p_{5.2}r_4 + p_{5.3}r_3 + p_{5.4}r_2 + p_{5.5}r_1)}{1 - (p_{5.1}r_1 + p_{5.2}r_2 + p_{5.3}r_3 + p_{5.4}r_4 + p_{5.5}r_5)}$$

In order to calculate these partial autocorrelations in between each of them, we have to make the following calculations:

$$p_{3.1} = p_{2.1} - p_{3.3}p_{2.2}$$

$$p_{3.2} = p_{2.2} - p_{3.3}p_{2.1}$$

$$p_{4.1} = p_{3.1} - p_{4.4}p_{3.3}$$

$$p_{4.2} = p_{3.2} - p_{4.4}p_{3.2}$$

$$p_{4.3} = p_{3.3} - p_{4.4}p_{3.1} \text{ etc.}$$

Or, for example, for $p_{6.6}$ the same calculations would include:

$$p_{6.1} = p_{5.1} - p_{6.6}p_{5.5}$$

$$p_{6.2} = p_{5.2} - p_{6.6}p_{5.4}$$

$$p_{6.3} = p_{5.3} - p_{6.6}p_{5.3}$$

$$p_{6.4} = p_{5.4} - p_{6.6}p_{5.2}$$

$$p_{6.5} = p_{5.5} - p_{6.6}p_{5.1}$$

To see how the functions look for some of the basic models: for AR(1), see Fig. 12.1(a)–(f); for AR(2), see Fig. 12.2(a)–(f); for MA(1), see Fig. 12.3(a)–(d); for MA(2), see Fig. 12.4(a)–(d); and for ARMA(1,1), see Fig. 12.5(a)–(j).

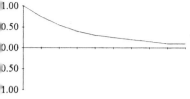

gure 12.1(a) AR(1) autocorrelations

Figure 12.1(b) AR(1) partial autocorrelations

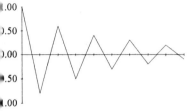

gure 12.1(c) AR(1) autocorrelations

Figure 12.1(d) AR(1) partial autocorrelations

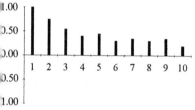

gure 12.1(e) AR(1) autocorrelations

Figure 12.1(f) AR(1) partial autocorrelations

We can see a variety of functions for every basic model which means that, ery often in practice, it will not be particularly easy to guess the model that ould fit our series the best. This is the reason why the Box–Jenkins method onsists of several steps, and model identification is just the first one. It is llowed by the model estimation step, as well as by diagnostic checking, before ctual forecasting is applied.

Table 12.1 summarizes the information that has been presented in the figures.

In Chapter 5, we calculated autocorrelations of our original series, as well s for the first and second differences. Let us now calculate partial autocorrelations, order to determine the order and model to fit to this series (see Figs 12.6, 2.7 and 12.8). In fact, the same series was used as an example in Chapters 6, and 9.

Before we make a graph, we should remember that, according to the stochastic eory, our series is just one possible realization out of an infinite number of ries. If, therefore, we treat it as a sample, we should calculate a standard error

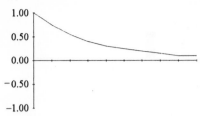

Figure 12.2(a) AR(2) autocorrelations

Figure 12.2(b) AR(2) partial autocorrelation

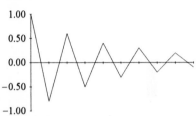

Figure 12.2(c) AR(2) autocorrelations

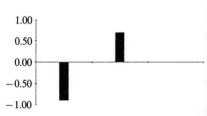

Figure 12.2(d) AR(2) partial autocorrelation

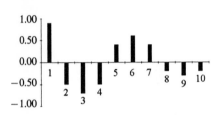

Figure 12.2(e) AR(2) autocorrelations

Figure 12.2(f) AR(2) partial autocorrelations

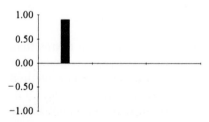

Figure 12.3(a) MA(1) autocorrelations

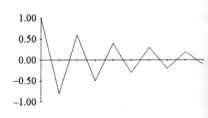

Figure 12.3(b) MA(1) partial autocorrelation

Figure 12.3(c) MA(1) autocorrelations

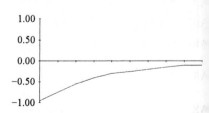

Figure 12.3(d) MA(1) partial autocorrelation

Figure 12.4(a) MA(2) autocorrelations

Figure 12.4(b) MA(2) partial autocorrelations

Figure 12.4(c) MA(2) autocorrelations

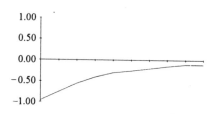

Figure 12.4(d) MA(2) partial autocorrelations

Table 12.1

Properties of functions	Autocorrelations	Partial autocorrelations
AR(p)	Infinite damped exponentials and/or damped sine wave (tails off)	Finite, cuts off
MA(q)	Finite, cuts off	Infinite dominated by damped exponentials and/or sine wave
ARMA(p,q)	Infinite damped exponentials and/or damped sine wave after first $q - p$ lags (tails off)	Infinite dominated by damped exponentials and/or sine wave after first $p - q$ lags
ARIMA($1,d,0$)	Decays exponentially	Only first one non-zero
ARIMA($0,d,1$)	Only first non-zero	Exponential decay
ARIMA($2,d,0$)	Mixture of exponentials or damped sine wave	Only first two non-zero
ARIMA($0,d,2$)	Only first two non-zero	Mixture of exponentials or damped sine wave
ARIMA($1,d,1$)	Decays exponentially from first lag	Decays exponentially from first lag

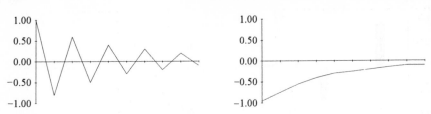

Figure 12.5(a) ARIMA(1,1) autocorrelations   **Figure 12.5(b)** ARIMA(1,1) partial autocorrelatio

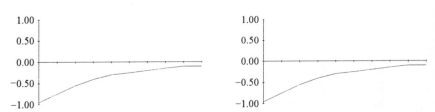

Figure 12.5(c) ARIMA(1,1) autocorrelations   **Figure 12.5(d)** ARIMA(1,1) partial autocorrelatio

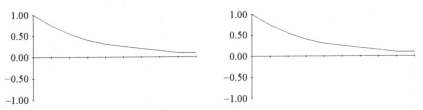

Figure 12.5(e) ARIMA(1,1) autocorrelations   **Figure 12.5(f)** ARIMA(1,1) partial autocorrelatio

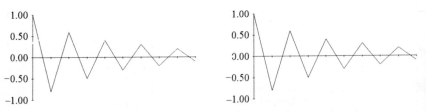

Figure 12.5(g) ARIMA(1,1) autocorrelations   **Figure 12.5(h)** ARIMA(1,1) partial autocorrelatio

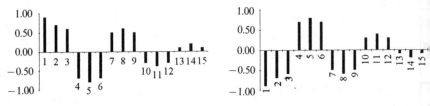

Figure 12.5(i) ARIMA(1,1) autocorrelations   **Figure 12.5(j)** ARIMA(1,1) partial autocorrelatio

Figure 12.6 table (original series):

LAG 'k'	AUTOCOR- RELATIONS	PARTIAL AUTOCORR.	k,1	k,2	k,3	k,4	k,5	k,6
A	B	C	D	E	F	G	H	I
1	0.40	0.40						
2	0.36	0.24	0.30					
3	0.21	0.01	0.30	0.24				
4	−0.02	−0.22	0.30	0.29	0.08			
5	0.15	0.20	0.35	0.28	0.02	−0.29		
6	0.08	0.08	0.33	0.30	0.01	−0.31	0.18	
7	−0.04	−0.19	0.35	0.33	−0.04	−0.30	0.24	0.14

Figure 12.6 Auto and partial autocorrelations: original series

Figure 12.7 table (first differences):

LAG 'k'	AUTOCOR- RELATIONS	PARTIAL AUTOCORR.	k,1	k,2	k,3	k,4	k,5	k,6
A	B	C	D	E	F	G	H	I
1	−0.49	−0.49						
2	0.02	−0.29	−0.63					
3	0.18	0.06	−0.62	−0.25				
4	−0.38	−0.34	−0.59	−0.34	−0.14			
5	0.17	−0.26	−0.68	−0.37	−0.23	−0.49		
6	0.13	0.04	−0.67	−0.35	−0.22	−0.48	−0.23	
7	−0.22	−0.09	−0.67	−0.37	−0.26	−0.50	−0.26	−0.02

Figure 12.7 Auto and partial autocorrelations: first differences of the series

LAG 'k'	AUTOCOR-RELATIONS	PARTIAL AUTOCORR.	k,1	k,2	k,3	k,4	k,5	k,6
A	B	C	D	E	F	G	H	I
1	−0.68	−0.68						
2	0.13	−0.61	−1.09					
3	0.23	−0.11	−1.15	−0.72				
4	−0.37	−0.24	−1.17	−0.89	−0.38			
5	0.22	−0.38	−1.27	−1.04	−0.72	−0.69		
6	0.08	−0.09	−1.30	−1.10	−0.79	−0.79	−0.50	
7	−0.26	−0.06	−1.31	−1.13	−0.83	−0.83	−0.56	−0.17

Figure 12.8 Auto and partial autocorrelations: second differences of the series

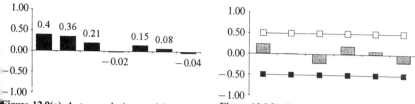

Figure 12.9(a) Autocorrelations: original series

Figure 12.9(b) Partial autocorrelations: original series

of estimate. Standard error of estimate for our autocorrelations is calculated as:

$$se(r_k) = \sqrt{\frac{2}{n}} = \sqrt{\frac{2}{7}} = \sqrt{0.28} = 0.53 \text{ for } k \geqslant p + 1$$

As it makes sense to calculate only $n/3$ autocorrelations and in our case we had a series of 20 observations, in the example above $n = 7$, which is approximately one third of 20 observations. The reason for calculating only $N/3$ autocorrelations is very simple. After approximately one third of the total number of autocorrelations that we could calculate, the autocorrelation function loses its theoretical properties and the results could be misleading. The reason for losing its theoretical properties is the relative shortness of actual series that represent just one practical sample, out of the total universe of the population of possible samples. Due to its imperfection and deviation from the theoretical infinite series, our actual series distorts and amplifies these deviations even further when autocorrelations are calculated for more than just one third of its original length. The whole phenomenon has its statistical interpretation but, for the sake of simplicity, we shall accept just this verbal explanation.

If we now make graphs of autocorrelations and partial autocorrelations for the original series, then they should appear as shown in Fig. 12.9(a) and (b). The same graphs for the first and second differences are as shown in Fig. 12.10(a) to (d).

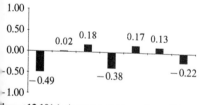

Figure 12.10(a) Autocorrelations: first differences

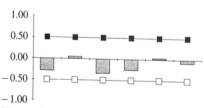

Figure 12.10(b) Partial autocorrelations: first differences

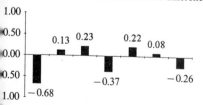

Figure 12.10(c) Autocorrelations: second differences

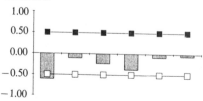

Figure 12.10(d) Partial autocorrelations: second differences

As we can see, there are several possible explanations. Judging by the graphs of the autocorrelations and the partial autocorrelations functions of the original series, we could say that it resembles ARMA(1,1). On the other hand, we know that it is a non-stationary series (confirmed by the original series autocorrelations graph which shows not a significant but a gradual drop in autocorrelations) and, according to the first differences graphs, we can say that ARIMA(1,1,1) is the most suitable.

This identification procedure leads us to only tentative models, and enables us to make only initial estimates for the parameters. The actual model estimation and diagnostic checking are further steps that we have to take when applying this method.

After we have decided which model to apply, we must then make initial estimates of parameters. The formulas to be used are as shown in Table 12.2.

Table 12.2

Model	Parameters	Region
AR(1)	$f_1 = r_1$	$-1 < f_1 < 1$
AR(2)	$f_1 = \dfrac{r_1(1 - r_2)}{1 - r_1^2}$	$f_2 + f_1 < 1$
	$f_2 = \dfrac{r_2 - r_1^2}{1 - r_1^2}$	$f_2 - f_1 < 1$ $-1 < f_2 < 1$
MA(1)	$r_1 = \dfrac{-t_1}{1 + t_1^2}$	$-1 < t_1 < 1$
	or $\quad r_1 t_1^2 + t_1 + r_1 = 0$	
	or $\quad t_1 = -\dfrac{-1 \pm \sqrt{1 - 4r_1^2}}{2r_1}$	
MA(2)	$r_1 = \dfrac{-t_1(1 - t_2)}{1 + t_1^2 + t_2^2}$	$t_2 + t_1 < 1$
	$r_2 = \dfrac{-t_2}{1 + t_1^2 + t_2^2}$	$t_2 - t_1 < 1$ $-1 < t_2 < 1$
ARMA(1,1)	$r_1 = \dfrac{(1 - f_1 t_1)(f_1 - t_1)}{1 + t_1^2 - 2f_1 t_1}$	$-1 < f_1 < 1$
	$r_2 = f_1 r_1$	$-1 < t_1 < 1$

We can see that, although it is easy to calculate the parameters of all AR as well as MA(1) models, the parameters of MA(2) and all ARMA models are much more difficult to calculate. However, there is a rather complicated general

outine for making initial estimates of all parameters for all models, which
is worth mentioning. In practice, when using computers and ready-made
ox–Jenkins forecasting packages (such as SPSS, for example), the package
applies even more complicated and mathematically more correct iterative
outines but, as we have from the beginning of this book advocated simplicity,
'e are going to use an abstract and much simplified routine.

Our simple procedure is as follows:

First we find $p + q + 1$ autocovariances of our series, the original if it is
stationary, or the appropriate differenced one if it is non-stationary. We
have elaborated autocorrelations, but let us just remind ourselves that
autocovariance is a measure that we had one stage before calculating
autocorrelations. If the autocorrelations formula was:

$$r_k = \frac{c_k}{c_0}$$

then autocovariance c_k is:

$$c_k = \frac{1}{N} \sum_{t=1}^{N-k} (z_t - z')(z_{t+k} - z')$$

where z is either original or transformed series observations and z' their mean
value.

Basically, we already have these values in our table (Fig. 12.11).
The next step is to find parameters f_1 and f_2 from the formula:

$$c_{q+p} = f_1 c_{q+p-1} + f_2 c_{q+p-2} + \ldots + f_p c_q$$

which results in:

$$c_2 = f_1 c_1$$

$$c_3 = f_1 c_2 + f_2 c_1$$

Or, alternatively, we can say that for a model of the first order:

$$f_1 = \frac{c_2}{c_1}$$

Or for a second order model:

$$f_2 = \frac{c_3 - f_1 c_2}{c_1}$$

We said that our series is an approximation of a theoretical stochastic model
with p parameters. This means that it could be developed into a temporary
model whose autocovariances are calculated as:

$$c'_j = \sum_{i=0}^{p} f_i^2 c_j + \sum_{i=1}^{p} (f_0 f_1 + f_0 f_{i+1} + \ldots + f_{p-i} f_p) d_j$$

PERIOD	SERIES	D=C-X'	E=D^2	F=D1*D2	G=D1*D3	H=D1*D4	I=D1*D5	J=D1*D6
0	1	0.85	0.72	-1.83	2.42	-0.13	-0.98	1.57
1	-2	-2.15	4.62	-6.13	0.32	2.47	-3.98	4.62
2	3	2.85	8.12	-0.43	-3.28	5.27	-6.13	8.12
3	0	-0.15	0.02	0.17	-0.28	0.32	-0.43	-0.13
4	-1	-1.15	1.32	-2.13	2.47	-3.28	-0.98	1.32
5	2	1.85	3.42	-3.98	5.27	1.57	-2.13	-3.98
6	-2	-2.15	4.62	-6.13	-1.83	2.47	4.62	-1.83
7	3	2.85	8.12	2.42	-3.28	-6.13	2.42	-6.13
8	1	0.85	0.72	-0.98	-1.83	0.72	-1.83	4.12
9	-1	-1.15	1.32	2.47	-0.98	2.47	-5.58	1.32
10	-2	-2.15	4.62	-1.83	4.62	-10.43	2.47	2.47
11	1	0.85	0.72	-1.83	4.12	-0.98	-0.98	2.42
12	-2	-2.15	4.62	-10.43	2.47	2.47	-6.13	6.77
13	5	4.85	23.52	-5.58	-5.58	13.82	-15.28	-5.58
14	-1	-1.15	1.32	1.32	-3.28	3.62	1.32	
15	-1	-1.15	1.32	-3.28	3.62	1.32		
16	3	2.85	8.12	-8.98	-3.28			
17	-3	-3.15	9.92	3.62				
18	-1	-1.15	1.32					
19								
20								
SUM	3		88.53	-43.50	1.73	15.61	-83.56	15.12
AVG	0.15							

Figure 12.11 Autocovariances of the first differences

	K	L	M	N
1				
2				
3	K=D1*D7	L=D1*D8	AUTOCORRE-	AUTOCOVAR-
4			LATIONS	IANCES
5	K	L	M	N
6				4.43
7	−1.83	2.42	−0.49	−2.17
8	−6.13	−1.83	0.02	0.09
9	2.42	−3.28	0.18	0.78
10	0.17	0.32	−0.38	−1.68
11	2.47	−0.98	0.17	0.76
12	1.57	−3.98	0.13	0.56
13	4.62	−10.43	−0.22	−0.97
14	13.82	−3.28		
15	−0.98	−0.98		
16	1.32	−3.28		
17	−6.13	8.77		
18	−2.68	−0.98		
19	2.47			
20				
21				
22				
23				
24				
25				
26				
27	11.14	19.48		
28				

Figure 12.11 *Continued*

where:

$$j = 0, 1, \ldots, q$$
$$d_j = c_{j+i} + c_{j-i}$$
$$f_0 = -1$$

which means that we can calculate:

$$c_0' = (1 + f_1^2)c_0 - 2f_1 c_1$$
$$c_1' = (1 + f_1^2)c_1 - f_1(c_2 + c_0)$$
$$c_2' = (1 + f_1^2)c_2 - f_1(c_3 + c_1), \text{ etc.}$$

4. Finally, on the basis of the previous autocovariance, we can calculate parameters t and residual variance σ_a^2. The general formula, with the convention that $t_0 = 0$, are:

$$\sigma_a^2 = \frac{c_0'}{1 + t_1^2 + \ldots + t_q^2}$$

$$t_j = -\left(\frac{c_j'}{\sigma_a^2} - t_1 t_{j+1} - t_2 t_{j+2} - \ldots - t_{q-j} t_q\right)$$

which effectively means that, for the first order process ($q = 1$), parameters σ_a^2 and t_1 are:

$$\sigma_a^2 = \frac{c_0'}{1 + t_1^2}$$

$$t_1 = -\left(\frac{c_1'}{\sigma_a^2}\right)$$

Or for the second order process:

$$\sigma_a^2 = \frac{c_0'}{1 + t_1^2 + t_2^2}$$

$$t_2 = -\left(\frac{c_2'}{\sigma_a^2}\right)$$

$$t_1 = -\left(\frac{c_1'}{\sigma_a^2} - t_1 t_2\right)$$

In both cases we find the above values through an iteration process, where we begin with parameters $t_1, t_2, \ldots, t_q$ equal to zero, find σ_a^2, then t_2, then t_1, then again σ_a^2 and the new t_1, t_2, etc., until the calculations do not show any further progress.

Basically, this is the end of the initial procedure of preliminary estimates of parameters. In our case we said that our series could be ARIMA(1,1,1), which makes life relatively easy. In Fig. 12.11 we have calculated autocovariances a mentioned earlier. You will notice that we have c_0, which is necessary for further calculations. We have then created another table (Fig. 12.12) to make things more presentable, and copied onto it autocovariances from the previous table. The next two columns calculate f_1 and the derived series autocovariances c', as described above. The following two columns again use the same 'trick' for iterations, described in Chapter 11. Basically, we assign an initial value of zero to t_1. This value is used to calculate σ_a^2, after which the new value for t_1 is calculated. After this first calculation σ_a^2 has a value of 4.26 and t_1 is 0.47. Now we change the tactics and activate the iterations option, which can be found in the Calculations sub-menu of the Options pop-down menu in the spreadsheet

	A	B	C	D	E	F
1		Autocovar-	Parameter	Derived series	Residual	Parameter
2		iances	f1	autocovar. c'	variance	t1
3	A	B	C	D	E	F
4	0	4.43		4.26		0
5	1	−2.17	−0.04	−2.00	2.87	0.70
6	2	0.09				
7	3	0.78				
8	4	−1.68				
9	5	0.76				
0	6	0.56				
1	7	−0.97				
2	Final				2.87	0.70

gure 12.12 Computation of initial estimates of parameters of ARIMA(1,1,1)

fter we have done this, we start using a new and constantly improving value
f t_1, as well as the new and constantly improving value of σ_a^2. In the end, the
ʳstem stops iterating as it converges to an optimal solution, and in our case
$_a^2 = 2.87$ and $t_1 = 0.70$. Just for the sake of an exercise to demonstrate the
rocedure, we have done the same calculations as if the series could be described
y the ARIMA(2,1,2) model (Fig. 12.13). However, we must emphasize that one
ɹould not get carried away with iterations and forget about the permissible
ᵉgions for both parameters f and t.

Now, if our series belongs to ARIMA(1,1,1) then our model could be described
s:

$$\nabla z_t + 0.04\nabla z_{t-1} = a_t - 0.70a_{t-1}$$

ʰhere ∇z_t is a differenced value.

In Chapter 13 we shall see how to use this formula for checking and forecasting.

xercises

2.1 Consider the following questions:

(a) The term *moving average* was employed previously in Chapter 8. How
   does the meaning of the term differ between these chapters?
(b) What is meant by a *stationary series* and how can a series with trend
   be transformed into a stationary series?
(c) Determine the family and order of the following models:
   (i) $x_t = 23 + 1.08e_{t-1} + e_t$
   (ii) $x_t = 15 + 1.08x_{t-1} + x_{t-2} + e_t$
   (iii) $x_t = 93 + 2.56x_{t-1} + 0.9x_{t-2} + 3.8e_{t-1} + e_t$

	A	B	C	D	E	F	G	H
1		Autocovar-iances	Parameters	Parameter	Derived series autocovar. c'	Residual variance	Parameter	Parameter
2			f1	f2			t2	t1
3	A	B	C	D	E	F	G	H
4	0	4.43			4.26		0	0
5	1	−2.17	−0.04	−0.36	−2.00	2.92	−0.01	0.68
6	2	0.09			0.03			
7	3	0.78						
8	4	−1.68						
9	5	0.76						
10	6	0.56						
11	7	−0.97						
12	Final					2.92	−0.01	0.68

Figure 12.13 Computation of initial estimates of parameters of ARIMA(2,1,2)

12.2   Consider the time series in Table 12.3.

Table 12.3

Time point	Series	Time point	Series
1	2.44	7	35.95
2	5.30	8	45.86
3	8.97	9	55.70
4	13.88	10	67.36
5	19.58	11	79.63
6	26.99	12	92.13

(a) Graph the time series and from the graph determine if the series exhibits trend.

(b) Determine the first four autocorrelation coefficients and produce a suitable graph. Does the autocorrelation graph suggest that the series exhibits trend?

(c) Determine the first four autocorrelation coefficients of the first and second differenced series, and add these coefficients to the above graph. What level of differencing is required to make the series stationary?

12.3   Consider the time series in Table 12.4.

Table 12.4

Time point	Series	Time point	Series
1	50.80	14	51.80
2	50.30	15	53.60
3	50.20	16	53.10
4	48.70	17	51.60
5	48.50	18	50.80
6	48.10	19	50.60
7	50.10	20	49.70
8	48.70	21	49.70
9	49.20	22	50.30
10	51.10	23	49.90
11	50.80	24	51.80
12	52.80	25	51.00
13	53.00		

(a) Produce a graph of the above time series, and comment on whether or not the series exhibits trend.

(b) Determine the first five autocorrelations corresponding to the above series.

(c) Having calculated the above autocorrelations determine from these the first five partial autocorrelations. Use a suitable graph to display both the partial and autocorrelations. What model would you suggest fitting?

12.4 Determine the coefficients of the AR(1) and AR(2) models when fitted to the time series considered in the previous problem. Which model would you suggest was more appropriate?

12.5 Consider the time series in Table 12.5.

Table 12.5

Time point	Series	Time point	Series
1	96.00	11	107.00
2	102.00	12	96.00
3	109.00	13	105.00
4	99.00	14	93.00
5	91.00	15	97.00
6	106.00	16	96.00
7	97.00	17	115.00
8	109.00	18	93.00
9	93.00	19	103.00
10	94.00	20	103.00

(a) Produce a suitable graph of the above data.
(b) Determine the first five autocorrelation coefficients, autocovariances and the first three derived autocovariances for the above data.
(c) Determine the coefficients of the MA(1) and MA(2) models when applied to this data.

13
Box–Jenkins forecasting

---

t the beginning of Chapter 12 we said that ARMA models could be described
'ith the formula:

$$z_t = f_1 z_{t-1} + \ldots + f_p z_{t-p} + a_t - t_1 a_{t-1} - \ldots - t_q a_{tq}$$

t the end of the very same chapter we described our ARIMA model as:

$$\nabla z_t + 0.04 \nabla z_t = a_t - 0.70 a_{t-1}$$

Ve have to explain this unexpected change of notation. A general formula
xpressing ARMA models is:

$$f(B)z_t = t(B)a_t$$

his is nothing but a little 'trick' of writing the same model in a more elegant
ay. In fact, B is called a *backward shift operator*, and so Bz_t is equal to z_{t-1}.
nother operator employed is a *backward difference operator*, ∇z_t, and math-
natically it is represented:

$$\nabla z_t = z_t - z_{t-1}$$

hich, again, could be related to the backward shift operator as:

$$\nabla z_t = z_t - z_{t-1} = (1 - B)z_t$$

It is worth repeating that ARIMA models have exactly the same formula as
RMA models, with one exception: they are represented by a differenced series
nd not the original one. The reason for this is that every non-stationary model
ould be made stationary by differencing the series d times, hence the word
itegrated' in ARIMA which means that by integrating, or summing, the
ationary process d times we can obtain a non-stationary process.

Before we proceed further, let us consider more formulas to make the matter
ven clearer. Using the notation from the beginning of this chapter we can say
iat the various models could be described with the formulas in Table 13.1.

Table 13.1

Model	Order	Formula
AR	$(p,0,0)$	$z_t = f_1 z_{t-1} + f_2 z_{t-2} + \ldots + f_p z_{t-p} + a_t$ or $(1 - f_1 B - f_2 B^2 - \ldots - f_p B^p) z_t = a_t$ or $f(B) z_t = a_t$
MA	$(0,0,q)$	$z_t = a_t - t_1 a_{t-1} - t_2 a_{t-2} - \ldots - t_q a_{t-q}$ or $z_t = (1 - t_1 B - t_2 B^2 - \ldots - t_q B^q) a_t$ or $z_t = t(B) a_t$
ARMA	$(p,0,q)$	$z_t = f_1 z_{t-1} + \ldots + f_p z_{t-p} + a_t - t_1 a_{t-1} - \ldots - t_q a_{t-q}$ or $(1 - f_1 B - \ldots - f_p B^p) z_t = (1 - t_1 B - \ldots - t_q B^q) a_t$ or $f(B) z_t = t(B) a_t$
ARIMA	(p,d,q)	$\nabla z_t = f_1 \nabla z_{t-1} + \ldots + f_p \nabla z_{t-p} - t_1 a_{t-1} - \ldots - t_q a_{t-q} + a$ or $f(B) \nabla^d z_t = t(B) a_t$

Table 13.2

Model	Order	Formula
ARIMA	$(0,1,1)$	$\nabla z_t = a_t - t_1 a_{t-1}$ or $\nabla z_t = (1 - t_1 B) a_t$
	$(0,2,2)$	$\nabla^2 z_t = a_t - t_1 a_{t-1} - t_2 a_{t-2}$ or $\nabla^2 z_t = (1 - t_1 B - t_2 B^2) a_t$
	$(1,1,1)$	$\nabla z_t - f_1 \nabla z_{t-1} = a_t - t_1 a_{t-1}$ $(1 - f_1 B) \nabla z_t = (1 - t_1 B) a_t$

In order to be practical let us show, as an example, just three specific model of the ARIMA process (Table 13.2).

Basically, if our series is an ARIMA $(p,1,0)$ model then it means that ever differenced value in our series is a sum of previously differenced values, correcte by some factor (parameters f). If our series is an ARIMA $(0,1,q)$ then this mean that any differenced value in our series is a result of some current shock value (errors in particular), minus the previous shock values corrected by some factor hence multiplying with t which are the parameters smaller than one. We shoul remember that the theory behind the exponential smoothing is very similar t that which we are elaborating in this chapter, although in a much simpler form However, exponentially weighted values from previous chapters are just on possible case out of a number of models covered by the Box–Jenkins theory.

Let us return to our example. According to the above, our ARIMA $(1,1,1$ model has an alternative formula:

$$(1 + 0.04B) \nabla z_t = (1 - 0.7B) a_t$$

ı this formula we have said that the sum between every consecutive two
ifferenced observations, of which one is reduced by the value of a factor
)arameter) f, has to be the same as the difference of the two consecutive random
1ocks, of which one is reduced by factor (parameter) t. By doing this we have
bviously linked our observations very closely to random shocks, which are
othing but forecasting errors. So let us elaborate the theory related to
)recasting and forecasting errors.

If we are standing in the period t, and the last observation in our series is
alled z_t, then we can make a forecast from this origin t for lead time l, and get
ny new forecasted value which we can call z_{t+l}. In the same manner as before,
/e can interpret this new forecasted value in either terms of z_t, i.e. observations,
r in terms of a_t, i.e. random shocks. Naturally, the third solution, where previous
bservations together with random shocks are involved, is also possible.

If the one step ahead forecast is $z_t^*(1)$, then the one step ahead forecast error is:

$$e_t(1) = z_{t+1} - z_t^*(1) = a_{t+1}$$

lternatively, we can also say that:

$$a_{t-1} = z_{t-1} - z_{t-2}^*(1)$$

Iere we can see the significance of random shocks. If forecasting errors are
othing but random shocks, then it means that they should not, under any
ircumstances, be correlated. If they are, they are not random and therefore
ur model does not adequately describe the series. However, this is true for
ne step ahead errors only, or, as we should say, the forecast errors at lead
me 1 must be uncorrelated. All the others, for longer lead times, will be
orrelated. To recapitulate, we can say that the forecast errors made from
ifferent origins will be correlated only for $l > 1$, i.e. lead times longer than 1.
.t the same time the forecast errors made from the same origin t at different
:ad times l will always be correlated.

If we now rewrite our forecast:

$$(1 + 0.04B)\nabla z_t = (1 - 0.7B)a_t$$

ıto:

$$\nabla z_t + 0.04\nabla z_{t-1} = a_t - 0.7a_{t-1}$$

nd then:

$$\nabla z_t = -0.04\nabla z_{t-1} - a_t - 0.7a_{t-1}$$

et us remember that we are dealing with a differenced series, and first differences
re defined as:

$$\nabla z_t = z_t - z_{t-1}$$

nd consequently:

$$\nabla z_{t-1} = z_{t-1} - z_{t-2}$$

Just a short digression. If we were, for example, dealing with the secon differences, then equally the second differences are defined as:

$$\nabla^2 z_t = \nabla z_t - \nabla z_{t-1}$$

Substituting the second differences in the above formula for the first difference we have

$$\nabla^2 z_t = z_t - z_{t-1} - z_{t-1} + z_{t-2} = z_t - 2z_{t-1} + z_{t-2}$$

This we might find useful when forecasting a series which has been difference twice, but let us now go back to our example.

Our series could be written, according to the above, as:

$$z_t - z_{t-1} = -0.04(z_{t-1} - z_{t-2}) + a_t - 0.7a_{t-1}$$

Or,

$$z_t = z_{t-1} - 0.04(z_{t-1} - z_{t-2}) + a_t - 0.7a_{t-1}$$

We can make a forecast for any lead time l:

$$z_{t+l} = z_t^*(l) = z_{t+l-1} - 0.04(z_{t+l-1} - z_{t+l-2}) + a_{t+l} - 0.7a_{t+l-1}$$

We have to remember that $a_t = z_t - z_{t-1}^*(1)$, which makes:

$$a_{20} = z_{20} - z_{19}^*(1)$$

$$a_{19} = z_{19} - z_{18}^*(1)$$

$$a_{18} = z_{18} - z_{17}^*(1)$$

We also have to say that all a_{t+j} for $j = 1, 2, \ldots$ which have not happened ye will be replaced by zeros in our forecasting formula.

If this is the case and if $t = 20$ and $l = 1, 2, 3$ then for z_{21}, z_{22}, z_{23} and z_2 we can use the notation $z_{20}^*(1), z_{20}^*(2), z_{20}^*(3), z_{20}^*(4)$ and make forecasts:

$$z_{20}^*(1) = z_{20} - 0.04(z_{20} - z_{19}) - 0.7a_{20}$$

$$z_{20}^*(2) = z_{20}^*(1) - 0.04[z_{20}^*(1) - z_{20}]$$

$$z_{20}^*(3) = z_{20}^*(2) - 0.04[z_{20}^*(2) - z_{20}^*(1)]$$

$$z_{20}^*(4) = z_{20}^*(3) - 0.04[z_{20}^*(3) - z_{20}^*(2)]$$

.

.

If $l = 3, 4, 5 \ldots$

$$z_t^*(l) = z_t^*(l-1) - 0.04[z_t^*(l-1) - z_t^*(l-2)]$$

There are some lessons we can learn from the above. We can start th

recasting process by assigning zero to all unknown a_t, as this is their expected
value. In case of having a model of either order p or q, the forecasts for up to
$(p$ or $q)$ will depend directly on actual z_t or a_t, while at longer lead time only
mplicitly. This is because it is true that $z_t^*(3)$ depends on $z_t^*(1)$ and $z_t^*(2)$, but,
on the other hand, $z_t^*(1)$ and $z_t^*(2)$ depend on z_t and/or a_t, which makes $z_t^*(3)$
mplicitly dependence on z_t and a_t.

It should be emphasized that this is just one way of forecasting, as the
ox–Jenkins method forecasts can be applied in three different ways. Nevertheless,
his one seems to be the less complicated from the notations point of view, so
e would be wise to use it.

We have managed thus far to follow through two difficult stages of applying
he Box–Jenkins method, which are model identification and forecasting. We
ave said that the method also includes a model estimation and diagnostic
hecking, so we must now look at some of the elements of these two steps. In
ct, this will enable us to make a back-forecast or, as we have previously called
, an ex-post forecast.

Before we start the practicalities of model estimation and ex-post forecasting,
e have to mention just one more convention. We used the backward shift
perator B, which was defined as $Bz_t = z_{t-1}$. There is also an inverse operation
nd, therefore, an inverse operator called forward shift operator F which is
efined as $Fz_t = z_{t+1}$. The relationship between these two operators is described
s $F = B^{-1}$. This basically means that every model could be described in terms
f either the backward shift or forward shift operator. It is interesting to know
hat forecasts will slightly differ, and so we must explain why. Before we start,
a order to avoid complicated ∇z_t notation, let us say that differences are
epresented by w_t, which, in case we have to difference the series once, means
hat $w_t = z_t - z_{t-1}$.

We mentioned earlier that a_t, which is a random shock element in a theoretical
nodel, could, in fact, be considered an error element in our practical model.
his was mentioned in the context of forward forecasting. If we apply backward
precasting, then we have to change the notation and call errors e_t. So, if we
ave an ARIMA $(1,d,1)$ process:

$$(1 - fB)w_t = (1 - tB)a_t$$

hen it could be expressed in terms of a_t as:

$$a_t = w_t - fw_{t-1} + ta_{t-1}$$

he same process could be written as the forward process:

$$(1 - fF)w_t = (1 - tF)e_t$$

r in terms of e_t as:

$$e_t = w_t - fw_{t+1} + te_{t+1}$$

ow do we use these formulas to produce ex-post forecasts? We should follow
he logic of the table in Fig. 13.1, where we have used our practical model to

	A	B	C	D	E	F	G	H	I	J
	PERIOD	TIME	SERIES	FIRST DIFFERENCES		f = −0.04			t = 0.7	
		t	z(t)	w(t)	.−0.04w(t−1)	0.04w(t+1)	0.7e(t+1)	e(t)	0.7a(t−1)	a(t)
	A	B	C	D	E	F	G	H	I	J
7		−3	11.18	0.00			0	0	0	0
8		−2	11.18	0.00	0.00	0.03	0	0	0	0
9		−1	11.14	0.03	0.00	−0.04	0	0	0	0
10	1	0	12	−0.86	0.00	0.08	0.82	0	0	−0.86
11	2	1	13	1.00	0.03	−0.12	0.20	1.17	−0.60	0.37
12	3	2	11	−2.00	−0.04	0.00	2.25	0.29	0.26	−1.70
13	4	3	14	3.00	0.08	0.04	0.30	3.22	−1.19	1.73
14	5	4	14	0.00	−0.12	−0.08	0.30	0.42	1.21	1.33
15	6	5	13	−1.00	0.00	0.08	1.43	0.43	0.93	−0.07
16	7	6	15	2.00	0.04	−0.12	0.09	2.05	−0.05	1.91
17	8	7	13	−2.00	−0.08	−0.04	2.04	0.12	1.34	−0.58
18	9	8	16	3.00	0.08	0.04	0.00	2.92	−0.41	2.51
19	10	9	17	1.00	−0.12	0.08	−1.13	−0.01	1.76	2.88
20	11	10	16	−1.00	−0.04	−0.04	−0.65	−1.61	2.02	1.06
21	12	11	14	−2.00	0.04	0.08	1.12	−0.92	0.74	−1.30
22	13	12	15	1.00	0.08	−0.04	0.67	1.59	−0.91	0.01
23	14	13	13	−2.00	−0.04	0.08	2.92	0.96	0.01	−1.95
24	15	14	18	5.00	0.08	−0.20	−0.75	4.17	−1.37	3.55
25	16	15	17	−1.00	−0.20	0.04	−0.27	−1.07	2.49	1.69
26	17	16	16	−1.00	0.04	0.04	0.66	−0.38	1.18	0.14
27	18	17	19	3.00	0.04	−0.12	−2.02	0.94	0.10	3.06
28	19	18	16	−3.00	−0.12	0.12	0	−2.88	2.14	−0.74
29	20	19	15	−1.00	0.12	0.04			−0.52	−1.64
30	21	20			0.04				−1.15	
31	22	21								

ιake all the calculations. As every column is named, the calculations have been ιade exactly in the order of appearance in the table; however, let us give a ιore detailed explanation.

Our series consists of 20 observations, but for the sake of calculations we ιve to rename the periods into time, t. It starts with the second observation hich means that, temporarily, we have to sacrifice the first observation in the ιries in order to calculate the first ex-post forecast. There are some other ιnventions and practical assumptions we have had to make too, but we shall ιplain them as we go along. Basically, we have done the following (make sure ι switch on the Iterations option in your Excel spreadsheet before any ιlculations are made):

Wherever in the table there is a zero as a single digit, this means that it was assigned to the cell and not calculated.

First, starting from $t = 0$ and moving downwards to $t = 19$, all w_t were calculated as $w_t = z_t - z_{t-1}$. We are going to explain later on what happened with w_t for $t < 0$. After that, all $-0.04w_{t-1}$ were calculated starting from $t = 2$ as well as all $-0.04w_{t+1}$ starting from $t = 0$.

The next step starts by moving backwards. For $t = 18$ we assign zero to $0.7e_{19}$, because we cannot calculate it and we are going to need it for our recursive calculations one step from the end of the series. As the title of the column suggests, in this column we are just multiplying e_t with parameter $f = 0.7$. The order of calculations is

for $t = 17$, $0.7 \times e_{18}$
for $t = 16$, $0.7 \times e_{17}$
.

.

.
for $t = 0$, $0.7 \times e_1$

We should not be concerned that we still do not have the following column, i.e. e_t, and that in our spreadsheet we are initially going to have zeros in the column '$0.7e_t$'. As soon as we fill in the next column the values will appear in this one too.

Unless we have done it initially, we now assign zeros to certain cells in the column e_t for $t < 0$ (remember, these are entered into the table as single digit zeros). The reason for assigning zeros to the unknown e_t is so that we make the smallest mistake. If the e_t are not known we can assign zeros to them, because they are distributed independently of w_t and, therefore, should be random. After that, we start recursive calculations again, using:

$$e_{18} = w_{18} + 0.04w_{19} + 0.7e_{19}$$

$$e_{17} = w_{17} + 0.04w_{18} + 0.7e_{18}$$

.

$$e_0 = w_0 + 0.04w_1 + 0.7e_1$$

We can see that the previous column is automatically filling in.

5. As zero was assigned to e_0, this means that from the above equation w_0 is equal to:

$$0 = w_0 + 0.04w_1 + 0.7e_1$$

$$w_0 = -0.04w_1 - 0.7e_1$$

We can now calculate w_t for $t < 0$. As expected the values die out after a while.

6. In the next column, where we have $0.7a_{t-1}$, we use the same 'trick' as with e_t, which means we assign zeros for all $0.7a_{t-1}$ if $t < 0$. The value of $0.7a$ will be used in the next column for calculating a_t.

7. The calculation of a_t is now easy and we start with:

$$a_0 = w_0 + 0.04w_{-1} + 0.7a_{-1}$$

$$a_1 = w_1 + 0.04w_0 + 0.7a_0$$

.

.

$$a_{18} = w_{18} + 0.04w_{17} + 0.7a_{17}$$

8. In our table, in the column for w_t, we even calculated the first differences for the non-existent values for $t < 0$. This means that we can, in fact, recursively calculate non-existent z_t using the derived formula where:

$$z_{t-1} = z_t - w_t$$

We can see these values become quickly constant, in fact, after the second recursive period.

If we now want to convert a_t into z_t, or to be more precise, into ex-post forecasts $z_t^*(l)$, then the result would be:

$$'z_2 = z_1^*(1) = z_1 - 0.04(z_1 - z_0) - 0.7a_1$$

.

.

$$'z_{20} = z_{19}^*(1) = z_{19} - 0.04(z_{19} - z_{18}) - 0.7a_{19}$$

We have, basically, come again to the forecasting point, as for the first period ahead we have:

$$'z_{21} = z_{20}^*(1) = z_{20} - 0.04(z_{20} - z_{19}) - 0.7a_{20}$$

√e may recall that this is the formula we used previously to describe the
•recasting process. However, there is still room for improvement as we should
e developing the forecast, not with initial values of parameters, but with the
nes called the *maximum likelihood estimates*. In any case, we are going to return
) this point.

Before we continue, let us use another example to make the procedure more
nderstandable. In fact, we are going to use the same series we used in Chapter
1. If you remember, this series was obviously a non-stationary one, with a
rong resemblance to a parabola-type function.

Let us start with determining the order of the process by calculating
utocorrelations and partial autocorrelations for the original series, as well as
)r the first and second differences. After these have been calculated, as shown
ι Figs 13.2(a) and (b), they should be presented in the usual graphic form (Fig.
3.3(a) to (f)).

PERIOD	AUTOCORRELATIONS		
	ORIGINAL	1ST DIFFER.	2ND DIFFER.
0	1.00	1.00	1.00
1	0.64	−0.63	−0.70
2	0.61	0.13	0.13
3	0.46	0.32	0.26
4	0.23	−0.34	−0.32
5	0.26	0.19	0.19
6	0.09	−0.05	−0.11
7	0.00	0.07	0.13

igure 13.2(a) Autocorrelations for original series, first and second differences

PERIOD	PART. AUTOCORRELATIONS		
	ORIGINAL	1ST DIFFER.	2ND DIFFER.
0	1.00	1.00	1.00
1	0.64	−0.63	−0.70
2	0.34	−0.43	−0.70
3	−0.03	0.34	−0.26
4	−0.31	0.30	−0.02
5	0.18	0.12	0.21
6	−0.05	−0.24	−0.10
7	−0.17	0.06	0.06

gure 13.2(b) Partial autocorrelations for original series, first and second differences

Analysing the graphs in Fig. 13.3, and comparing them to the theoretical
aphs in Chapter 12, we can see that this series is definitely a non-stationary
ιe, and that we would have to difference the values before we make it stationary.

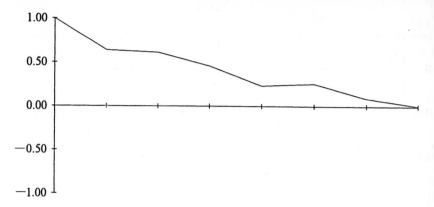

Figure 13.3(a) Original series autocorrelations

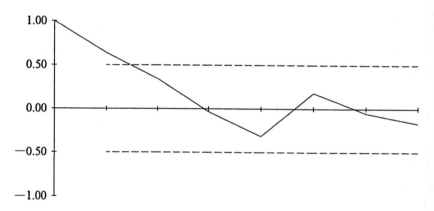

Figure 13.3(b) Original partial autocorrelations

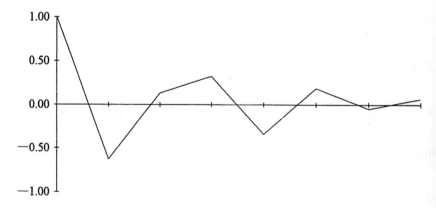

Figure 13.3(c) First differences autocorrelations

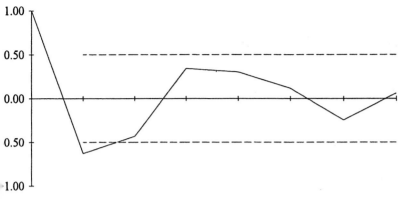

gure 13.3(d) First differences partial autocorrelations

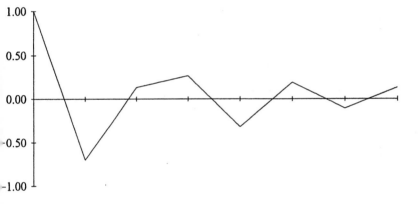

gure 13.3(e) Second differences autocorrelations

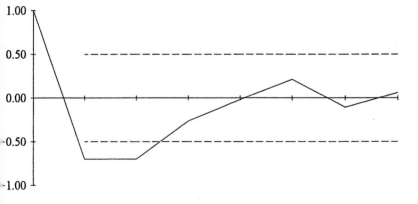

gure 13.3(f) Second differences partial autocorrelations

Several possible models could be explored, and for the sake of these exercises shall choose ARIMA (1,1,0), (1,1,1), (2,1,0) and (2,1,1).

Following exactly the same procedure for calculating the initial values parameters as described in Chapter 12, we establish that initial values of parameters can start with the following values:

f_1	f_2	t_1	t_2
-0.21	-0.56	-0.14	0.72

In order to demonstrate the consequences of different models, we have produ forecasts for several different models and the results can be graphica represented as in Figs 13.4 to 13.7. These forecasts were calculated on the ba of optimized parameters, and, of course, for each model different values optimized parameters were calculated.

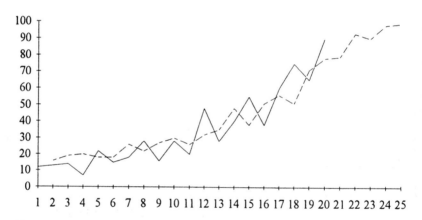

Figure 13.4 ARIMA (1,1,0) forecast

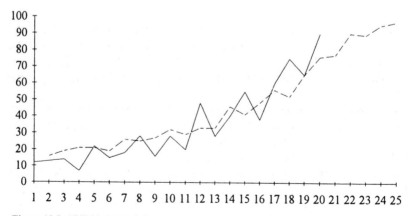

Figure 13.5 ARIMA (1,1,1) forecast

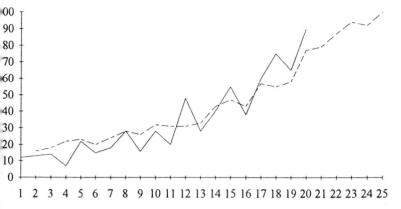

Figure 13.6 ARIMA (2,1,0) forecast

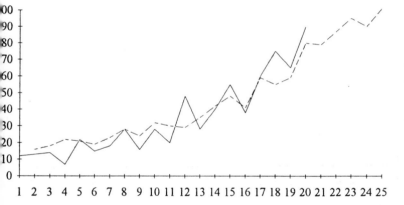

Figure 13.7 ARIMA (2,1,1) forecast

Just a visual inspection of these three graphs suggests that (1,1,0) fits the series reasonably well, but loses 'breath' closer to the end of the series. An almost identical conclusion applies to (1,1,1). Models (2,1,0) and (2,1,1) show similar tendencies, and in particular in the third quarter of the series they show quite good fits.

Perhaps it is too early to comment on some of the properties of every forecast, since this is going to be the subject of Chapter 15, but let us just make a brief comparison of each forecast. In terms of metric properties, the above forecasts exhibit the performance shown in Table 13.3.

Let us give a very brief explanation of every criterion. AIC is Akaike Information Criterion, the smaller the better. SBC is Schwartz Bayesian Criterion, the smaller the value the better the model describes the series. MSE Mean Square Error, again the smaller the better. RMS is Root Mean Square

Table 13.3

	ARIMA			
	(1,1,0)	(1,1,1)	(2,1,0)	(2,1,1)
AIC	147.7	147.4	144.7	146.0
SBC	149.6	150.2	147.5	149.8
MSE	122.3	113.3	96.8	98.9
RMS	11.0	10.6	9.8	9.9
MPE	−11.9	−20.3	−20.8	−19.3

Error or Standard Error, the smaller the better. MPE is Mean Percentage Erro
the smaller the better.

We are going to explain in later chapters the relevance of every statistic, b
let us concentrate here on a simple criterion: the smaller the value of eac
statistic, the better the model is suited to our series. No doubt we have som
mixed feelings. According to the first three criteria it seems that ARIMA (2,1,
fits better than the others. However, one of the recommendations of Box an
Jenkins is that, when in doubt, overfit the model. In other words, apply mo
parameters than seems necessary. As it is obvious that we have to differen
the values, and on the other hand it is unnecessary to difference it twice, let
apply the model with the maximum practical number of parameters, i.e. ARIM
(2,1,2). In reality we would not attempt to go through such laborious an
time-consuming experimenting.

Let us proceed with this ARIMA (2,1,2) model and see what the outcome
If ARIMA (2,1,2) has a shape as:

$$(1 - f_1B - f_2B^2)\nabla z_t = (1 - t_1B - t_2B^2)a_t$$

Then, using initial values of parameters our series could be described as:

$$(1 + 0.21B + 0.56B^2)\nabla z_t = (1 + 0.14B - 0.72B^2)a_t$$

which could be rewritten as:

$$\nabla z_t + 0.21\nabla z_{t-1} + 0.56\nabla z_{t-2} = a_t + 0.14a_{t-1} - 0.72a_{t-2}$$

We have said that:

$$\nabla z_t = z_t - z_{t-1}$$

and, therefore, we can rewrite our ARIMA (2,1,2) model as:

$$z_t - z_{t-1} + 0.21(z_{t-1} - z_{t-2}) + 0.56(z_{t-2} - z_{t-3}) = a_t + 0.14a_{t-1} - 0.72a_{t-2}$$

or in explicit form:

$$z_t = z_{t-1} - 0.21(z_{t-1} - z_{t-2}) - 0.56(z_{t-2} - z_{t-3}) + a_t + 0.14a_{t-1} - 0.72a_{t-2}$$

Figure 13.8 shows the calculations for this model, although with the final, not initial value of parameters.

In this case, forecasts for (2,1,2) are:

$$z_{20}^*(1) = z_{20} - 0.21(z_{19} - z_{18}) - 0.56(z_{18} - z_{17}) + 0.14a_{20} - 0.72_{t19}$$

$$z_{20}^*(2) = z_{20}^*(1) - 0.21(z_{20} - z_{19}) - 0.56(z_{19} - z_{18}) - 0.72_{t20}$$

$$z_{20}^*(3) = z_{20}^*(2) - 0.21(z_{20}^*(1) - z_{19}) - 0.56(z_{20} - z_{19})$$

$$z_{20}^*(4) = z_{20}^*(3) - 0.21(z_{20}^*(2) - z_{20}^*(1)) - 0.56(z_{20}^*(1) - z_{20})$$

$$z_{20}^*(5) = z_{20}^*(4) - 0.21(z_{20}^*(3) - z_{20}^*(2)) - 0.56(z_{20}^*(2) - z_{20}^*(1))$$

And for $l = 6, 7, 8 \ldots$

$$z_{20}^*(1) = z_{20}^*(l - 1) - 0.21(z_{20}^*(l - 2) - z_{20}^*(l - 3)) - 0.56(z_{20}^*(l - 3) - z_{20}^*(l - 4))$$

Before we actually produce the forecast, let us elaborate just one more point.

Firstly we have to explain why we have bothered with all these recursive calculations if, as stated at the beginning of this chapter, we could have calculated ex-post forecasts very easily from z_t by starting with zeros for all unknown a_t. Well, we could have, indeed, and then we would have a *conditional sum of squares* function, which is defined as:

$$S^*(f,t) = \sum_{t=1}^{n} a_t^2$$

This conditional sum of squares function is based on conditionally assigning zeros to all unknown a_t and w_t. However, we learn from other people's experience, and from theoretical properties, that we can only afford to do this if we have a very large series, and if the model proposed is not near its boundaries. If either of these two is not the case, then we are better off using an *unconditional sum of squares*, where we apply recursive calculations of a_t and w_t, in order to find initial estimates for ex-post forecasting. The unconditional sum of squares function is also

$$S(f,t) = \sum_{t=1-Q}^{n} a_t^2$$

Of course, a_t is now based on a recursive calculations basis, and could differ from a_t calculated with a conditional method. We can also see that t does not start from 1 but from $1 - Q$, where Q is a reasonable number after which w_t becomes equal to zero. In fact, this is the reason for introducing the column time t', and starting calculations from the time equal to -7.

So, we can say that our aim is to achieve the 'maximum likelihood estimate' of parameters f and t. Where the least square estimates of parameters makes our unconditional sum of squares function minimum, we can say that, for this model, we have the best possible approximation of our series. This takes us one step further, as it means that we have to calculate a sum of all a_t^2, as the

	A	B	C	D	E	F	G	H	I
1									
2									
3	PERIOD	TIME	SERIES	FIRST	f1= 0.22		f2= 0.25		
4				DIFFERENCE			t2= -0.95		
5		t	z(t)	w(t)	0.22w(t-1)	0.25w(t-2)	0.22w(t+1)	0.25w(t+2)	0.85e(t+1
6	A	B	C	D	E	F	G	H	
7		-7	-35.92	-0.60			-0.22	-0.38	0
8		-6	-34.91	-1.01	-0.13		-0.33	-0.68	0
9		-5	-33.39	-1.51	-0.22	-0.15	-0.60	-0.92	0
10		-4	-30.68	-2.71	-0.33	-0.25	-0.81	-1.90	0
11		-3	-27.01	-3.67	-0.38	-0.68	-1.67	-2.00	0
12		-2	-19.40	-7.61	-0.81	-0.68	-1.76	-5.85	0
13		-1	-11.41	-7.99	-1.67	-0.92	-5.15	0.25	0
14	1	0	12	-23.41	-1.76	-1.90	0.22	0.25	-2.77
15	2	1	13	1.00	-5.15	-2.00	0.22	-1.75	-23.84
16	3	1	14	1.00	0.22	-5.85	-1.54	3.75	-16.16
17	4	2	7	-7.00	0.22	0.25	3.30	-1.75	9.56
18	5	3	22	15.00	-1.54	0.25	-1.54	0.75	17.91
19	6	4	15	-7.00	3.30	-1.75	0.66	2.50	20.09
20	7	5	18	3.00	-1.54	3.75	2.20	-3.00	-9.97
21	8	6	28	10.00	0.66	-1.75	-2.64	3.00	-26.66
22	9	7	16	-12.00	2.20	0.75	2.64	-2.00	-4.74
23	10	8	28	12.00	-2.64	2.50	-1.76	7.00	12.51
24	11	9	20	-8.00	2.64	-3.00	6.16	-5.00	22.24
25	12	10	48	28.00	-1.76	3.00	-4.40	3.00	-1.47
26	13	11	28	-20.00	6.16	-2.00	2.64	3.75	1.58
27	14	12	40	12.00	-4.40	7.00	3.30	-4.25	-20.65
28	15	13	55	15.00	2.64	-5.00	-3.74	5.50	-8.55
29	16	14	38	-17.00	3.30	3.00	4.84	3.75	25.93
30	17	15	60	22.00	-3.74	3.75	3.30	-2.50	9.31
31	18	16	75	15.00	4.84	-4.25	-2.20	6.25	0.00
32	19	17	65	-10.00	3.30	5.50	5.50		
33	20	18	90	25.00	-2.20	3.75			
34	21	19							
35	22	20							
36	23	21							
37	24	22							
38	25	23							

Figure 13.8 Forecast using Box–Jenkins method; ARIMA (2,1,2) model

above formula suggests, and then compare it with several other sums for differen values of parameters. There is a routine for doing this but, for the sake o simplicity, let us say that it would be sufficient to experiment and alter value of parameters in our spreadsheet, until we get the smallest possible unconditiona sum of squares. However, let us not be carried away with experiments, an assign values to the parameters which would bring them out of the permissibl region.

In our particular ARIMA (2,1,2) case we started a model approximatio procedure with initial values of $f_1 = -0.21$, $f_2 = -0.56$, $t_1 = -0.14$ an $t_2 = 0.72$, which gave us a conditional sum of squares equal to $S(f,t) = 8226.1$ Through the process of model estimation procedure we experimented with th different values of f_1, f_2, t_1 and t_2, which finally brought us to the paramete

	J	K	L	M	N	O
1						
2						
3						FORECAST
4						
5	-0.95e(t+2)	e(t)	0.85a(t-1)	-0.95a(t-2)	a(t)	Z*(t)
6		I			J	K
7	0	0			0	
8	0	0			0	
9	0	0		0.00	0	
10	0	0	0.00	0.00	-4.13	
11	0	0	-3.51	0.00	-5.70	
12	0	0	-4.84	3.92	-5.94	
13	3.09	0	-5.05	5.41	-3.96	
14	26.65	0	-3.37	5.64	-13.99	
15	18.06	-3.25	-11.89	3.77	-1.49	11.48
16	-10.68	-28.05	-1.27	13.29	12.55	7.90
17	-20.02	-19.01	10.67	1.42	6.38	8.76
18	-22.45	11.24	5.42	-11.92	6.95	19.16
19	11.14	21.07	5.91	-6.06	-9.36	14.34
20	29.80	23.64	-7.96	-6.60	-10.47	21.30
21	5.30	-11.72	-8.90	8.90	7.05	23.96
22	-13.99	-31.37	5.99	9.95	4.08	19.09
23	-24.86	-5.58	3.46	-6.69	9.13	28.22
24	1.64	14.72	7.76	-3.87	-5.35	18.40
25	-1.77	26.16	-4.55	-8.67	10.62	45.08
26	23.08	-1.73	9.02	5.08	-8.49	29.56
27	9.56	1.86	-7.22	-10.09	-2.94	44.96
28	-28.98	-24.29	-2.50	8.07	14.26	46.34
29	-10.40	-10.06	12.12	2.80	-2.09	44.29
30	0.00	30.51	-1.78	-13.55	6.08	59.42
31	0.00	10.95	5.17	1.98	13.36	66.79
32		0	11.35	-5.78	-5.98	72.25
33		0	-5.08	-12.69	7.23	91.55
34						81.17
35						92.35
36						92.61
37						95.46
38						96.15

Figure 13.8 *Continued*

values of $f_1 = 0.22, f_2 = 0.25$, $t_1 = 0.85$ and $t_2 = -0.95$. These parameters give $S(f,t) = 1625.32$ (see Fig. 13.9).

If our forecast is presented in a form of a graph, then it looks as shown in Fig. 13.10.

It is interesting to see that, by applying the Box–Jenkins method, we have not only managed to extrapolate this quadratic function, but obtain a forecast that suggests that the immediate future of the forecasted phenomenon will not necessarily continue in a form of a parabola, but will slow down for a while, and even change shape into a logistic curve. If we recall our adaptive forecasting forecast, we can see that this is a competely different one.

This is a good example for demonstrating that, when making decisions about the future, we should not be led only by the findings discovered through statistical

		A	B	C	D	E	F	G	H
42									
43		PERIOD	TIME	f1 = -0.21	t1 = -0.14	f1 = -0.20	t1 = 0.10	f1 = 0.22	t1 = 0.85
44				f2 = -0.56	t2 = 0.72	f2 = -0.30	t2 = -.80	f2 = 0.25	t2 = -.95
45			t	a(t)	a^2(t)	a(t)	a^2(t)	a(t)	a^2(t)
46		A	B	C	D	E	F	G	H
47			-4	-4.13	17.06	-4.13	17.06	-4.13	17.06
48			-3	8.63	74.50	-1.22	1.48	-5.70	32.46
49			-2	0.17	0.03	3.42	11.69	-5.94	35.25
50			-1	-9.82	96.51	3.84	14.76	-3.96	15.71
51		1	0	-0.27	0.07	-4.82	23.24	-13.99	195.77
52		2	1	-3.20	10.21	-3.12	9.76	-1.49	2.23
53		3	2	2.02	4.08	5.04	25.44	12.55	157.55
54		4	3	-10.49	110.12	-5.10	25.97	6.38	40.69
55		5	4	17.15	294.26	11.36	128.94	6.95	48.27
56		6	5	-10.03	100.54	1.31	1.72	-9.36	87.69
57		7	6	13.46	181.30	-7.45	55.54	-10.47	109.62
58		8	7	4.68	21.86	11.10	123.31	7.05	49.65
59		9	8	0.12	0.01	-4.33	18.73	4.08	16.61
60		10	9	11.15	124.31	1.48	2.20	9.13	83.36
61		11	10	-4.43	19.67	-2.39	5.71	-5.35	28.64
62		12	11	38.05	1447.69	29.77	886.50	10.62	112.73
63		13	12	-17.04	290.35	-10.71	114.72	-8.49	72.10
64		14	13	33.10	1095.64	-16.49	271.93	-2.94	8.67
65		15	14	7.97	63.48	28.52	813.36	14.26	203.47
66		16	15	10.55	111.24	0.14	0.02	-2.09	4.36
67		17	16	21.36	456.25	-1.50	2.25	6.08	37.01
68		18	17	35.07	1230.14	24.33	592.16	13.36	178.36
69		19	18	6.77	45.82	-3.87	14.94	-5.98	35.73
70		20	19	49.31	2431.00	5.15	26.48	7.23	52.29
71									
72		S(f,t)			8226.14		3187.95		1625.32

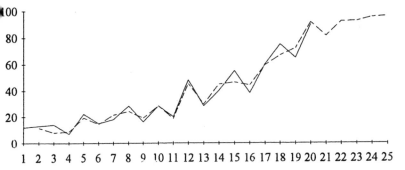

Figure 13.10 ARIMA (2,2,2) forecast with optimized parameters

analysis, but also by other elements that will be mentioned in later chapters. All of these factors together will help us in deciding which of the two possible developments we should accept as the most accurate forecast.

Now, although we are going to elaborate error measurement in Chapter 14, let us just mention a quick technique for measuring the model adequacy, as proposed by Box and Jenkins.

It was stated earlier that, provided our model describes the series adequately, there should be no pattern apparent in the residuals. Basically, if we call the residuals everything that is outside of our model, i.e. the difference between the actual observations and ex-post forecasts, then we have to calculate the autocorrelations of these residuals.

If:

$$'z_t = z^*_{t-1}(1) \text{ and } 'a_t = z_t - 'z_t$$

then $'a$'s represent actual residuals with their own peculiar behaviour somewhat different from the theoretical one.

In our case the graph of the residuals has the form shown in Figs 13.11 and 13.12. The autocorrelations and partial autocorrelations function of the residuals has the shape shown in Figs 13.13 and 13.14.

It looks as though the graph of autocorrelations of residuals is showing no pattern left over in the residuals, and that they are now following a random walk pattern within the two standard errors limit of:

$$\pm\sqrt{\frac{2}{n}}$$

In fact, the second partial autocorrelation is a little bit outside the boundaries, but as this example is artificially short, we can tolerate this. Once we are sure of this, we can calculate the so-called 'Box–Pierce' statistic Q as:

$$Q = n\sum_{k=1}^{K} r_k^2('a)$$

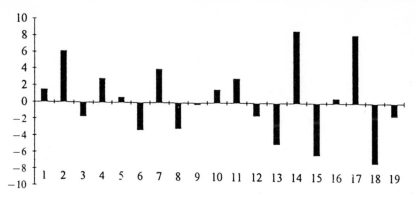

Figure 13.11 Absolute value of errors

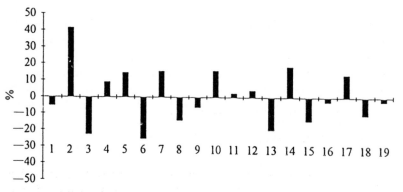

Figure 13.12 Percentage errors

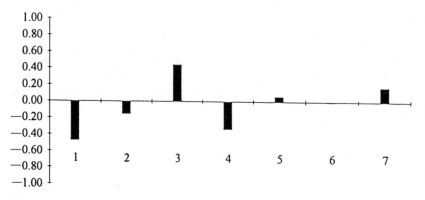

Figure 13.13 Residuals autocorrelations

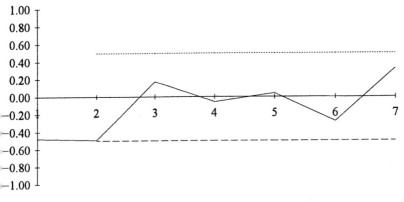

Figure 13.14 Residuals partial autocorrelations

where:

K = number of autocorrelations
$n = N - d$
N = number of observations
d = degree of differencing
$r_k(a)$ = residual autocorrelations

In our case the residual autocorrelations were:

r_1	r_2	r_3	r_4	r_5	r_6	r_7
−0.48	−0.15	0.45	−0.34	0.06	−0.01	0.17

The sum of all the squared autocorrelations values above is 0.59. As we had only 19 ex-post forecasts and a first level of differencing, n is equal to 18. This leads us to $Q = 10.77$.

This statistic is compared with the table values of χ^2 (chi square) for particular or desired percentage points. Only if it is below the table value for the percentage point of χ^2, can we say that our model is adequate. In our case, for three degrees of freedom (these are simply calculated as $df = K - p - q$), the table value for 0.1 is 6.25 (this is the level of significance of one per cent). For 0.05, or five per cent level of significance, the table value is 7.81. We can make a conclusion that our model is not adequate on any of these two levels of significance. As the next largest value from our Q is 12.8 and this is on the level of 0.0005, we can say that our model is acceptable at a very low level of significance. However, let us not forget that our example has forced us to use the absurd value of only three degrees of freedom.

So, we have finally come to the end of one of the most complicated chapters of forecasting theory and practice. One might say that it is still too complicated to be understood, but this should not be a problem as, with a little bit of homework and refreshing of 'A'-level maths and basic statistics, the method

can easily become clear and usable. A much bigger problem can arise if on
says that it is not complicated at all, and therefore one would feel too confiden
in applying the method. In this case we would offer a word of warning becaus
the method is somewhat complex and should be respected as such. On th
other hand, if you feel that the complexity is not causing difficulties, this coul
be a good sign as it means that with just a little more reading of the origina
work of Box and Jenkins you can apply the method with full confidence.

We said, at the beginning, that we were going to make some abstraction
and deviations from the general corridors covered by this method, and, indeed
we have. For the sake of some exercises we have used an inappropriately shor
series. In practice the series should have at least 50 observations to be used
We have not even mentioned seasonal models, although they are also very wel
suited to this method. We have not explored the various different and, for som
specific cases, more appropriate ways of presenting and forecasting a series. W
have also frequently ignored the difference between the theoretical behaviou
of a process and our practical model. However, despite this, we have not change
the 'spirit' of the method and, with very simple spreadsheet tools, have mad
it understandable and available to many with a very limited quantitativ
background.

Exercises

13.1 (a) Apply the AR(1) model with parameter 0.7133 and the AR(2) mode
with parameters 0.9024 and 0.0976 to the time series given in Exercis
12.3. (The mean of this time series is 50.648.)
(b) Produce a suitable graph of the original time series along with th
AR(1) and AR(2) models.

13.2 (a) Apply the MA(1) model with parameter 0.7248 and the AR(2) mode
with parameters 0.7049 and -0.0091 to the time series given i
Exercise 12.5. (The mean of this time series is 100.2.)
(b) Produce a suitable graph of the original time series along with th
MA(1) and AR(2) models.

13.3 Consider the ARIMA (0,1,1) model:

$$z_t = -\theta_1 e_{t-1} + e_t$$

where $z_t = x_t - x_{t-1}$.

(a) Rewrite the above formula in terms of the original x series.
(b) Given that $e_t = x_t - x^*_{t-1}(1)$ and $e_{t+1} = 0$, show that the answer to (a
can be written as

$$x^*_{t-1}(1) = (1 - \theta_1)x_{t-1} + \theta_1 x^*_{t-2}(1)$$

(c) Compare this equation to that for exponential smoothing in Chapter 9. How are the smoothing constant α and θ_1 related?

13.4 Consider the ARIMA $(2,1,1)$ model:

$$z_t = \phi_1 z_{t-1} + \phi_2 z_{t-2} - \theta_1 e_{t-1} + e_t$$

$$\text{where } z_t = x_t - x_{t-1}$$

(The x series represents the original undifferenced series.)

Show that the above ARIMA model can be rewritten in terms of the original x series using the definition of $z_t = x_t - x_{t-1}$ to give:

$$x_t = (1 + \phi_1)x_{t-1} + (\phi_2 - \phi_1)x_{t-2} - \phi_2 x_{t-3} - \theta_1 e_{t-1} + e_t$$

14

Tips for using the Box–Jenkins method

It seems appropriate to summarize the method and mention some tips and 'tricks of the trade', as well as the jargon that we have failed to include so far. Even if one is going to be using one of the standard statistical packages for forecasting (like SPSS, for example), the understanding of the jargon and of the basic principles is more than vital.

We said that the first step in time series analysis is to establish whether the series is stationary. If it is not, it has to be differenced in order to be made stationary. If one level of differencing is not enough, we can take the second differences. In practice we should not go beyond the second differences. However, there are situations where even after second differencing our series still appears to be non-stationary. This happens in particular with the series whose underlying trend is changing over time. If the magnitude of variations of the series is changing, very often we cannot remove the trend with simple differencing. Differences will, in this case, make the series mean stationary, while the variance remains non-stationary. The solution to this problem is to transform the series.

In the same way as, after the differencing, we used this newly created series as the basis for any further calculations, we can now use the transformed series. Transformations are very simple and most of the time are just logarithm values of the series. For example, series z_t could be a transformation of the original series x_t as:

$$z_t = \log x_t$$

or,

$$z_t = \ln x_t$$

We have said that, after the series has been differenced or transformed and turned into a stationary series, normally we would expect the mean value of this stationary series to be zero. This applies in particular to the series which are stationary in original form. However, in practice most stationary series have on-zero mean value. If it happens that the series has non-zero mean value, we should do a simple transformation where every observation is replaced by its difference from the mean value. In other words, we create a new series z_t where:

$$z_t = x' - x_t$$

and x' is the mean value of the series.

If our series could be formulated as:

$$x_t - x_{t-1} = e_t$$

In other words, the differences between the consecutive observations are nothing but random errors (a good example is the stock exchange), then this series is, in jargon, called a *random walk*. Using the Box–Jenkins notation it could be described as an ARIMA (0,1,0) model with no constant term. Random walk has no AR, MA nor constant parameter present. If it happens that there is a constant term present in the model, then it is called a *random walk with a drift*. This means that the fluctuations will continue to be random, but at a different level that is determined by the constant.

One term we have not mentioned is *invertibility*, and it is very likely that every standard text on the Box–Jenkins method will make reference to it. In relation to MA models we often hear this term invertibility. We should remember that AR models are clearly defined with a unique shape of autocorrelations function. Unfortunately, MA models are not so 'clear cut'. In order to recognize an MA model from the autocorrelation function, we have to impose certain restrictions. The basic restriction, called invertibility, is that the sum of all q parameters f is smaller than one, i.e.:

$$f_1 + f_2 + \ldots + f_q < 1.$$

It also means that every invertible MA model of order q (in other words, with limited number of parameters), could be represented by an infinite order AR model. One might ask, if MA models are just different types of AR models, why have we bothered with MA models at all? Well, the reason for having MA models is called *parsimony*. We have already described parsimony as a principle that dictates that every series should be fitted with the smallest possible number of parameters, and this is the reason for introducing MA models, rather than dealing with the infinite number of parameters of AR models in certain cases.

Sometimes in the literature you will find models that include a constant, and we have referred to such in the context of transformations, e.g.:

$$z_t = 12.3 + 0.75z_{t-1} - 0.12z_{t-2} + e_t$$

In this example, 12.3 is the constant or a trend parameter, as referred to in some sources. The biggest questions are, when do we include this constant into our model and how do we calculate it? The general rule is, if our series is non-stationary in its original form and we had to difference it to make it stationary, then the constant is not needed and it could stay at zero. If the original series is stationary, and we have a significantly large mean (whic effectively means $x' \pm \sigma_x > 1$), the constant is necessary. If our model does nc have an AR component, then the constant is equal to the mean value of th series. If our model has an AR component then the constant is equal to:

$$c_0 = x'\left(1 - \sum_{i=1}^{p} f_p\right)$$

If we do not have the constant in our model then our series is sometimes calle stochastic. The models with the constant are called deterministic model: Generally speaking, deterministic models have $q \geq 1$ as well as $d \geq 1$. A every complex series could be fitted with a polynomial of a certain degree, i this context d corresponds to the degree of polynomial function.

Something that we have not mentioned is the question of model parameter correlation. We have said that our aim is to build the parsimonious model, i.' the model with the smallest number of parameters. As sometimes we do nc know which model represents our series, we might enter into identification an estimation procedure with several alternative models. Chapter 15 will tell u how to compare the results from various models and methods, but at thi moment we want, even before comparing the models, to eliminate those tha are statistically redundant. The best method is to measure correlation betwee the parameters in the model. We can build a small table (Table 14.1) wher every parameter in one model is correlated with all the others in the sam model, and if any of them shows high correlation, then the parsimony has bee violated. In fact, as the correlation coefficients are presented in the form of matrix, it will be quite clear which parameters are correlated with the others an therefore redundant.

The example in Table 14.1 shows large correlation between f_1 and f_2. Ther is no need, therefore, to have two AR parameters and we can successfully f the series with just one AR parameter—ARIMA $(1,0,2)$ or ARIMA $(1,1,2)$ fc example.

Table 14.1

	f_1	f_2	t_1	t_2
f_1	1.00	0.87	0.68	-0.44
f_2	0.87	1.00	0.60	-0.16
t_1	0.68	0.60	1.00	-0.65
t_2	-0.44	-0.16	-0.65	1.00

Another method available for eliminating parsimonious models is measurin the significance of parameters. If a parameter is not significant, there is no nee to have it in the model. The significance is easily calculated from the confidenc limit. We have not discussed it, but the parameter confidence limit is a standar element on the printouts of any forecasting package. If the value of the parameter plus or minus its confidence limit is less than $+1$ or -1, then the parameter is not significant and we should take it out of our model.

Another tool, besides correlation matrix and parameter significance, is the residuals. In relation to these there is one point that deserves amplifying. In Chapter 13 we said that the residuals should be below the significance level, and should appear to be random. We have to say also that the residual mean should be zero, or close to zero, as otherwise our forecast is biased. An important statistic for testing that the residual mean is non-zero, is residual standard error. We shall see in the next chapter that standard error is calculated as:

$$SE = \sqrt{\frac{\sum_{t=1}^{n} (e_t - e')^2}{n}}$$

If the residual mean (RM) is greater than two standard errors divided by the square root of the number of residuals, then we can say that it is significantly non-zero:

$$RM > \frac{2SE}{\sqrt{n}}$$

There is a possibility that some packages using the Box–Jenkins method apply some other statistics and jargon, but basically what has been mentioned in this chapter covers most of the standard terminology related to this method.

15
Error measurement

We have described the various methods and stressed the strong points of eac and every one of them. Unfortunately, if you think it will be easy to choose th right method for your requirements on the basis of what has been said i previous chapters, you are mistaken. There will be many occasions when w are not going to be certain which method is the best one or, alternatively, the will be situations where it will appear that several methods could do the jo quite successfully. Even if we are certain of how to make a decision, we migl work with different parameters and generate several forecasts, which will, agai raise the question of the best forecast. What do we do in cases like this?

In the same way that we analysed the original series (input series) in ord to determine underlying characteristics, we can also examine the result of ot work (output series) so that we can draw helpful conclusions. In fact, we a implicitly examining the series of forecasts, as our prime interest is to measu how closely the forecasts fit the original series.

So, the decision for choosing an optimum forecast from the several availab is based on measuring the deviations of the ex-post forecasts from the actu series. The deviation is, in fact, an error and there are quite a few different typ of error measurement. To be even more precise, we can say that it is possib to measure not only errors, but quite a few other things in forecasting; let be more specific about this.

Forecasting, as a discipline, should satisfy the following criteria, which w often call the *metric criteria*:

- Objectivity
- Validity
- Reliability
- Accuracy
- Confidence
- Sensitivity

The reason we call these criteria 'metric' is because they are measurable and quantifiable. We need to explain each of these metric characteristics.

Objectivity is a requirement that stipulates that the result of a forecasting process should depend entirely on the data, and not on the person conducting the forecast. This is a particularly important requirement as it eliminates speculations but, unfortunately, even some of the most sophisticated methods (such as Box–Jenkins) require quite a few subjective interventions and decisions. By satisfying this requirement, in general we can say that we are upgrading forecasting from being an art or skill, to being a science.

Validity is a requirement that says that the forecast is valid only if it approximates the series that is the subject of our interest. In other words, we can produce a forecast, basically a series of numbers, that does not represent the phenomenon that we want to forecast. Statistically speaking, we have generated a series that is representing, i.e. approximating, some other phenomenon out of thousands possible, and not our time series. To prove that an ex-post forecast validly represents an original time series we can, among other things, measure the correlation between these two series. If the correlation is high, there is no doubt that the forecast is valid.

Reliability is a term that is more connected with a method than with a result produced by the method. We can say that the reliability of the method is measured by the consistency of the results produced by it. A good example could be forecasting from different starting points in the series, and measuring ex-post forecasts generated from these different origins. The more consistent the results, the more reliable the method is.

Accuracy is closely related to validity, although only in one direction. A method or the result could be valid, but not particularly accurate. On the other hand, it is not possible to have an accurate forecast that is not valid. Therefore, accuracy is a measure of the fitness of the forecast.

Confidence is a criterion which is telling us with what probability we should accept the results of forecasting. Some forecasts can be fairly accurate, especially towards the end of the series, which should indicate that we found the correct model to approximate the more recent pattern of the series. But, because of the more distant history of the series, the interval within which it is probable that the result will take place, could be so wide that we might suspect that our model is adequate for long-term forecasting. To be fair, we must say that this criterion reflects more the nature of the data than the method itself.

And, finally, the *sensitivity* is, as is the reliability, more related to the method than to the results. We can say that the more scattered the results of a method are (if we use different types of data), the more sensitive the method is. It is quite obvious that it is a positive step to have very sensitive methods, as otherwise we would get the same result no matter what the input was.

So, to summarize, we can say that we should be pleased with our result if we use a sensitive and reliable method, which is producing valid and accurate forecasts, which are placed within an acceptable narrow confidence interval.

As we are going to see in Chapter 16, some of these criteria could be artificia
if the forecast is not related to some other policy matters.

One way or other, it seems we are going to have to introduce some statistic
that will help us in measuring the quality of our forecasts. More or less all c
these statistics are based on different types of forecasting error.

Forecasting error is, basically, a difference between the actual and th
forecasted observations or, in other words:

$$e_t = x_t - F_t$$

where it is understood that:

x_t = actual observation in the original series in the moment t
F_t = forecast for the period t

Later we are going to show other symbols, so perhaps we should define the
straightaway. In our formulas we are going to use:

n = number of errors that we are measuring (in a series of errors)
e' = mean value of all errors in the series
x' = mean value of all original observations in the series
F' = mean value of all forecasts in the series

Before we get into the practicalities of error measurement, let us mentio
some of the forecasting errors properties. First of all, forecasting error shoul
be a random variable. This means that, if our forecasts are really well representin
the original series, the differences (errors) between the series and forecasts shoul
be random. If there is any pattern in the series of errors, then it definitely mean
that we have missed out the pattern of the series, and have used either a wron
method or wrong parameters. In order to prove the randomness of errors, w
can always use a simple autocorrelation analysis, which we elaborated in earlie
chapters when describing the analytical tools of the input series. Another poir
worth mentioning, beside randomness, is that it is desirable that the errors d
not jump up and down too much. If they do, then this is a sign of too great
variance, and it means that our forecast is quite valid, but not accurate enough.

Before getting into different types of errors and elaborating their meanin
let us also mention two simple graphical methods for analysing errors. If w
put the actual values of the series on axis X and forecasted values on axis Y
and if our forecasts are perfect after we connect each actual value with it
forecast, they should all be aligned along a straight line at an angle of 45°. C
course, in practice this will never happen, but the closer the scatter diagram i
to this ideal line, the better our result is.

Another simple graphic method is to divide each forecast with its correspondin
actual observation, and then multiply it by 100. By doing so we produce inde
numbers which tell us that, if the actual series is equal to the number one, the
the variations of forecasts from this value will be represented by values belo
or above one. This is, at the same time, a percentage for which the foreca

misses out the actual observation. If we use a simple graph (Fig. 15.1), where he centre is a straight line representing the value of one, and where all forecasts are drawn as variations around this central line, we can easily see if our forecasts are showing a tendency to digress from this line. Again, this is a sign that errors are not random, and therefore that the forecast is not correct.

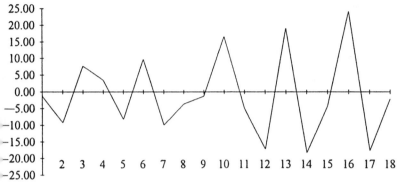

Figure 15.1 Error fluctuations around actual series

In the above example we can, in fact, see a divergence, as obviously the model fits the series more appropriately at the beginning, but later—instead of 'catching up' with the changes, and showing a tendency to reduce the amplitude of errors, as well as standardizing variations proportionally above and below the series line—it shows obvious instability.

Let us now see which statistics we can derive from the errors, in order to draw some further conclusions.

The most common statistic is called a *mean error* (ME) and it is calculated as:

$$ME = \frac{\sum_{t=1}^{n} e_t}{n}$$

Mean error shows us if our forecast is systematically biased in either a positive or a negative direction. As, by definition, it eliminates all positive deviations with the negative ones, even if we have dramatic fluctuations in both directions, the end result, i.e. ME, could be zero despite the fluctuations. Because of this problem, this measure is never used independently for accessing results, and is just an introduction to more appropriate measures. This statistic is shown in cell D28 of Fig. 15.2.

Mean absolute error or *deviation* (MAE or MAD) has a formula:

$$MAD = \frac{\sum_{t=1}^{n} |e_t|}{n}$$

A	B	C	D	E	F	G	H	I	J
PERIOD	SERIES	FORECAST	MEAN ERROR ME	ABSOLUTE ERROR MAD	MEAN SQUARE ERROR MSE	ROOT MEAN SQUARE ERROR RMS	RELAT. ROOT MEAN SQUARE ERROR(RRMS)	ERROR VARIANCE S	
A	B	C	D	E	F	G	H	I	
1	12								
2	13								
3	14	15.27	−1.27	1.27	1.61	1.61	0.11	74.77	
4	7	16.25	−9.25	9.25	85.52	85.52	12.22	0.45	
5	22	14.28	7.72	7.72	59.59	59.59	2.71	4.82	
6	15	11.53	3.47	3.47	12.01	12.01	0.80	41.61	
7	18	26.28	−8.28	8.28	68.55	68.55	3.81	2.68	
8	28	18.26	9.74	9.74	94.85	94.85	3.39	0.03	
9	16	25.87	−9.87	9.87	97.44	97.44	6.09	0.00	
10	28	31.57	−3.57	3.57	12.74	12.74	0.46	40.28	
11	20	21.26	−1.26	1.26	1.59	1.59	0.08	74.93	
12	48	31.38	16.62	16.62	276.20	276.20	5.75	44.93	
13	28	32.94	−4.94	4.94	24.40	24.40	0.87	24.77	
14	40	57.13	−17.13	17.13	293.52	293.52	7.34	52.08	
15	55	35.90	19.10	19.10	364.83	364.83	6.63	84.36	
16	38	56.19	−18.19	18.19	330.91	330.91	8.71	68.48	
17	60	64.21	−4.21	4.21	17.72	17.72	0.30	32.56	
18	75	50.76	24.24	24.24	587.57	587.57	7.83	205.18	
19	65	82.58	−17.58	17.58	309.14	309.14	4.76	58.78	
20	90	92.05	−2.05	2.05	4.20	4.20	0.05	61.86	
SUM	692.00	683.72	−16.72	178.48	2642.39	2642.39	71.90	872.57	
AVG	34.60	34.19	−0.93	9.92	146.80	146.80	3.99	48.48	
ROOT						12.12	2.00	6.96	
STATISTIC						35.02		70.22	

150

PERIOD	SERIES	FORECAST	MEAN PERCENTAGE ERROR (MPE)	MEAN ABS. PERCENTAGE ERROR (MAPE)	THEIL U1	COEFFICIENT	CORRELATION r	COEFFICIENTS OF CORRELATION	DETERMINAT. R
A	B	C	D	E	F	G	H	I	J
1	12								
2	13								
3	14	15.27	−9.06	9.06	196.00	233.13	389.69	424.36	357.86
4	7	16.25	−132.11	132.11	49.00	263.99	495.09	761.76	321.78
5	22	14.28	35.09	35.09	484.00	203.93	250.81	158.76	396.23
6	15	11.53	23.10	23.10	225.00	133.05	443.96	384.16	513.07
7	18	26.28	−46.00	46.00	324.00	690.61	131.25	275.56	62.51
8	28	18.26	34.78	34.78	784.00	333.46	105.11	43.56	253.61
9	16	25.87	−61.69	61.69	256.00	669.32	154.65	345.96	69.13
10	28	31.57	−12.75	12.75	784.00	996.62	17.27	43.56	6.85
11	20	21.26	−6.30	6.30	400.00	451.96	188.73	213.16	167.09
12	48	31.38	34.62	34.62	2304.00	984.76	−37.59	179.56	7.87
13	28	32.94	−17.64	17.64	784.00	1084.99	8.23	43.56	1.55
14	40	57.13	−42.83	42.83	1600.00	3264.12	123.91	29.16	526.55
15	55	35.90	34.73	34.73	3025.00	1288.77	34.96	416.16	2.94
16	38	56.19	−47.87	47.87	1444.00	3157.43	74.82	11.56	484.22
17	60	64.21	−7.02	7.02	3600.00	4122.86	762.60	645.16	901.42
18	75	50.76	32.32	32.32	5625.00	2576.59	669.60	1632.16	274.71
19	65	82.58	−27.05	27.05	4225.00	6819.84	1471.25	924.16	2342.22
20	90	92.05	−2.28	2.28	8100.00	8473.30	3205.70	3069.16	3348.32
SUM			−217.95	607.24	34209.00	35748.74	8490.04	9601.48	10037.93
AVG			−12.11	33.74	1900.50	1986.04			
ROOT					43.59	44.57		9817.28	
STATISTIC						0.14	0.86		0.75

Figure 15.2 Various forecasting errors

151

This error measures deviations from the series in absolute terms, which means, regardless of whether the errors are positive or negative, we should take them as positive. In fact, a typical error tells us by how much our forecast is biased. This measure is one of the most common ones used for analysing the quality of different forecasts, and the statistic is shown in cell E28 of Fig. 15.2.

Mean square error (MSE) is calculated as:

$$MSE = \frac{\sum_{t=1}^{n} e_t^2}{n}$$

Beside MAD, a mean square error is one of the most often used statistics. It has a tendency to prefer a series of small errors, and penalizes forecasts if there are one or two large errors in the series. In other words, it encourages safe forecasting that produces smoother forecasting lines, rather than a bolder approach which tries to follow the dynamic pattern of the series, even at the expense of making one or two bigger mistakes. This statistic is shown in cell F28 of Fig. 15.2.

Another often-used error statistic is the *root mean square error* (RMS):

$$RMS = \sqrt{\frac{\sum_{t=1}^{n} e_t^2}{n}}$$

This measure is sometimes more easily understood than MSE, the reason being that it is expressed in the same units as the original series. In other words, if the original series represents a series of pounds per square inch, then RMS is also a number of pounds per square inch. This statistic is also called a variance or, more precisely, standard deviation, because the root value is calculated as it measures dispersion—although in this case not a dispersion from its mean value, but from the original series. RMS is shown in cell G29 of Fig. 15.2.

A statistic derived from RMS is called a *variation coefficient* (V):

$$V = \frac{RMS}{\sum_{t=1}^{n} \frac{x_t}{n}} 100$$

The variation coefficient, as presented here, tells us by what percentage our forecast deviates from the mean value of the original series. In a way, this tells us how well the forecasting model represents the actual series. This statistic is shown in cell G30 of Fig. 15.2.

The following error is a *relative root mean square error* (RRMS):

$$RRMS = \sqrt{\frac{\sum_{t=1}^{n} \frac{e_t^2}{x_t}}{n}}$$

As the term implies, RRMS is a relative error and, as such, is without a real dimension in terms of actual units. It is used as an indicator for the comparison of results generated by different methods (like MSE). This statistic is shown in cell H29 Fig. 15.2.

If we want to measure a real dispersion (variance) of our errors then we could use a statistic called an *error variance*. The formula is:

$$SE = \sqrt{\frac{\sum_{t=1}^{n} (e_t - e')^2}{n}}$$

In fact, error variance is given at the second degree, so it is s^2 and, when presented as above, it is called standard deviation. The reason we mention this measure is because of an interesting relationship. Basically, by using the above formula we are measuring the dispersion of errors, not around zero (actual observations), but around its mean value. The above formula tells us that $s^2 = \text{MSE} - e'^2$. Or, if we rearrange it, then it is $\text{MSE} = s^2 + e'^2$. This is telling us that the mean square error is a sum of the two factors, one of which is measuring how much our errors are biased, and another which is measuring the variability of errors around their mean value. As stated before, this is significant because although we do not want our errors to be too far from the original values, we do not want to see them fluctuating too much either. In this respect, we have a confirmation that MSE is a statistic with real statistical properties.

Error variance is also used for determining the confidence interval of our forecast, as it gives us a plus/minus figure which, if we add or deduct from the mean value, gives a corridor within which the majority of our forecasts should be based. The mean plus/minus three times standard deviation should cover almost 100 per cent of all variations.

If we do the following:

$$SER = \frac{SE}{x'} 100$$

SER is a relative standard error, in fact a proper variation coefficient, and it expresses in percentages an average deviation from the mean value of the actual series. Variance is shown in cell I28, standard deviation in cell I29 and variation coefficient in cell I30 (Fig. 15.2).

A very interesting and understandable error is a *mean percentage error* (MPE):

$$MPE = \frac{\sum_{t=1}^{n} \frac{e_t}{x_t} 100}{n}$$

This error gives us an average percentage deviation of our forecast from the actual series. It is a common fact that every relative measure prefers underestimated values and, as such, is somewhat biased. MPE is shown in cell D64 of Fig. 15.2.

An error derived from the previous one is a *mean absolute percentage error* (MAPE):

$$MAPE = \frac{\sum_{t=1}^{n} \left| \frac{e_t}{x_t} \right| 100}{n}$$

This error shows, as does the previous one, percentage deviations of our forecast from the original series. However, it does not take into account positive or negative variations, but rather a typical percentage deviation expressed in relative (percentage) numbers. MAPE is shown in cell E64 of Fig. 15.2.

The next measure to mention is the *Theil's U1* statistic:

$$U1 = \frac{\sqrt{\frac{\sum_{t=1}^{n} e_t^2}{n}}}{\left(\sqrt{\frac{\sum_{t=1}^{n} F_t^2}{n}} + \sqrt{\frac{\sum_{t=1}^{n} x_t^2}{n}} \right)}$$

Although it looks complicated, this statistic is not difficult to calculate and can be very useful. Basically, it compares the changes in actual observations with the changes taking place with the forecasting values. As it is a coefficient, it implies that it can take values between zero and one. The closer to zero, the more accurate the forecast is. Theil's U_1 statistic is shown in cell G66 of Fig. 15.2.

If we consider coefficients, then we should certainly mention the *correlation coefficient* (r) as a serious measure of successful forecasting. The formula is:

$$r = \sqrt{\frac{\sum_{t=1}^{n} (F_t - x')^2}{\sum_{t=1}^{n} (x_t - x')^2}}$$

However, the above formula is usually used when we are dealing with a regression line, i.e. where forecasts are calculated on the basis of the least square method. As the parameters of many of our forecasting methods are not based on the least square principle, we should use the following formula for correlations:

$$r = \frac{\sqrt{\sum_{t=1}^{n} (x_t - x')(F_t - x')}}{\sqrt{\left(\sum_{t=1}^{n} x_t^2 \right) \left(\sum_{t=1}^{n} F_t^2 \right)}}$$

Again, the value can be anything between -1 and $+1$. The closer the value to $+1$, the more closely are the two series, actual series and ex-post forecasts, correlated. The closer the value to -1, the more we have failed in our forecast as the two series are, in this case, completely opposite to each other. If the value is close to zero there is no correlation whatsoever, and, again, this means failure for us, as we have not produced a valid forecast. This statistic is shown in cell I66 of Fig. 15.2.

Another derived statistic is called the *determination coefficient* (R). It represents the squared correlation coefficient:

$$R = r^2$$

The determination coefficient gives us a proportion of described variance, i.e. all our deviations from the actual series. If we multiply it by 100, we are presenting it in a relative form, and it tells us the percentage of deviations of forecasts from the actual series described by the connection, i.e. the forecasting model. In other words, if the result is 0.97, we can say that 97 per cent of all deviations from the actual series are caused by some inherent reasons built into our forecasting formula. Only 3 per cent of all errors happened for some other reasons that we cannot mathematically define. This statistic is shown in cell I66 of Fig. 15.2.

16
Forecast selection

In Chapter 15 we briefly discussed many statistics that are available for th
purposes of forecast assessment. Although the list is far from exhaustive, th
statistics mentioned are more than enough to draw competent conclusions abou
the quality of our forecasts. Nevertheless, we shall take an even more detaile
look at these statistics, with a more practical approach, to avoid giving th
impression that they were only mentioned for the sake of their theoretica
implications. Thus, first we shall repeat the actual meaning of every measur
described so far and, after that, apply them to a hypothetical case, which assume
that we have produced three different forecasts and now have to support ou
decision for choosing an optimum result.

Let us assume that one example we used in Chapter 15 describes sales c
ceramic tiles in one particular market, throughout a period of 20 years, an
that the figures show thousands of square feet. As we can see, when th
phenomenon was recorded for the first time the sales were only 12 000 squar
feet, and reached the volume of 90 000 square feet in the last year. We mad
an ex-post forecast which showed some discrepancies from the actual serie:
The actual series shows an annual average sale of 34 600 square feet, while th
forecast shows an average of 34 190 square feet. These two figures are nc
particularly relevant, as we are obviously dealing with a non-stationary serie
with an upward trend, so the actual average is of very little meanin
Nevertheless, we have to calculate both averages as we are going to use thes
figures for calculating some other measures. If we refer to Fig. 15.2, we ca
describe each measure as follows.

ME has the value of -0.93, and tells us that our forecast has bee
systematically underneath the line of the actual series, at an average of 93
square feet. This is not a bad performance as it represents a very small erro
The fact that our error is negative means that our model is just a little too slo
for the actual series, and that it shows a conservative tendency of slow reactio
to dynamic changes taking place in the real series. On the other hand, it als

tells us that our positive errors are well compensated by our negative errors, and no matter how many of them we make, they have balanced well.

MAD has the value of 9.92 which tells us that, although we balanced our errors well around the original series, we have still made an average error of 9920 square feet, which is a typical error. This is the measure of perfection of our model, i.e. the method applied, as it is telling us how biased the model is. We should not be dissatisfied with the model as the value of MAD is almost four times below the average error, so, all in all, it is not a bad performance.

MSE shows a value of 146.80, and we cannot assign any units to this figure. This measure will be very useful for comparing different alternative models, so in this particular instance we cannot comment, as it has no reference point for comparison.

RMS has the value of 12.12 and this means 12 120 square feet. Still, we cannot say too much about this measure, as we have to compare it with another series to see which one is lower. However, we can derive from this measure another one, a variation coefficient that shows a value of 35.02, or in its relative terms, 35.02 per cent. As we have derived a coefficient of variation on the basis of the discrepancies between the forecast and the actual series, we can say that the average discrepancy of our forecast is 35.02 per cent from the average value of the actual series. This is not a particularly good figure but, bearing in mind that we are dealing with a non-stationary series, we should not be concerned as it is obvious that we are comparing a dynamic figure with a static figure.

RRMS is 2.00, and it can be used only for the comparison of several alternative series, so, as such, is not relevant in this context.

S stands for standard deviation, which is the best known measure of dispersion. If we measure a dispersion of errors around their average value (the mean), we can get some useful information. Variance of our forecasting errors is 48.48. Standard deviation is 6.96 or 6960 square feet. If we add and deduct three times 6960 to 9920 (average absolute forecasting error, i.e. MAD, as we calculated the variance from this typical error), we are going to get a limit of + 30 880 to − 10 960; this is a corridor within which all our errors have to be distributed (in fact, 99.99 per cent). As we can see, this interval is fairly large and even goes into negative figures because of high standard deviation which, in turn, is high due to the non-stationarity of the series. From standard deviation we derived another statistic, variation coefficient. In our case it is 70.22, which means that our average forecasting error deviates for 70.22 per cent from the average value of the series. Again, due to the non-stationarity of the series it is not a particularly relevant interpretation.

MPE is telling us what we already knew from ME, but is now expressing it in relative figures. It is − 12.11, which means that our forecast is constantly below the actual series by 12.11 per cent.

MAPE again repeats the message carried by MAD, which is that our forecasts are missing the actual figures by an average of 33.74 per cent. This is not a good sign.

U1 shows a value of 0.14 which is very satisfactory (remember, the closer to zero, the better). This Theil coefficient is telling us that our model is showing similar dynamism to the actual series and that, although we can see from the previous statistics that our forecast is not too accurate, at least our method is sensitive and certainly not a bad choice. This statistic should encourage us to use the method, but to try to increase its accuracy by changing parameters.

r is 0.86 and, as correlation coefficient, could be either positive or negative (remember, from -1 to $+1$). It is a good sign that it has this value; this indicates that the original series and ex-post forecast are correlated to a great degree.

R, or determination coefficient, is 0.75 which means that 75 per cent of the total deviations from the actual series could be interpreted by the model. This is a reasonable percentage, as it indicates that one quarter of all errors happened not because of the model inadequacy, but for some unexplained reasons.

As we were not able to interpret some of the statistics, due to the fact that we have not had a reference value, and as we were not sure whether we should be satisfied with some of the statistics, let us now take one normal and two extreme cases, to conduct a simulation of a real analysis. Very often the more obvious the extremes are, the easier it is to see the differences, and this is the reason for taking these two artificially extreme cases. We have seen so far that various methods show a tendency to fall behind the actual series. In other words, when the actual series changes direction it is reflected in our ex-post forecast one period behind. This shifting will not necessarily happen in the future but, nevertheless, as it is a part of ex-post forecasts, it affects our analysis. Let us assume a hypothetical case, where our model shows exactly opposite values from the original series—so that, although we should have no doubts that a pattern exists, it is shifted one period from the actual event. We can say that the model is shifted in phase.

We can take another hypothetical example where, again, we managed to simulate the pattern of the original series but for some reason failed to use adequate parameters, which resulted in a systematic forecasting error. Our forecast, in this case, systematically underestimates the actual series.

If this happens we must ask ourselves which one of the two is the more acceptable forecast. Let us first see them both in graphic format. A phase shifted forecast could look like Fig. 16.1, while a forecast with a systematic error could look like Fig. 16.2.

It is obvious that both of the two forecasts have exactly the same pattern as the original series but, at the same time, both of them show some big deficiencies in approximating the original series. The first forecast is, with every period, going in a completely opposite direction to the original series, but at least it is crossing the values of the curve. The second forecast is a perfect match, except that it does not have any common points with the actual series.

Of course, the above two examples are deliberate extremes that will help us in seeing some aspects of error measurement, which we would otherwise not be able to see. To make the whole comparison more realistic, let us also use an

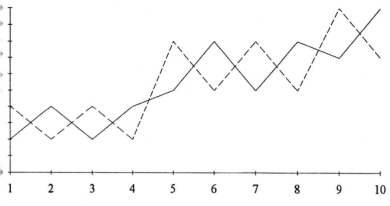

gure 16.1 Phase shifted series

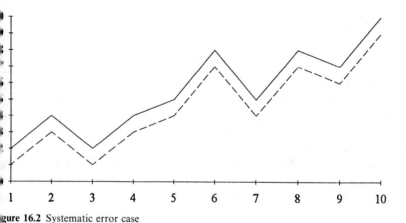

gure 16.2 Systematic error case

ample of something that we could call a 'normal' forecast. This could appear
shown in Fig. 16.3.

We are now going to conduct an error measurement procedure in between
e three forecasts. For the sake of clarity, let us compile all error statistics in
e table (Fig. 16.4), and let us call the three forecasts cases I, II and III.

From the comparison, we can see that ME confirms exactly what we warned
earlier. The best results are shown with series II and, in fact, it shows no
ean error at all. By looking at the graphs we can see that errors exist in all
ree cases, and in particular in case II. What has happened is that all positive
rors have been compensated by negative errors and, therefore, ME is 0.00.
nis statistic would suggest we accept case II as the most optimal one.

MAD tells us that case III is the best one by its criteria, although case I is
ceptable too. Again, we know for sure that case III cannot be the best one

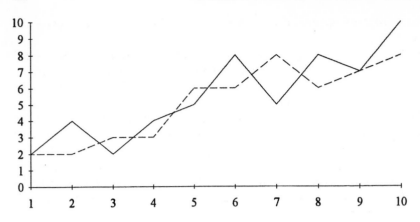

Figure 16.3 Normal forecast

ERROR MEASUREMENT	NORMAL SERIES case I	PHASE SHIFTED CASE case II	SYSTEMATIC ERROR CASE case III	RANK case I	II	III
Mean Error	0.40	0.00	1.00	2	1	3
Mean Absolute Error	1.40	2.60	1.00	2	3	1
Mean Square Error	2.80	7.00	1.00	2	3	1
Root Mean Square Error	1.67	2.65	1.00	2	3	1
Relative Root Mean Square Error	0.72	1.18	0.49	2	3	1
Error Variance	0.84	0.24	0.00	3	2	1
Standard deviation	0.92	0.49	0.00	3	2	1
Variation coefficient	65.47	18.84	0.00	3	2	1
Mean Percentage Error	1.5	−15.79	23.93	1	2	3
Mean Absolute Percentage Error	27.5	56.79	23.93	2	3	1
Theil Coefficient	0.14	0.22	0.09	2	3	1
Correlation Coefficient	0.78	0.46	1.00	2	3	1
Determination Coefficient	0.6	0.21	1.00	2	3	1

Figure 16.4 Error comparison

due to a constant and systematic error, so we shall ignore the clues suggested by MAD.

MSE repeats the findings of the MAD and supports case III. We mentioned earlier that MSE is a statistic that prefers more small deviations, and is particularly sensitive to one or two larger deviations. This is confirmed here, as case II is by far the worst one.

RMS is, again, supporting case III and penalizing case II. On the other hand, RMS takes a more realistic view, and although it ranks the series in the same order, does not judge them so dramatically by showing them as extremes.

The next three statistics, variance, standard deviation and variation coefficient, again show a great favouritism towards smaller deviations and, therefore, prefer case III. It is interesting to see that, according to these three statistics, case II more acceptable than case I.

MPE confirms the findings of ME and prefers case I. Equally, MAPE confirms MAD and prefers case III.

The Theil coefficient shows interesting results. It supports case III as the best one and, after that, suggests that case I is the second best. We should remember that this statistic measures the dynamism of both the original and the ex-post forecasted series, and implicitly ignores errors. As series III is identical to the original series, it should show a low Theil value.

Correlation and determination coefficients tell us that case III is the best one, followed by case I. We are once more obtaining a confirmation that smaller errors are preferred to the larger ones.

What can we say as a resumé? According to the ex-post analysis of our three hypothetical cases, of which two were deliberately exaggerated, it seems that the best forecast is one of the two exaggerated ones. Should we agree with this? Definitely not. The statistics mentioned above are to be used not as a decision tool, but as an inference tool. This means that by calculating them and acknowledging their values, we may draw certain conclusions on the basis of what they show, but under no circumstances should we be misled into making decisions solely on the basis of their values. Common sense should have at least the same weight as statistics. However, the problem we may face if we depend too much on common sense is the problem of the validity of our forecasts, in which case we eliminate the factor of exactness that we were promoting heavily throughout earlier chapters. This means that we have to take some other factors into consideration, before making any judgements or making any decisions that will affect the future.

17
Systems approach to forecasting

In order to put the results of the forecasting procedures elaborated throughou Chapter 16 into a useful and practical perspective, we have to move one ste away from the statistics. At the very beginning of this book, we said that w must not make the mistake of equating forecasting with statistics, so the nex few chapters will, hopefully, help us to take a pragmatic view of forecastin, Just as we have thus far used statistical tools to develop certain results an achieve given aims, so we are now going to use some of the tools that will hel us to give the right interpretation of the results, developed by the statistics. Th tools we are referring to are very well-known postulates from general system theory, and should definitely help us to see a completely new dimension c forecasting.

The computer sciences, as such, include one more or less abstract theor which is called the *systems theory*. It is absolutely vital for the understandin of many things that surround us, and without it computer systems would neve have been developed. The systems theory starts with a simple premise that ever problem we encounter can be treated as a system and, therefore, as a theor it is interested in achieving control and management of this system. A systen is defined as a collection of individual elements that are interacting in order t achieve a common goal. If we take these elements out of the system, they wi act in a different way, as they would then acquire different characteristics an move towards a different aim. In the same way, when a system loses some c its elements, it will no longer have the same characteristics and, therefore, wi achieve a different aim. Another vital point is that a system does not consist c the elements only, but that the elements very often comprise something els too, which is called a sub-system. A sub-system can act almost independentl; but only within the framework and aim given by the system. If a system consist of sub-systems, then we can equally assume that any system could also be part of a larger or wider system—so, in fact, it is also acting as a sub-systen Any changes in the performance affect the components of the system, and the

y to react to correct the general direction of the system in order to achieve
e same given aim. It actually sounds like intelligent behaviour but, in fact, is
ly what we call a feedback principle, which is one of the most elementary
inciples of computer operation, without which systems cannot exist.

The general systems theory, when analysing different problems or phenomena,
ways tries to extract: the aim and the performance measure of the phenomenon;
e components from which this phenomenon is created; what is surrounding
e phenomenon; how the phenomenon is generated; and how to control the
ovements of this phenomenon. If we can define these parameters, we can equate
e problem that we are dealing with to a system. Basically, everything that
rrounds us, and every activity that we undertake, is determined by its
aracteristics, its environment and the performances anticipated. It does not
ke too much imagination to apply this way of thinking to forecasting.

If we can say that every system is defined by its input, its output, certain
ansformation functions (process), and the feedback principle, then we can
sume that a system should perform better (or give better results) than would
 the expected behaviour of every component of the system. In fact, if we add
e performance of all the components of the system together, assuming that
ey act independently, the result should be inferior to the result that they could
hieve if they acted interactively, as system elements. This is called a synergism,
here a simultaneous action of the separate but mutually interactive elements
t with the same aim, producing the total effect, which is greater than a sum
 effects achieved by every individual element acting independently. What is
ry important when talking about systems is: the number of elements that are
cluded in a system; the number of attributes assigned to every individual
ement; the number of interactions between the elements; and finally, the level
 organization of the system. Basically, we cannot achieve the synergism if we
ve got one of the above principles wrong. It is very important to say that one
ould not play safe, and, in the case of doubt, include one or two extra elements
 the system, or one or two more safety attributes. As when determining the
mber of parameters in the forecasting model, where we were following the
rsimonious principle, we are now following similar principles in the systems
finition procedure. However, system redundancy is equally as dangerous as
stem abundancy, so synergy is only possible in carefully designed systems.

It is quite obvious that, before we build a system, we should analyse the
oblem in hand in order to understand it properly. Indeed, this phase of the
stem building is called the *systems analysis*, which no doubt everybody has
ard about. A systems analyst is a person who is not only analysing the
oblem, but also is defining the parameters that will turn this problem into a
stem's solution. In order to do so, an analyst should know exactly: what the
quirements (aims) are; what elements could be included in the system; how
ese elements should be interrelated; how they are going to behave; what is
rrounding the elements; and finally, what results are expected, and how these
sults are going to affect the behaviour of the system. Once a clear view of

these aspects is achieved, the system should be easily defined, and should produce much better results than the partial solutions.

Before we start talking specifically about forecasting problems, we must make one or two more principal suggestions. Let us start with the environmental aspects of the forecasting system. If we can say that forecasting could be treated from the general systems theory point of view, and we are going to be more precise later on, then it means that, providing we define forecasting as a system, we can expect quite beneficial results from it. At the same time, if forecasting is a system then it has an environment that is not only surrounding it, but partially defining it too. As we are talking about forecasting in the business and management context, then, no doubt, forecasting is just one of the marketing functions. This is a very important statement, as it automatically neutralizes possible over-emphasis on the statistics—although admittedly we have spent most of our time in this book dealing with statistics, which might imply that is of prime importance for forecasting. If the forecasting function has its place and full meaning only in the context of marketing, then it is worthwhile spending just a little time within this context.

Marketing, as a concept, was developed to assist in sales activities in order to increase the profitability of a company, as opposed to the concept of a given production line, a given product mix, and the attempt to get the maximum out of the product by using different selling techniques. Marketing has turned the concept upside-down. It says that what we think we should be selling is not important; rather, what is important, and what should influence us, is what the potential customers think that they should be buying. If we can figure this out we can tune our production and our product mix accordingly, and not only have happy and satisfied customers but healthy profit margins too. Basically by analysing customers' needs and interpreting them correctly, we are able to use this information as the most important factor in determining: how our production is going to be organized; which products we are going to manufacture; how they are going to be priced; how we are going to sell them; which channels we are going to use; what support in terms of advertising and promotion we are going to use, and so on. Once we have defined all of this, we shall be interested in how we are going to perform not only today, but tomorrow as well, which is where forecasting fits into marketing. However, before we can be ready to develop forecasts and interpret them, we have to understand some of the marketing environment.

If customers are the centre of the universe according to the marketing concept, then we should know something about them or, at least, have a clear view of the topology of customers. First of all we should understand the difference between the customer and the end user. These two are often represented by the same person, but they are not necessarily the same. What we should be interested in is, who is the decision maker—the best example being products for children. Think about them and try to define who is who in the process of buying a product for a child. Not easy! Another problem is that the population of customers is not always available to us in full. The population of consumers is divided into: the *absolute non-consumers* (people who are not and will never be our potential target, for whatever reason); the *relative non-consumers* (the ones not yet representing actual consumers but who potentially could) and the *actual consumers*. Needless to say, actual consumers represent not only our consumers but those using competitive products, and are, therefore, only potential consumers. When working on forecasts, these factors should be taken seriously into consideration—otherwise forecasts could be misleading, as will be elaborated later.

If we concentrate on actual consumers only, we might ask ourselves why somebody is buying (or not buying) our product, and what should be changed to attract potential consumers. This question is closely related to the consumer behaviour theory, which can really be a jungle where it is difficult to see the path. Beside the various psychological factors that determine behaviour, there are a number of social factors to consider. We could spend a lot of time discussing details of these theories, but this is not the purpose of this book. What we should remember is that this area of marketing is very important, and should never be forgotten in the context of forecasting. The subsequent thought is, after we have made changes in products and our activities, how many customers can we expect to have; this is much closer to our interest.

One way or other, it seems that forecasting, as a marketing function, is designed to provide answers to two basic questions: firstly, how we are going to perform tomorrow, provided we continue to follow the marketing pattern that we have followed so far; and secondly, what results can we expect to achieve if we change the mix? Whenever we talk about changes, these are always related to decisions, so really we can say that forecasting should be a function integrated into our marketing policy for the sake of decision-making purposes. Now we have come very close to the point of treating the forecasting function as a system.

18
Forecasting, planning and decision making

One of the points to be clarified about the role of the forecasting function within marketing is, what are we really, from a practical point of view, trying to achieve If we say that forecasting provides the basis for decision making, and decision making is related to future events which we can only assume and assess, the it means that the forecasting function has to produce satisfactory results within the conditions of extreme uncertainty. In fact, this function attempts to bridge two different moments of time: the past, which we know well but have no guarantees of continuation, and the future, of which we know nothing but would like to continue on the basis of the past. This point brings us to a very common mistake, when we are not sure what we are forecasting. In our attempts to extrapolate from the past and make the future less uncertain, we forecast the sales and then expect our sales force to fulfil it. Is this a good procedure? Is our job to forecast what is possible to sell or to sell what we have forecasted. If we adopt the latter case, then we cannot talk of the marketing concept Forecasting is not the central point or the aim, it is the consequence. We can say that it is realistic to achieve a certain sales level that we have forecasted and we should, indeed, try to reach it, but our forecasts should not become law and they should always be subject to critical reviews and revisions. This is, in fact, a feedback principle that we have mentioned already.

So, our forecasts could obviously treat two closely related, but at the same time different, matters. One is a forecast of what it is possible to sell, and the other is a forecast of what we actually will sell. Both of them are subject to change, In fact, if we interpret these two forecasts from the marketing point of view, and treat forecasts as a marketing function, then there should be no confusion. If other marketing functions are working correctly, then no doubt what we are going to sell is going to be very close to what it is possible to sell However, it is not up to the forecast function to equate these two things. In other words, let us not expect what is not realistic. It is up to forecasting to open the corridors and specify what is possible, and up to other marketing functions to make it reality. If we have a clear view of this, there is no possibility of falling into a trap.

There are certain things that discourage people, in particular those in management, from forecasting. Besides the fact that sometimes they think certain competences have been taken away from them by the introduction of the forecasting function into the organization, they have a much more serious complaint. They say that forecasts are usually not accurate. Quite right! If we kept on fulfilling our forecasts, as we mentioned in the previous example, then something would definitely be wrong with our forecasts. The whole point of forecasting is that we are dealing with situations of uncertainty, and there is no way the future can be made certain. We can reduce uncertainty by careful planning and clever implementation of other marketing tools, or by using superior statistical methods, but we are never going to eliminate error and our forecasts are bound to show discrepancies from actuality.

It would be interesting to expand a little on the theme of planning and its relationship with forecasting. As opposed to forecasting, which deals with anticipating the future, planning attempts to introduce certain measures and actions to achieve the aims, which will be coordinated with an anticipated future. As it is obvious that planning aims to change the future, it would be interesting to know which comes first. Do we forecast first and them make plans to change the future, or do we make plans about possible changes and then forecast? It is difficult to say. The obvious answer is that these two functions are interactive, and that, once again, we have to respect the feedback principle. Once we have produced a forecast, other marketing functions, through planning and other measures, will try either to stick to the forecast or to change it in their favour. After we see the results, the forecasting function again assesses the future, to give us a basis for planning and decision making. Basically, it is a continuous process in which one function influences another, and vice versa. To summarize we can say that if forecasting did not exist in our company and we suddenly decided to introduce it, and if, after that, our planning of the future and the decision-making process remained the same, then we would not have to bother to forecast at all. Forecasting, like any other function, only makes sense if we believe in it, and if it influences other functions in the company or reflects the changes in other functions.

There is no doubt that planning and forecasting are closely related, and that the actual basis of planning is a decision-making process. This automatically gives a particular significance to forecasting, as it is obvious that forecasting exists for the sake of decision making. Although everybody is interested in the future, quite frankly nobody would bother to forecast it except that we are forced to make decisions today that will affect the future. So really, forecasting provides a basis for decision making. What do we mean by decision making? If we are dealing with a conflict situation, or a situation with multiple scenarios, and we want to resolve this situation in order to achieve the best possible result for our company, then we are getting involved in decision making. We are, in fact, trying to extract several quantitative or qualitative possibilities which when implemented, will produce the result that we want to see. If this extraction of possibilities is based just on our experience and common sense, then we are making intuitive decisions. If it is based not only on facts, but on information derived from these facts by applying certain scientific apparatus, then this is called scientific decision making.

Besides the technicalities behind scientific decision making, there are a few very simple and sound principles. First of all, our decisions have to be integral which means solving the whole problem and not only parts of it. This is one of the elementary principles of systems analysis, and we should really stick to it if we want to make our decisions on a higher level. Whatever scientific methods we apply in order to derive information, we should never use methods just for the sake of using them. They have to be a direct function of the decision-making process, otherwise we can only call them pseudo-scientific in the business context. Another natural consideration is that the decision has to provide an optimal solution. If our decision is not balanced, in terms of maximum achievements expected, then it is not based on scientific principles. It would mean that we have made subjective interventions in the decision-making process, for whatever reason, and that we cannot expect objective and optimal results. We can also say that the only way to know that there are several solutions, and to know which one is the optimal one, is by modelling the problem and simulating solutions. Therefore, we can say that modelling and simulations are integral parts of scientific decision making. And finally, if we are going to model something and derive further, hidden information for the sake of decision making, then it is obvious that we need data to make models. We all know that scientific methods are based on verified and reliable data, so if we are not sure that our data can be verified, we had better not even start complicated modelling exercises.

So, forecasting in general has the purpose of reducing the uncertainty factor, which then enables us to make competent and sound decisions that will produce optimal results for our company. If forecasting is made within the marketing environment, then the uncertainty factor is particularly high. We are not only dealing with problems within our company which, at the end of the day, affect our marketing, but we are also dealing with external influences, which are going to affect us. By external influences we do not only mean the government's and other global and macro-economic measures, but our competitors too. The marketing function, as such, is exposed to all sorts of disturbance factors, and decisions made within its context take the company directly on the road to success, or directly into disaster. No wonder that the decision-making process within it is very sensitive! Forecasting should make the decision-making process in marketing an easier task, or at least as easy as possible; it should reduce the risk factor involved and take responsibility away from an individual, which he or she should not be carrying in the first place.

It would be correct to say that every decision is based on certain assumptions and expectations. If we are not capable of articulating either of the two, our decisions are bound to be very defective. Forecasting helps us in recognizing both components. It confirms the assumptions on the basis of analysing past data, and provides the expectations by extrapolating the past into the future. As such, it is almost a condition without which competent and scientifically based decision making is not possible.

If we refer to our introductory chapters where we discussed the need to introduce forecasting into large corporations as a method of balancing the circumstances and decreasing uncertainty, we may also be reminded of the smaller companies and ask ourselves how they handle forecasting. One of the things that happened in the past in large corporations was that forecasters, and other scientifically orientated specialists, started to develop the rules of the game on their own. Instead of developing functional excellence for the sake of pursuing business strategies, functional strategies started to create their own logic. A consequence was almost intolerable conflict between them and the real decision makers. Both sides had the feeling that the other group was taking away part of their responsibilities and stealing recognition they wanted for themselves. On the other hand certain functions were left undone, as each party considered less attractive jobs to be the responsibility of the other side. No matter who was right or wrong, forecasting practice certainly did not benefit from this. In smaller companies things like this are far from being a problem. A much bigger problem is recognizing that forecasting, as a measure of reducing future risks, is a necessity. Even if this is realized, we still have the problem of how to apply, in practice, relatively complex methods, how to use and interpret results and, finally, how to implement the findings. We are going to assume that if one is reading this book the problem has been recognized and, hopefully, the book has revealed the details of quite a few complex methods in an accessible way, and has defined the way of using, i.e. interpreting and implementing data.

Going back to our idea of adopting a general systems theory concept in dealing with this problem, we can stress that it would mean treating a forecasting function as a sub-system within the marketing system. This would mean approaching the building of this system in a modular way, in order to achieve a complex solution once everything is defined—which in turn would mean adopting a practical approach whereby the system has to justify its existence; it has to be economical and efficient. Equally it has to produce information that is new to decision makers, but that does not create confusion in terms of information abundance. All in all, quite complicated requirements, but not impossible to achieve.

19

Implementing a forecasting system

If we make a decision that a forecasting function is exactly what we need in our company to help us to cope with uncertainty and maximize our results, and, assuming that we agree that the only proper way to do it is to incorporate it into our marketing activities, then we should spend some time in learning the know-how.

The first and the most elementary requirement of implementing forecasting is to have adequate data. If we have no data to use, everything else is in vain. The data that we need could be of various natures, depending on what we want to forecast. Usually they consist of data containing the phenomenon that we are directly interested in forecasting, like the sales of one of our product ranges; data of similar or competitive products; data of some complementary phenomena (if we are in the ceramic tiles business, obviously we are going to be interested in general construction figures, bath fittings in general, etc.); and, finally, data containing general business and economic figures affecting our particular business. We are not trying to suggest that one should have all these data bases. Data necessary for forecasting will be determined by our aims and the level of complexity up to which we are willing to go. In many cases in small to medium companies, we are going to be satisfied with just our own sales figures, and there is nothing wrong with this. Obviously, data are readily available within our own organization, and we do not have to make an effort to gather them or to keep them updated.

Assuming that we have the data, and assuming that we know what we want to forecast, and that we have learned how to apply some of the forecasting methods, the question is, do we just go ahead and make a forecast? In principle the answer is yes, but we must bear in mind certain elements. One of the very important parameters is who is going to 'consume' the forecast. If we are doing it for ourselves, then we should, naturally, be aware of our requirements. If we are doing it for somebody else, we should seriously take into consideration what the other person's expectations are, and how deeply he or she is capable of following our approach. In other words, the end-result has to be tailored to provide useful information and not confusion. We also have to be aware of the consequences that our forecast is going to have. It is important to know how the forecast will affect other functions in the company. If the consequences are serious, we had better pay proper attention to the forecast and not do it superficially. We also have to be aware of the possible errors that our forecasts could generate. We have to be able to answer whether these errors are originating in the data available, and whether they are arising because we aggregated or derived data in the wrong way. We have to know whether they are originating as a result of using the wrong methods, whether they are caused by the wrong interpretation of results or, perhaps, by interpretation in the wrong context, etc. These are all possible traps that we have to be aware of.

On the basis of what we have just said we can recapitulate that our informal (or formal) forecasting system should be based on four elements:

1. Series of data to be forecasted
2. General knowledge of the phenomenon that we are forecasting
3. General information about the environment surrounding the phenomenon that we are forecasting
4. Aims and targets that we are trying to achieve, and for which our forecasts will be used as a basis for decision making

It would be interesting to speculate about what exactly we expect as a result of the forecasting process, naturally, assuming that we are not doing it for ourselves but that somebody else is producing it for us. Is it a series of numbers with the inevitable graphs, or is it a page or two of verbal description of expected future developments—and if so, how much do we trust the numbers generated by our quantitative forecasts? Well, first of all we should trust our figures completely, because it is assumed that we have used appropriate methods and treated data in the correct manner. If this assumption is correct, then no matter how much we do not like the forecast, it is the only valid and objective outcome. We cannot discount the results, as otherwise we are moving a step backwards towards intuitive decision making. Now, if because of other information and knowledge we have, we suspect that the forecasts are not too realistic, then we have a duty to intervene and interpret the forecast. So, basically, the end-result should be a piece of paper with figures on it, but equally it should contain verbal justification for accepting this solution. The figures should contain more than one series—in other words, we have to have options. The options will either contain results acquired by using different methods, or the results obtained by one method, but with a certain confidence limit giving us a corridor of expected development of the series.

We must mention one more parameter, immanent in the general systems philosophy, which we had in mind when talking of implementing a forecasting system in our company. This parameter is called a control and it is achieved through the feedback principle. Forecasting is a continuous process, and, as

such, only becomes valuable for decision-making purposes. We have to monitor
the results and analyse their discrepancies from reality, as this is the only way
to correct the forecast and improve it for future applications. If we notice that
we are systematically making mistakes, then we should analyse the whole set
of assumptions that we have used before entering the forecasting process. Some
of the questions we can ask ourselves are:

- Are the data adequate, and have we understood the properties of the series
  properly?
- Do we know what we can expect from the methods used?
- Have the models applied been correctly estimated and tested (remember
  parsimony)?
- Can we improve the model, or must we, perhaps, change the method
  altogether?
- Should we do more experimenting and simulation with various possibilities
  in order to understand our data, methods and models better?
- Do we know the reasons why the forecasting errors have happened in the
  past and have we done anything to eliminate them?
- Do we understand the purpose of this particular forecasting study?
- Do we know enough of the product that we are forecasting, in terms of its
  life cycle, position in the market and the consumers' perception of it?
- Do we know the parameters surrounding our phenomenon, and do we
  understand the market as well as global trends?
- Do we know the targets and aims to which we would contribute by producing
  our forecast?
- Do we know who the decision makers are, and what their expectations are?
- Do we know which measures were implemented last time, as a result of our
  forecasting?
- Do we know the effects of these measures on the performance of our product?
- Have we thought of either changing the measures or the aims, if it appears
  that there are no faults in the forecasting procedure?

These are some of the questions that we have to keep asking ourselves all the
time. If we continue to do so, we can say that we have a 'system' which is
continuously and integrally providing solutions as a basis for our decisions. By
doing so in the manner that we have described, we are operating this system
fully in accordance with the principles of scientific management.

Appendix 1
Spreadsheet solutions

	A	B	C	D	E	F	G	H
1								
2								
3								
4	PERIOD	SERIES	FIRST DIFFERENCES	SECOND DIFFERENCES	LOGARITHMS	LOG DIFFERENCES	RECIPROCAL VALUES	REC. VALUES DIFFERENCES
5								
6	A	B	C	D	E	F	G	H
7	1	12			=LOG(B7)		=1/B7	
8	2	13	=B8-B7		=LOG(B8)	=E8-E7	=1/B8	=G8-G7
9	3	11	=B9-B8	=C9-C8	=LOG(B9)	=E9-E8	=1/B9	=G9-G8
10	4	14	=B10-B9	=C10-C9	=LOG(B10)	=E10-E9	=1/B10	=G10-G9
11	5	14	=B11-B10	=C11-C10	=LOG(B11)	=E11-E10	=1/B11	=G11-G10
12	6	13	=B12-B11	=C12-C11	=LOG(B12)	=E12-E11	=1/B12	=G12-G11
13	7	15	=B13-B12	=C13-C12	=LOG(B13)	=E13-E12	=1/B13	=G13-G12
14	8	13	=B14-B13	=C14-C13	=LOG(B14)	=E14-E13	=1/B14	=G14-G13
15	9	16	=B15-B14	=C15-C14	=LOG(B15)	=E15-E14	=1/B15	=G15-G14
16	10	17	=B16-B15	=C16-C15	=LOG(B16)	=E16-E15	=1/B16	=G16-G15
17	11	16	=B17-B16	=C17-C16	=LOG(B17)	=E17-E16	=1/B17	=G17-G16
18	12	14	=B18-B17	=C18-C17	=LOG(B18)	=E18-E17	=1/B18	=G18-G17
19	13	15	=B19-B18	=C19-C18	=LOG(B19)	=E19-E18	=1/B19	=G19-G18
20	14	13	=B20-B19	=C20-C19	=LOG(B20)	=E20-E19	=1/B20	=G20-G19
21	15	18	=B21-B20	=C21-C20	=LOG(B21)	=E21-E20	=1/B21	=G21-G20
22	16	17	=B22-B21	=C22-C21	=LOG(B22)	=E22-E21	=1/B22	=G22-G21
23	17	16	=B23-B22	=C23-C22	=LOG(B23)	=E23-E22	=1/B23	=G23-G22
24	18	19	=B24-B23	=C24-C23	=LOG(B24)	=E24-E23	=1/B24	=G24-G23
25	19	16	=B25-B24	=C25-C24	=LOG(B25)	=E25-E24	=1/B25	=G25-G24
26	20	15	=B26-B25	=C26-C25	=LOG(B26)	=E26-E25	=1/B26	=G26-G25

Figure 4.5 Solution

	A	B	C	D	E	F
1						
2						
3						
4	PERIOD	SERIES	Moving averages – 3	Moving averages – 5	Moving averages – 10	Moving averages – 20
5						
6	A	B	C	D	E	F
7	1	12				
8	2	13	=SUM(B7:B9)/3			
9	3	11	=SUM(B8:B10)/3			
10	4	14	=SUM(B9:B11)/3			
11	5	14	=SUM(B10:B12)/3	=SUM(B7:B11)/5	=SUM(B7:B16)/10	
12	6	13	=SUM(B11:B13)/3	=SUM(B8:B12)/5		
13	7	15	=SUM(B12:B14)/3	=SUM(B9:B13)/5		
14	8	13	=SUM(B13:B15)/3	=SUM(B10:B14)/5		
15	9	16	=SUM(B14:B16)/3	=SUM(B11:B15)/5		
16	10	17	=SUM(B15:B17)/3	=SUM(B12:B16)/5		=SUM(B7:B26)/20
17	11	16	=SUM(B16:B18)/3	=SUM(B13:B17)/5		
18	12	14	=SUM(B17:B19)/3	=SUM(B14:B18)/5		
19	13	15	=SUM(B18:B20)/3	=SUM(B15:B19)/5		
20	14	13	=SUM(B19:B21)/3	=SUM(B16:B20)/5		
21	15	18	=SUM(B20:B22)/3	=SUM(B17:B21)/5	=SUM(B17:B26)/10	
22	16	17	=SUM(B21:B23)/3	=SUM(B18:B22)/5		
23	17	16	=SUM(B22:B24)/3	=SUM(B19:B23)/5		
24	18	19	=SUM(B23:B25)/3	=SUM(B20:B24)/5		
25	19	16	=SUM(B24:B26)/3	=SUM(B21:B25)/5		
26	20	15		=SUM(B22:B26)/5		

Figure 4.8 Solution

	A	B	C	D	E	F	G
1							
2							
3		PERIOD	SERIES	D=C-X'	E=D^2	F=D1*D2	G=D1*D3
4							
5	A	B	C	D	E	F	G
6		1	12	=C6-$C$27	=D6^2	=D6*D7	=D6*D8
7		2	13	=C7-$C$27	=D7^2	=D7*D8	=D7*D9
8		3	11	=C8-$C$27	=D8^2	=D8*D9	=D8*D10
9		4	14	=C9-$C$27	=D9^2	=D9*D10	=D9*D11
10		5	14	=C10-$C$27	=D10^2	=D10*D11	=D10*D12
11		6	13	=C11-$C$27	=D11^2	=D11*D12	=D11*D13
12		7	15	=C12-$C$27	=D12^2	=D12*D13	=D12*D14
13		8	13	=C13-$C$27	=D13^2	=D13*D14	=D13*D15
14		9	16	=C14-$C$27	=D14^2	=D14*D15	=D14*D16
15		10	17	=C15-$C$27	=D15^2	=D15*D16	=D15*D17
16		11	16	=C16-$C$27	=D16^2	=D16*D17	=D16*D18
17		12	14	=C17-$C$27	=D17^2	=D17*D18	=D17*D19
18		13	15	=C18-$C$27	=D18^2	=D18*D19	=D18*D20
19		14	13	=C19-$C$27	=D19^2	=D19*D20	=D19*D21
20		15	18	=C20-$C$27	=D20^2	=D20*D21	=D20*D22
21		16	17	=C21-$C$27	=D21^2	=D21*D22	=D21*D23
22		17	16	=C22-$C$27	=D22^2	=D22*D23	=D22*D24
23		18	19	=C23-$C$27	=D23^2	=D23*D24	=D23*D25
24		19	16	=C24-$C$27	=D24^2	=D24*D25	
25		20	15	=C25-$C$27	=D25^2		
26	SUM		=SUM(C6:C25)		=SUM(E6:E25)	=SUM(F6:F25)	=SUM(G6:G25)
27	X'=sum(C)/n		=C26/20				

Figure 5.1 Solution

	H=D1*D4	I=D1*D5	J=D1*D6	K=D1*D7	L=D1*D8	AUTOCORRE-LATIONS
1						
2						
3						
4						
5	H	I	J	K	L	M
6	=D6*D9	=D6*D10	=D6*D11	=D6*D12	=D6*D13	=F26/$E$26
7	=D7*D10	=D7*D11	=D7*D12	=D7*D13	=D7*D14	=G26/$E$26
8	=D8*D11	=D8*D12	=D8*D13	=D8*D14	=D8*D15	=H26/$E$26
9	=D9*D12	=D9*D13	=D9*D14	=D9*D15	=D9*D16	=I26/$E$26
10	=D10*D13	=D10*D14	=D10*D15	=D10*D16	=D10*D17	=J26/$E$26
11	=D11*D14	=D11*D15	=D11*D16	=D11*D17	=D11*D18	=K26/$E$26
12	=D12*D15	=D12*D16	=D12*D17	=D12*D18	=D12*D19	=L26/$E$26
13	=D13*D16	=D13*D17	=D13*D18	=D13*D19	=D13*D20	
14	=D14*D17	=D14*D18	=D14*D19	=D14*D20	=D14*D21	
15	=D15*D18	=D15*D19	=D15*D20	=D15*D21	=D15*D22	
16	=D16*D19	=D16*D20	=D16*D21	=D16*D22	=D16*D23	
17	=D17*D20	=D17*D21	=D17*D22	=D17*D23	=D17*D24	
18	=D18*D21	=D18*D22	=D18*D23	=D18*D24	=D18*D25	
19	=D19*D22	=D19*D23	=D19*D24	=D19*D25		
20	=D20*D23	=D20*D24	=D20*D25			
21	=D21*D24	=D21*D25				
22	=D22*D25					
23						
24						
25						
26	=SUM(H6:H25)	=SUM(I6:I25)	=SUM(J6:J25)	=SUM(K6:K25)	=SUM(L6:L25)	
27						

Figure 5.1 Solution *Continued*

177

	A	B	C	D
1				
2				
3		PERIOD	SERIES	D=B*C
4				
5	A	B	C	D
6		1	12	=B6*C6
7		2	13	=B7*C7
8		3	11	=B8*C8
9		4	14	=B9*C9
10		5	14	=B10*C10
11		6	13	=B11*C11
12		7	15	=B12*C12
13		8	13	=B13*C13
14		9	16	=B14*C14
15		10	17	=B15*C15
16		11	16	=B16*C16
17		12	14	=B17*C17
18		13	15	=B18*C18
19		14	13	=B19*C19
20		15	18	=B20*C20
21		16	17	=B21*C21
22		17	16	=B22*C22
23		18	19	=B23*C23
24		19	16	=B24*C24
25		20	15	=B25*C25
26	SUM	=SUM(B6:B25)	=SUM(C6:C25)	=SUM(D6:D25)
27	X'=sum(B)/n		=C26/20	
28	b=(n*sum(D)-	=(20*D26-B26*C26)/(20*E26-B26^2)		
29	sum(B)*sum			
30	(C))/(n*sum			
31	(E)-sum(B)^2)			
32	a=sum(C)/n-	=C26/20-$B$28*B26/20		
33	b*sum(B)/n			

	E = B^2	FUTURE PERIODS	LINEAR FORECAST
	E	F	G
6	=B6*B6		=$B$32+$B$28*B6
7	=B7*B7		=$B$32+$B$28*B7
8	=B8*B8		=$B$32+$B$28*B8
9	=B9*B9		=$B$32+$B$28*B9
10	=B10*B10		=$B$32+$B$28*B10
11	=B11*B11		=$B$32+$B$28*B11
12	=B12*B12		=$B$32+$B$28*B12
13	=B13*B13		=$B$32+$B$28*B13
14	=B14*B14		=$B$32+$B$28*B14
15	=B15*B15		=$B$32+$B$28*B15
16	=B16*B16		=$B$32+$B$28*B16
17	=B17*B17		=$B$32+$B$28*B17
18	=B18*B18		=$B$32+$B$28*B18
19	=B19*B19		=$B$32+$B$28*B19
20	=B20*B20		=$B$32+$B$28*B20
21	=B21*B21	21	=$B$32+$B$28*B21
22	=B22*B22	22	=$B$32+$B$28*B22
23	=B23*B23	23	=$B$32+$B$28*B23
24	=B24*B24	24	=$B$32+$B$28*B24
25	=B25*B25	25	=$B$32+$B$28*B25
26	=SUM(E6:E25)	26	=$B$32+$B$28*(20+B6)
27		27	=$B$32+$B$28*(20+B7)
28		28	=$B$32+$B$28*(20+B8)
29			=$B$32+$B$28*(20+B9)
30			=$B$32+$B$28*(20+B10)
31			=$B$32+$B$28*(20+B11)
32			=$B$32+$B$28*(20+B12)
33			=$B$32+$B$28*(20+B13)

Figure 6.1 Solution *Continued*

	A	B	C	D	E	F	G
1							
2							
3	PERIOD	SERIES	TREND	Eliminating trend	Eliminating irregulars	Typical cycles	Recomposition
5	A	B	C	D	E	F	G
6	1	12	=$B$27+$B$28*A6	=B6/C6		1.02	=C6*F6
7	2	13	=$B$27+$B$28*A7	=B7/C7	=SUM(D6:D8)/3	1.06	=C7*F7
8	3	11	=$B$27+$B$28*A8	=B8/C8	=SUM(D7:D9)/3	1.08	=C8*F8
9	4	14	=$B$27+$B$28*A9	=B9/C9	=SUM(D8:D10)/3	1.04	=C9*F9
10	5	14	=$B$27+$B$28*A10	=B10/C10	=SUM(D9:D11)/3	1	=C10*F10
11	6	13	=$B$27+$B$28*A11	=B11/C11	=SUM(D10:D12)/3	0.96	=C11*F11
12	7	15	=$B$27+$B$28*A12	=B12/C12	=SUM(D11:D13)/3	0.98	=C12*F12
13	8	13	=$B$27+$B$28*A13	=B13/C13	=SUM(D12:D14)/3	1.02	=C13*F13
14	9	16	=$B$27+$B$28*A14	=B14/C14	=SUM(D13:D15)/3	1.06	=C14*F14
15	10	17	=$B$27+$B$28*A15	=B15/C15	=SUM(D14:D16)/3	1.08	=C15*F15
16	11	16	=$B$27+$B$28*A16	=B16/C16	=SUM(D15:D17)/3	1.04	=C16*F16
17	12	14	=$B$27+$B$28*A17	=B17/C17	=SUM(D16:D18)/3	1	=C17*F17
18	13	15	=$B$27+$B$28*A18	=B18/C18	=SUM(D17:D19)/3	0.96	=C18*F18
19	14	13	=$B$27+$B$28*A19	=B19/C19	=SUM(D18:D20)/3	0.98	=C19*F19
20	15	18	=$B$27+$B$28*A20	=B20/C20	=SUM(D19:D21)/3	=(E20+E13)/2	=C20*F20
21	16	17	=$B$27+$B$28*A21	=B21/C21	=SUM(D20:D22)/3	=(E21+E14)/2	=C21*F21
22	17	16	=$B$27+$B$28*A22	=B22/C22	=SUM(D21:D23)/3	=(E22+E15)/2	=C22*F22
23	18	19	=$B$27+$B$28*A23	=B23/C23	=SUM(D22:D24)/3	=(E23+E16)/2	=C23*F23
24	19	16	=$B$27+$B$28*A24	=B24/C24	=SUM(D23:D25)/3	=(E24+E17+E10)/3	=C24*F24
25	20	15	=$B$27+$B$28*A25	=B25/C25		=(E18+E11)/2	=C25*F25
26	21		=$B$27+$B$28*A26			=(E19+E12)/2	=C26*F26
27	a =	12.32					
28	b =	0.24					

Figure 7.1 Solution

180

	A	B	C	D	E	F	G
1							
2	DESCRIPTION	PERIOD	SERIES	TREND	INDEX E=C/D	DESEASONALIZED VALUES	RESIDUAL INDICES
3							
4							
5	A	B	C	D	E	F	G
6	Jan 1986.	1	55	=$B$55+$B$56*B6	=(C6/D6)*100	=(C6/G4)*100	=(F6/D6)*100
7	Feb	2	53	=$B$55+$B$56*B7	=(C7/D7)*100	=(C7/G5)*100	=(F7/D7)*100
8	Mar	3	61	=$B$55+$B$56*B8	=(C8/D8)*100	=(C8/G6)*100	=(F8/D8)*100
9	Apr	4	95	=$B$55+$B$56*B9	=(C9/D9)*100	=(C9/G7)*100	=(F9/D9)*100
10	May	5	118	=$B$55+$B$56*B10	=(C10/D10)*100	=(C10/G8)*100	=(F10/D10)*100
11	Jun	6	153	=$B$55+$B$56*B11	=(C11/D11)*100	=(C11/G9)*100	=(F11/D11)*100
12	Jul	7	253	=$B$55+$B$56*B12	=(C12/D12)*100	=(C12/G10)*100	=(F12/D12)*100
13	Aug	8	289	=$B$55+$B$56*B13	=(C13/D13)*100	=(C13/G11)*100	=(F13/D13)*100
14	Sep	9	240	=$B$55+$B$56*B14	=(C14/D14)*100	=(C14/G12)*100	=(F14/D14)*100
15	Oct	10	136	=$B$55+$B$56*B15	=(C15/D15)*100	=(C15/G13)*100	=(F15/D15)*100
16	Nov	11	92	=$B$55+$B$56*B16	=(C16/D16)*100	=(C16/G14)*100	=(F16/D16)*100
17	Dec	12	92	=$B$55+$B$56*B17	=(C17/D17)*100	=(C17/G15)*100	=(F17/D17)*100
18	Jan 1987.	13	59	=$B$55+$B$56*B18	=(C18/D18)*100	=(C18/G4)*100	=(F18/D18)*100
19	Feb	14	65	=$B$55+$B$56*B19	=(C19/D19)*100	=(C19/G5)*100	=(F19/D19)*100
20	Mar	15	94	=$B$55+$B$56*B20	=(C20/D20)*100	=(C20/G6)*100	=(F20/D20)*100
21	Apr	16	147	=$B$55+$B$56*B21	=(C21/D21)*100	=(C21/G7)*100	=(F21/D21)*100
22	May	17	194	=$B$55+$B$56*B22	=(C22/D22)*100	=(C22/G8)*100	=(F22/D22)*100
23	Jun	18	315	=$B$55+$B$56*B23	=(C23/D23)*100	=(C23/G9)*100	=(F23/D23)*100
24	Jul	19	422	=$B$55+$B$56*B24	=(C24/D24)*100	=(C24/G10)*100	=(F24/D24)*100
25	Aug	20	469	=$B$55+$B$56*B25	=(C25/D25)*100	=(C25/G11)*100	=(F25/D25)*100
26	Sep	21	428	=$B$55+$B$56*B26	=(C26/D26)*100	=(C26/G12)*100	=(F26/D26)*100
27	Oct	22	222	=$B$55+$B$56*B27	=(C27/D27)*100	=(C27/G13)*100	=(F27/D27)*100
28	Nov	23	145	=$B$55+$B$56*B28	=(C28/D28)*100	=(C28/G14)*100	=(F28/D28)*100
29	Dec	24	101	=$B$55+$B$56*B29	=(C29/D29)*100	=(C29/G15)*100	=(F29/D29)*100

Figure 7.7 Solution

	A	B	C	D	E	F	G
30	Jan 1988.	25	97	=$B$55+$B$56*B30	=(C30/D30)*100	=(C30/G4)*100	=(F30/D30)*100
31	Feb	26	112	=$B$55+$B$56*B31	=(C31/D31)*100	=(C31/G5)*100	=(F31/D31)*100
32	Mar	27	123	=$B$55+$B$56*B32	=(C32/D32)*100	=(C32/G6)*100	=(F32/D32)*100
33	Apr	28	247	=$B$55+$B$56*B33	=(C33/D33)*100	=(C33/G7)*100	=(F33/D33)*100
34	May	29	327	=$B$55+$B$56*B34	=(C34/D34)*100	=(C34/G8)*100	=(F34/D34)*100
35	Jun	30	414	=$B$55+$B$56*B35	=(C35/D35)*100	=(C35/G9)*100	=(F35/D35)*100
36	Jul	31	572	=$B$55+$B$56*B36	=(C36/D36)*100	=(C36/G10)*100	=(F36/D36)*100
37	Aug	32	624	=$B$55+$B$56*B37	=(C37/D37)*100	=(C37/G11)*100	=(F37/D37)*100
38	Sep	33	542	=$B$55+$B$56*B38	=(C38/D38)*100	=(C38/G12)*100	=(F38/D38)*100
39	Oct	34	304	=$B$55+$B$56*B39	=(C39/D39)*100	=(C39/G13)*100	=(F39/D39)*100
40	Nov	35	154	=$B$55+$B$56*B40	=(C40/D40)*100	=(C40/G14)*100	=(F40/D40)*100
41	Dec	36	127	=$B$55+$B$56*B41	=(C41/D41)*100	=(C41/G915)*100	=(F41/D41)*100
42	Jan 1989.	37	157	=$B$55+$B$56*B42	=(C42/D42)*100	=(C42/G4)*100	=(F42/D42)*100
43	Feb	38	102	=$B$55+$B$56*B43	=(C43/D43)*100	=(C43/G5)*100	=(F43/D43)*100
44	Mar	39	202	=$B$55+$B$56*B44	=(C44/D44)*100	=(C44/G6)*100	=(F44/D44)*100
45	Apr	40	309	=$B$55+$B$56*B45	=(C45/D45)*100	=(C45/G7)*100	=(F45/D45)*100
46	May	41	353	=$B$55+$B$56*B46	=(C46/D46)*100	=(C46/G8)*100	=(F46/D46)*100
47	Jun	42	560	=$B$55+$B$56*B47	=(C47/D47)*100	=(C47/G9)*100	=(F47/D47)*100
48	Jul	43	741	=$B$55+$B$56*B48	=(C48/D48)*100	=(C48/G10)*100	=(F48/D48)*100
49	Aug	44	842	=$B$55+$B$56*B49	=(C49/D49)*100	=(C49/G11)*100	=(F49/D49)*100
50	Sep	45	689	=$B$55+$B$56*B50	=(C50/D50)*100	=(C50/G12)*100	=(F50/D50)*100
51	Oct	46	445	=$B$55+$B$56*B51	=(C51/D51)*100	=(C51/G13)*100	=(F51/D51)*100
52	Nov	47	182	=$B$55+$B$56*B52	=(C52/D52)*100	=(C52/G14)*100	=(F52/D52)*100
53	Dec	48	187	=$B$55+$B$56*B53	=(C53/D53)*100	=(C53/G15)*100	=(F53/D53)*100
54	a=	75.47					
55	b=	7.73				*NOTE:	
						Cells G4:G15 from Fig.7.10	

Figure 7.7 Solution *Continued*

Top table — columns: Month | 86 | YE 87 | AR 88 | 89 | Average | Seasonal Indices

		YE	AR			Seasonal
		87	88	89	Average	Indices
Month	86					
Jan	34	36	43	66	=(C4+D4)/2	=F4*$F$17
Feb	28	35	41	58	=(C5+D5)/2	=F5*$F$17
Mar	43	49	54	62	=(C6+D6)/2	=F6*$F$17
Apr	74	80	85	89	=(C7+D7)/2	=F7*$F$17
May	90	94	103	109	=(C8+D8)/2	=F8*$F$17
Jun	126	135	140	147	=(C9+D9)/2	=F9*$F$17
Jul	182	182	190	195	=(C10+D10)/2	=F10*$F$17
Aug	193	203	204	211	=(C11+D11)/2	=F11*$F$17
Sep	163	164	165	180	=(C12+D12)/2	=F12*$F$17
Oct	89	90	90	103	=(C13+D13)/2	=F13*$F$17
Nov	41	45	57	57	=(C14+D14)/2	=F14*$F$17
Dec	36	39	42	55	=(C15+D15)/2	=F15*$F$17
SUM					=SUM(F4:F15)	=SUM(G4:G15)
					=1200/F16	

Figure 7.10 Solution

Bottom table:

	A	B	C	D	E
	DESCRIPTION	FUTURE PERIODS	TREND FORECAST	TYPICAL INDICES	RECOMPOSITION I.E. FORECAST
18	DESCRIPTION	FUTURE	TREND	TYPICAL	RECOMPOSITION
19		PERIODS	FORECAST	INDICES	I.E. FORECAST
20	Jan 1990.	49	=$B$32+$B$33*B20	40	=C20*D20/100
21	Feb	50	=$B$32+$B$33*B21	39	=C21*D21/100
22	Mar	51	=$B$32+$B$33*B22	52	=C22*D22/100
23	Apr	52	=$B$32+$B$33*B23	84	=C23*D23/100
24	May	53	=$B$32+$B$33*B24	100	=C24*D24/100
25	Jun	54	=$B$32+$B$33*B25	139	=C25*D25/100
26	Jul	55	=$B$32+$B$33*B26	189	=C26*D26/100
27	Aug	56	=$B$32+$B$33*B27	206	=C27*D27/100
28	Sep	57	=$B$32+$B$33*B28	167	=C28*D28/100
29	Oct	58	=$B$32+$B$33*B29	91	=C29*D29/100
30	Nov	59	=$B$32+$B$33*B30	52	=C30*D30/100
31	Dec	60	=$B$32+$B$33*B31	41	=C31*D31/100
32	a=	75.47			
33	b=	7.73			

Figure 7.14 Solution

183

	A	B	C	D	E	F	G	H
1								
2								
3								
4	PERIOD	SERIES	Single moving averages	Double moving averages	Parameter "a"	Parameter "b"	Forecast by single moving averages	Forecast by double moving averages
5								
6								
7	A	B	C	D	E	F	G	H
8	1	12						
9	2	13						
10	3	11	=SUM(B8:B10)/3					
11	4	14	=SUM(B9:B11)/3				=C10	
12	5	14	=SUM(B10:B12)/3	=SUM(C10:C12)/3	=2*C12-D12	=2/2*(C12-D12)	=C11	
13	6	13	=SUM(B11:B13)/3	=SUM(C11:C13)/3	=2*C13-D13	=2/2*(C13-D13)	=C12	=E12+F12
14	7	15	=SUM(B12:B14)/3	=SUM(C12:C14)/3	=2*C14-D14	=2/2*(C14-D14)	=C13	=E13+F13
15	8	13	=SUM(B13:B15)/3	=SUM(C13:C15)/3	=2*C15-D15	=2/2*(C15-D15)	=C14	=E14+F14
16	9	16	=SUM(B14:B16)/3	=SUM(C14:C16)/3	=2*C16-D16	=2/2*(C16-D16)	=C15	=E15+F15
17	10	17	=SUM(B15:B17)/3	=SUM(C15:C17)/3	=2*C17-D17	=2/2*(C17-D17)	=C16	=E16+F16
18	11	16	=SUM(B16:B18)/3	=SUM(C16:C18)/3	=2*C18-D18	=2/2*(C18-D18)	=C17	=E17+F17
19	12	14	=SUM(B17:B19)/3	=SUM(C17:C19)/3	=2*C19-D19	=2/2*(C19-D19)	=C18	=E18+F18
20	13	15	=SUM(B18:B20)/3	=SUM(C18:C20)/3	=2*C20-D20	=2/2*(C20-D20)	=C19	=E19+F19
21	14	13	=SUM(B19:B21)/3	=SUM(C19:C21)/3	=2*C21-D21	=2/2*(C21-D21)	=C20	=E20+F20
22	15	18	=SUM(B20:B22)/3	=SUM(C20:C22)/3	=2*C22-D22	=2/2*(C22-D22)	=C21	=E21+F21
23	16	17	=SUM(B21:B23)/3	=SUM(C21:C23)/3	=2*C23-D23	=2/2*(C23-D23)	=C22	=E22+F22
24	17	16	=SUM(B22:B24)/3	=SUM(C22:C24)/3	=2*C24-D24	=2/2*(C24-D24)	=C23	=E23+F23
25	18	19	=SUM(B23:B25)/3	=SUM(C23:C25)/3	=2*C25-D25	=2/2*(C25-D25)	=C24	=E24+F24
26	19	16	=SUM(B24:B26)/3	=SUM(C24:C26)/3	=2*C26-D26	=2/2*(C26-D26)	=C25	=E25+F25
27	20	15	=SUM(B25:B27)/3	=SUM(C25:C27)/3	=2*C27-D27	=2/2*(C27-D27)	=C26	=E26+F26
28							=C27	=E27+F27

Figure 8.1 Solution

	A	B	C	D	E	F
1						
2						
3	PERIOD	SERIES	Single exponential smoothing values	Double exponential smoothing values	Triple exponential smoothing values	Double smoothing "a"
4						
5						
6	A	B	C	D	E	F
7	1	12	=$B$7	=$B$7	=$B$7	
8	2	13	=0.3*B8+(1-0.3)*C7	=0.3*C8+(1-0.3)*D7	=0.3*D8+(1-0.3)*E7	=2*C8-D8
9	3	11	=0.3*B9+(1-0.3)*C8	=0.3*C9+(1-0.3)*D8	=0.3*D9+(1-0.3)*E8	=2*C9-D9
10	4	14	=0.3*B10+(1-0.3)*C9	=0.3*C10+(1-0.3)*D9	=0.3*D10+(1-0.3)*E9	=2*C10-D10
11	5	14	=0.3*B11+(1-0.3)*C10	=0.3*C11+(1-0.3)*D10	=0.3*D11+(1-0.3)*E10	=2*C11-D11
12	6	13	=0.3*B12+(1-0.3)*C11	=0.3*C12+(1-0.3)*D11	=0.3*D12+(1-0.3)*E11	=2*C12-D12
13	7	15	=0.3*B13+(1-0.3)*C12	=0.3*C13+(1-0.3)*D12	=0.3*D13+(1-0.3)*E12	=2*C13-D13
14	8	13	=0.3*B14+(1-0.3)*C13	=0.3*C14+(1-0.3)*D13	=0.3*D14+(1-0.3)*E13	=2*C14-D14
15	9	16	=0.3*B15+(1-0.3)*C14	=0.3*C15+(1-0.3)*D14	=0.3*D15+(1-0.3)*E14	=2*C15-D15
16	10	17	=0.3*B16+(1-0.3)*C15	=0.3*C16+(1-0.3)*D15	=0.3*D16+(1-0.3)*E15	=2*C16-D16
17	11	16	=0.3*B17+(1-0.3)*C16	=0.3*C17+(1-0.3)*D16	=0.3*D17+(1-0.3)*E16	=2*C17-D17
18	12	14	=0.3*B18+(1-0.3)*C17	=0.3*C18+(1-0.3)*D17	=0.3*D18+(1-0.3)*E17	=2*C18-D18
19	13	15	=0.3*B19+(1-0.3)*C18	=0.3*C19+(1-0.3)*D18	=0.3*D19+(1-0.3)*E18	=2*C19-D19
20	14	13	=0.3*B20+(1-0.3)*C19	=0.3*C20+(1-0.3)*D19	=0.3*D20+(1-0.3)*E19	=2*C20-D20
21	15	18	=0.3*B21+(1-0.3)*C20	=0.3*C21+(1-0.3)*D20	=0.3*D21+(1-0.3)*E20	=2*C21-D21
22	16	17	=0.3*B22+(1-0.3)*C21	=0.3*C22+(1-0.3)*D21	=0.3*D22+(1-0.3)*E21	=2*C22-D22
23	17	16	=0.3*B23+(1-0.3)*C22	=0.3*C23+(1-0.3)*D22	=0.3*D23+(1-0.3)*E22	=2*C23-D23
24	18	19	=0.3*B24+(1-0.3)*C23	=0.3*C24+(1-0.3)*D23	=0.3*D24+(1-0.3)*E23	=2*C24-D24
25	19	16	=0.3*B25+(1-0.3)*C24	=0.3*C25+(1-0.3)*D24	=0.3*D25+(1-0.3)*E24	=2*C25-D25
26	20	15	=0.3*B26+(1-0.3)*C25	=0.3*C26+(1-0.3)*D25	=0.3*D26+(1-0.3)*E25	=2*C26-D26
27	21					
28	22					
29	23					
30	24					
31	25					

Figure 9.1 Solution

	G	H	I
1			
2			
3	Exponential Parameters "b"	Triple Parameters "a"	Exponential "b"
4			
5			
6	G	H	I
7			
8	= 0.3/0.7*(C8-D8)	= 3*C9-3*D8+E8	= (0.3/(2^0.7^2)*((6-5*0.3)*C8-2*(5-4*0.3)*D8+(4-3*0.3)*E8))
9	= 0.3/0.7*(C9-D9)	= 3*C9-3*D9+E9	= (0.3/(2^0.7^2)*((6-5*0.3)*C9-2*(5-4*0.3)*D9+(4-3*0.3)*E9))
10	= 0.3/0.7*(C10-D10)	= 3*C10-3*D10+E10	= (0.3/(2^0.7^2)*((6-5*0.3)*C10-2*(5-4*0.3)*D10+(4-3*0.3)*E10))
11	= 0.3/0.7*(C11-D11)	= 3*C11-3*D11+E11	= (0.3/(2^0.7^2)*((6-5*0.3)*C11-2*(5-4*0.3)*D11+(4-3*0.3)*E11))
12	= 0.3/0.7*(C12-D12)	= 3*C12-3*D12+E12	= (0.3/(2^0.7^2)*((6-5*0.3)*C12-2*(5-4*0.3)*D12+(4-3*0.3)*E12))
13	= 0.3/0.7*(C13-D13)	= 3*C13-3*D13+E13	= (0.3/(2^0.7^2)*((6-5*0.3)*C13-2*(5-4*0.3)*D13+(4-3*0.3)*E13))
14	= 0.3/0.7*(C14-D14)	= 3*C14-3*D14+E14	= (0.3/(2^0.7^2)*((6-5*0.3)*C14-2*(5-4*0.3)*D14+(4-3*0.3)*E14))
15	= 0.3/0.7*(C15-D15)	= 3*C15-3*D15+E15	= (0.3/(2^0.7^2)*((6-5*0.3)*C15-2*(5-4*0.3)*D15+(4-3*0.3)*E15))
16	= 0.3/0.7*(C16-D16)	= 3*C16-3*D16+E16	= (0.3/(2^0.7^2)*((6-5*0.3)*C16-2*(5-4*0.3)*D16+(4-3*0.3)*E16))
17	= 0.3/0.7*(C17-D17)	= 3*C17-3*D17+E17	= (0.3/(2^0.7^2)*((6-5*0.3)*C17-2*(5-4*0.3)*D17+(4-3*0.3)*E17))
18	= 0.3/0.7*(C18-D18)	= 3*C18-3*D18+E18	= (0.3/(2^0.7^2)*((6-5*0.3)*C18-2*(5-4*0.3)*D18+(4-3*0.3)*E18))
19	= 0.3/0.7*(C19-D19)	= 3*C19-3*D19+E19	= (0.3/(2^0.7^2)*((6-5*0.3)*C19-2*(5-4*0.3)*D19+(4-3*0.3)*E19))
20	= 0.3/0.7*(C20-D20)	= 3*C20-3*D20+E20	= (0.3/(2^0.7^2)*((6-5*0.3)*C20-2*(5-4*0.3)*D20+(4-3*0.3)*E20))
21	= 0.3/0.7*(C21-D21)	= 3*C21-3*D21+E21	= (0.3/(2^0.7^2)*((6-5*0.3)*C21-2*(5-4*0.3)*D21+(4-3*0.3)*E21))
22	= 0.3/0.7*(C22-D22)	= 3*C22-3*D22+E22	= (0.3/(2^0.7^2)*((6-5*0.3)*C22-2*(5-4*0.3)*D22+(4-3*0.3)*E22))
23	= 0.3/0.7*(C23-D23)	= 3*C23-3*D23+E23	= (0.3/(2^0.7^2)*((6-5*0.3)*C23-2*(5-4*0.3)*D23+(4-3*0.3)*E23))
24	= 0.3/0.7*(C24-D24)	= 3*C24-3*D24+E24	= (0.3/(2^0.7^2)*((6-5*0.3)*C24-2*(5-4*0.3)*D24+(4-3*0.3)*E24))
25	= 0.3/0.7*(C25-D25)	= 3*C25-3*D25+E25	= (0.3/(2^0.7^2)*((6-5*0.3)*C25-2*(5-4*0.3)*D25+(4-3*0.3)*E25))
26	= 0.3/0.7*(C26-D26)	= 3*C26-3*D26+E26	= (0.3/(2^0.7^2)*((6-5*0.3)*C26-2*(5-4*0.3)*D26+(4-3*0.3)*E26))
27			
28			
29			
30			
31			

Figure 9.1 Solution *Continued*

	Smoothing "c"	Single Exponential Smoothing Forecast	Double Exponential Smoothing Forecast	Triple Exponential Smoothing Forecast
	J	K	L	M
8	=(0.3^2/(2*(0.7^2))*(C8-2*D8+E8))	=C7	=F8+G8	=H8+I8+J8
9	=(0.3^2/(2*(0.7^2))*(C9-2*D9+E9))	=C8	=F9+G9	=H9+I9+J9
10	=(0.3^2/(2*(0.7^2))*(C10-2*D10+E10))	=C9	=F10+G10	=H10+I10+J10
11	=(0.3^2/(2*(0.7^2))*(C11-2*D11+E11))	=C10	=F11+G11	=H11+I11+J11
12	=(0.3^2/(2*(0.7^2))*(C12-2*D12+E12))	=C11	=F12+G12	=H12+I12+J12
13	=(0.3^2/(2*(0.7^2))*(C13-2*D13+E13))	=C12	=F13+G13	=H13+I13+J13
14	=(0.3^2/(2*(0.7^2))*(C14-2*D14+E14))	=C13	=F14+G14	=H14+I14+J14
15	=(0.3^2/(2*(0.7^2))*(C15-2*D15+E15))	=C14	=F15+G15	=H15+I15+J15
16	=(0.3^2/(2*(0.7^2))*(C16-2*D16+E16))	=C15	=F16+G16	=H16+I16+J16
17	=(0.3^2/(2*(0.7^2))*(C17-2*D17+E17))	=C16	=F17+G17	=H17+I17+J17
18	=(0.3^2/(2*(0.7^2))*(C18-2*D18+E18))	=C17	=F18+G18	=H18+I18+J18
19	=(0.3^2/(2*(0.7^2))*(C19-2*D19+E19))	=C18	=F19+G19	=H19+I19+J19
20	=(0.3^2/(2*(0.7^2))*(C20-2*D20+E20))	=C19	=F20+G20	=H20+I20+J20
21	=(0.3^2/(2*(0.7^2))*(C21-2*D21+E21))	=C20	=F21+G21	=H21+I21+J21
22	=(0.3^2/(2*(0.7^2))*(C22-2*D22+E22))	=C21	=F22+G22	=H22+I22+J22
23	=(0.3^2/(2*(0.7^2))*(C23-2*D23+E23))	=C22	=F23+G23	=H23+I23+J23
24	=(0.3^2/(2*(0.7^2))*(C24-2*D24+E24))	=C23	=F24+G24	=H24+I24+J24
25	=(0.3^2/(2*(0.7^2))*(C25-2*D25+E25))	=C24	=F25+G25	=H25+I25+J25
26	=(0.3^2/(2*(0.7^2))*(C26-2*D26+E26))	=C25		
27		=C26	=$F$26+$G$26*1	=$H$26+$I$26*1+$J$26*1^2
28			=$F$26+$G$26*2	=$H$26+$I$26*2+$J$26*2^2
29			=$F$26+$G$26*3	=$H$26+$I$26*3+$J$26*3^2
30			=$F$26+$G$26*4	=$H$26+$I$26*4+$J$26*4^2
31			=$F$26+$G$26*5	=$H$26+$I$26*5+$J$26*5^2

Figure 9.1 Solution *Continued*

187

	A	B	C	D	E
1					
2	PERIOD	SERIES	TREND	INDEX	a
3					
4	A	B	C	D	E
5	1	12	=$B$32+$B$33*A5	=B5/C5	
6	2	13	=$B$32+$B$33*A6	=B6/C6	
7	3	14	=$B$32+$B$33*A7	=B7/C7	
8	4	7	=$B$32+$B$33*A8	=B8/C8	
9	5	22	=$B$32+$B$33*A9	=B9/C9	20
10	6	24	=$B$32+$B$33*A10	=B10/C10	=$E$32*(B10/G6)+(1-$E$32)*(E9+F9)
11	7	27	=$B$32+$B$33*A11	=B11/C11	=$E$32*(B11/G7)+(1-$E$32)*(E10+F10)
12	8	24	=$B$32+$B$33*A12	=B12/C12	=$E$32*(B12/G8)+(1-$E$32)*(E11+F11)
13	9	35	=$B$32+$B$33*A13	=B13/C13	=$E$32*(B13/G9)+(1-$E$32)*(E12+F12)
14	10	37	=$B$32+$B$33*A14	=B14/C14	=$E$32*(B14/G10)+(1-$E$32)*(E13+F13)
15	11	41	=$B$32+$B$33*A15	=B15/C15	=$E$32*(B15/G11)+(1-$E$32)*(E14+F14)
16	12	40	=$B$32+$B$33*A16	=B16/C16	=$E$32*(B16/G12)+(1-$E$32)*(E15+F15)
17	13	50	=$B$32+$B$33*A17	=B17/C17	=$E$32*(B17/G13)+(1-$E$32)*(E16+F16)
18	14	52	=$B$32+$B$33*A18	=B18/C18	=$E$32*(B18/G14)+(1-$E$32)*(E17+F17)
19	15	52	=$B$32+$B$33*A19	=B19/C19	=$E$32*(B19/G15)+(1-$E$32)*(E18+F18)
20	16	52	=$B$32+$B$33*A20	=B20/C20	=$E$32*(B20/G16)+(1-$E$32)*(E19+F19)
21	17	61	=$B$32+$B$33*A21	=B21/C21	=$E$32*(B21/G17)+(1-$E$32)*(E20+F20)
22	18	65	=$B$32+$B$33*A22	=B22/C22	=$E$32*(B22/G18)+(1-$E$32)*(E21+F21)
23	19	69	=$B$32+$B$33*A23	=B23/C23	=$E$32*(B23/G19)+(1-$E$32)*(E22+F22)
24	20	71	=$B$32+$B$33*A24	=B24/C24	=$E$32*(B24/G20)+(1-$E$32)*(E23+F23)
25	21		=$B$32+$B$33*A25		
26	22		=$B$32+$B$33*A26		
27	23		=$B$32+$B$33*A27		
28	24		=$B$32+$B$33*A28		
29	25		=$B$32+$B$33*A29		
30	26		=$B$32+$B$33*A30		
31	27		=$B$32+$B$33*A31		
32	a =	3.3			0.1

	F (b)	G (I')	H (FORECAST)
5		1.07	
6		1.03	
7		1.01809982869161	
8		0.92	
9	=B32	=$G$32*(B9/E9)+(1-$G$32)*G5	=(E9+F9)*G6
10	=$F$32*(E10-E9)+(1-$F$32)*F9	=$G$32*(B10/E10)+(1-$G$32)*G6	=(E10+F10)*G7
11	=$F$32*(E11-E10)+(1-$F$32)*F10	=$G$32*(B11/E11)+(1-$G$32)*G7	=(E11+F11)*G8
12	=$F$32*(E12-E11)+(1-$F$32)*F11	=$G$32*(B12/E12)+(1-$G$32)*G8	=(E12+F12)*G9
13	=$F$32*(E13-E12)+(1-$F$32)*F12	=$G$32*(B13/E13)+(1-$G$32)*G9	=(E13+F13)*G10
14	=$F$32*(E14-E13)+(1-$F$32)*F13	=$G$32*(B14/E14)+(1-$G$32)*G10	=(E14+F14)*G11
15	=$F$32*(E15-E14)+(1-$F$32)*F14	=$G$32*(B15/E15)+(1-$G$32)*G11	=(E15+F15)*G12
16	=$F$32*(E16-E15)+(1-$F$32)*F15	=$G$32*(B16/E16)+(1-$G$32)*G12	=(E16+F16)*G13
17	=$F$32*(E17-E16)+(1-$F$32)*F16	=$G$32*(B17/E17)+(1-$G$32)*G13	=(E17+F17)*G14
18	=$F$32*(E18-E17)+(1-$F$32)*F17	=$G$32*(B18/E18)+(1-$G$32)*G14	=(E18+F18)*G15
19	=$F$32*(E19-E18)+(1-$F$32)*F18	=$G$32*(B19/E19)+(1-$G$32)*G15	=(E19+F19)*G16
20	=$F$32*(E20-E19)+(1-$F$32)*F19	=$G$32*(B20/E20)+(1-$G$32)*G16	=(E20+F20)*G17
21	=$F$32*(E21-E20)+(1-$F$32)*F20	=$G$32*(B21/E21)+(1-$G$32)*G17	=(E21+F21)*G18
22	=$F$32*(E22-E21)+(1-$F$32)*F21	=$G$32*(B22/E22)+(1-$G$32)*G18	=(E22+F22)*G19
23	=$F$32*(E23-E22)+(1-$F$32)*F22	=$G$32*(B23/E23)+(1-$G$32)*G19	=(E23+F23)*G20
24	=$F$32*(E24-E23)+(1-$F$32)*F23	=$G$32*(B24/E24)+(1-$G$32)*G20	
25			=($E$24+$F$24*1)*G21
26			=($E$24+$F$24*2)*G22
27			=($E$24+$F$24*3)*G23
28			=($E$24+$F$24*4)*G24
29			=($E$24+$F$24*5)*G21
30			=($E$24+$F$24*6)*G22
31			=($E$24+$F$24*7)*G23
32	0.1	0.3	
33	Gamma	Beta	

Figure 10.1 Solution *Continued*

189

	A	B	C	D	E	F	G
1							
2	SEASONAL	INTERVAL 1	INTERVAL 2	INTERVAL 3	INTERVAL 4	INTERVAL 5	AVERAGE
3	MOMENT						
4	1	1.81	1.1	1.05	1.07	1.01	1.07
5	2	1.3	1.03	1.01	1.04	1.02	1.03
6	3	1.05	1.01	1.02	0.97	1.03	=SUM(B6:F6)/5
7	4	0.42	0.8	0.92	0.92	1.01	0.92

Figure 10.4 Solution

	A	B	C	D	E
1					
2	PERIOD	SERIES	FORECAST	FORECAST ERROR	WEIGHT 1
3			k = 0.1		w = 0.05
4					
5	A	B	C	D	E
6	1	12			= E25
7	2	13			= E7 + (2 * 0.1 * D8/I8 * B7/I8)
8	3	14	= (E7 * B7) + (F7 * B6)	= B8-C8	= E8 + (2 * 0.1 * D9/I9 * B8/I9)
9	4	7	= (E8 * B8) + (F8 * B7)	= B9-C9	= E9 + (2 * 0.1 * D10/I10 * B9/I10)
10	5	22	= (E9 * B9) + (F9 * B8)	= B10-C10	= E10 + (2 * 0.1 * D11/I11 * B10/I11)
11	6	15	= (E10 * B10) + (F10 * B9)	= B11-C11	= E11 + (2 * 0.1 * D12/I12 * B11/I12)
12	7	18	= (E11 * B11) + (F11 * B10)	= B12-C12	= E12 + (2 * 0.1 * D13/I13 * B12/I13)
13	8	28	= (E12 * B12) + (F12 * B11)	= B13-C13	= E13 + (2 * 0.1 * D14/I14 * B13/I14)
14	9	16	= (E13 * B13) + (F13 * B12)	= B14-C14	= E14 + (2 * 0.1 * D15/I15 * B14/I15)
15	10	28	= (E14 * B14) + (F14 * B13)	= B15-C15	= E15 + (2 * 0.1 * D16/I16 * B15/I16)
16	11	20	= (E15 * B15) + (F15 * B14)	= B16-C16	= E16 + (2 * 0.1 * D17/I17 * B16/I17)
17	12	48	= (E16 * B16) + (F16 * B15)	= B17-C17	= E17 + (2 * 0.1 * D18/I18 * B17/I18)
18	13	28	= (E17 * B17) + (F17 * B16)	= B18-C18	= E18 + (2 * 0.1 * D19/I19 * B18/I19)
19	14	40	= (E18 * B18) + (F18 * B17)	= B19-C19	= E19 + (2 * 0.1 * D20/I20 * B19/I20)
20	15	55	= (E19 * B19) + (F19 * B18)	= B20-C20	= E20 + (2 * 0.1 * D21/I21 * B20/I21)
21	16	38	= (E20 * B20) + (F20 * B19)	= B21-C21	= E21 + (2 * 0.1 * D22/I22 * B21/I22)
22	17	60	= (E21 * B21) + (F21 * B20)	= B22-C22	= E22 + (2 * 0.1 * D23/I23 * B22/I23)
23	18	75	= (E22 * B22) + (F22 * B21)	= B23-C23	= E23 + (2 * 0.1 * D24/I24 * B23/I24)
24	19	65	= (E23 * B23) + (F23 * B22)	= B24-C24	= E24 + (2 * 0.1 * D25/I25 * B24/I25)
25	20	90	= (E24 * B24) + (F24 * B23)	= B25-C25	
26	21		= ($E$25 * B25) + ($F$25 * B24)		
27	22		= ($E$25 * C26) + ($F$25 * B25)		
28	23		= ($E$25 * C27) + ($F$25 * C26)		
29	24		= ($E$25 * C28) + ($F$25 * C27)		
30	25		= ($E$25 * C29) + ($F$25 * C28)		
31	26		= ($E$25 * C30) + ($F$25 * C29)		
32	27		= ($E$25 * C31) + ($F$25 * C30)		
33	28		= ($E$25 * C32) + ($F$25 * C31)		

Figure 11.1 Solution

	F	G	H	I
1				
2	WEIGHT 2	SQUARED	SUMMED	SQUARE
3		SERIES	SQUARE	ROOTS
4	w = 0.05	B^2	VALUES	SQRT H
5	F	G	H	I
6	= F25	= B6^2		
7		= B7^2	= G7 + G6	
8	= F7 + (2*0.1*D8/I8*B6/I8)	= B8^2	= G8 + G7	= SQRT(H8)
9	= F8 + (2*0.1*D9/I9*B7/I9)	= B9^2	= G9 + G8	= SQRT(H9)
10	= F9 + (2*0.1*D10/I10*B8/I10)	= B10^2	= G10 + G9	= SQRT(H10)
11	= F10 + (2*0.1*D11/I11*B9/I11)	= B11^2	= G11 + G10	= SQRT(H11)
12	= F11 + (2*0.1*D12/I12*B10/I12)	= B12^2	= G12 + G11	= SQRT(H12)
13	= F12 + (2*0.1*D13/I13*B11/I13)	= B13^2	= G13 + G12	= SQRT(H13)
14	= F13 + (2*0.1*D14/I14*B12/I14)	= B14^2	= G14 + G13	= SQRT(H14)
15	= F14 + (2*0.1*D15/I15*B13/I15)	= B15^2	= G15 + G14	= SQRT(H15)
16	= F15 + (2*0.1*D16/I16*B14/I16)	= B16^2	= G16 + G15	= SQRT(H16)
17	= F16 + (2*0.1*D17/I17*B15/I17)	= B17^2	= G17 + G16	= SQRT(H17)
18	= F17 + (2*0.1*D18/I18*B16/I18)	= B18^2	= G18 + G17	= SQRT(H18)
19	= F18 + (2*0.1*D19/I19*B17/I19)	= B19^2	= G19 + G18	= SQRT(H19)
20	= F19 + (2*0.1*D20/I20*B18/I20)	= B20^2	= G20 + G19	= SQRT(H20)
21	= F20 + (2*0.1*D21/I21*B19/I21)	= B21^2	= G21 + G20	= SQRT(H21)
22	= F21 + (2*0.1*D22/I22*B20/I22)	= B22^2	= G22 + G21	= SQRT(H22)
23	= F22 + (2*0.1*D23/I23*B21/I23)	= B23^2	= G23 + G22	= SQRT(H23)
24	= F23 + (2*0.1*D24/I24*B22/I24)	= B24^2	= G24 + G23	= SQRT(H24)
25	= F24 + (2*0.1*D25/I25*B23/I25)	= B25^2		= SQRT(H25)
26				
27				
28				
29				
30				
31				
32				
33				

	A	B
1		
2	LAG	AUTOCORRELATIONS
3	'k'	
4	A	B
5	1	0.396989447548107
6	2	0.361328367473619
7	3	0.212073246430788
8	4	-0.024084419615459
9	5	0.147579143389199
10	6	0.083364369956487
11	7	-0.0373370577281192
12		
13	LAG	AUTOCORRELATIONS
14	'k'	
15	A	B
16	1	-0.491316257660049
17	2	0.019570190053938
18	3	0.176329389172856
19	4	-0.379119482646635
20	5	0.170737906300302
21	6	0.125864844257434
22	7	-0.220044618903 73
23		
24	LAG	AUTOCORRELATIONS
25	'k'	
26	A	B
27	1	-0.676636870654748
28	2	0.129727251890901
29	3	0.232447092978837
30	4	-0.370769348307739
31	5	0.218618687447475
32	6	0.083734433493 7734
33	7	-0.257047902819161

Figures 12.6, 12.7 and 12.8 Solutions

193

	C
1	
2	PARTIAL
3	AUTOCORR.
4	C
5	= B5
6	= (B6-(C5*B5))/(1-C5*B5)
7	= (B7-(D6*B6 + C6*B5))/(1-(D6*B5 + C6*B6))
8	= (B8-(D7*B7 + E7*B6 + C7*B5))/(1-(D7*B5 + E7*B6 + C7*B7))
9	= (B9-(D8*B8 + E8*B7 + F8*B6 + C8*B5))/(1-(D8*B5 + E8*B6 + F8*B7 + C8*B8))
10	= (B10-(D9*B9 + E9*B8 + F9*B7 + G9*B6 + C9*B5))/(1-(D9*B5 + E9*B6 + F9*B7 + G9*B8 + C9*B9))
11	= (B11-(D10*B10 + E10*B9 + F10*B8 + G10*B7 + H10*B6 + C10*B5))/(1-(D10*B5 + E10*B6 + F10*B7 + G10*B8 + H10*B9 + C10*B10))
12	
13	PARTIAL
14	AUTOCORR.
15	C
16	= B16
17	= (B17-(C16*B16))/(1-C16*B16)
18	= (B18-(D17*B17 + C17*B16))/(1-(D17*B16 + C17*B17))
19	= (B19-(D18*B18 + E18*B17 + C18*B16))/(1-(D18*B16 + E18*B17 + C18*B18))
20	= (B20-(D19*B19 + E19*B18 + F19*B17 + C19*B16))/(1-(D19*B16 + E19*B17 + F19*B18 + C19*B19))
21	= (B21-(D20*B20 + E20*B19 + F20*B18 + G20*B17 + C20*B16))/(1-(D20*B16 + E20*B17 + F20*B18 + G20*B19 + C20*B20))
22	= (B22-(D21*B21 + E21*B20 + F21*B19 + G21*B18 + H21*B17 + C21*B16))/(1-(D21*B16 + E21*B17 + F21*B18 + G21*B19 + H21*B20 + C21*B21))
23	
24	PARTIAL
25	AUTOCORR.
26	C
27	= B27
28	= (B28-(C27*B27))/(1-C27*B27)
29	= (B29-(D28*B28 + C28*B27))/(1-(D28*B27 + C28*B28))
30	= (B30-(D29*B29 + E29*B28 + C29*B27))/(1-(D29*B27 + E29*B28 + C29*B29))
31	= (B31-(D30*B30 + E30*B29 + F30*B28 + C30*B27))/(1-(D30*B27 + E30*B28 + F30*B29 + C30*B30))
32	= (B32-(D31*B31 + E31*B30 + F31*B29 + G31*B28 + C31*B27))/(1-(D31*B27 + E31*B28 + F31*B29 + G31*B30 + C31*B31))
33	= (B33-(D32*B32 + E32*B31 + F32*B30 + G32*B29 + H32*B28 + C32*B27))/(1-(D32*B27 + E32*B28 + F32*B29 + G32*B30 + H32*B31 + C32*B32))

	D	E	F	G	H	I
1						
2						
3	k,1	k,2	k,3	k,4	k,5	k,6
4	D	E	F	G	H	I
5						
6	=C5-(C6*C5)					
7	=D6-(C7*C6)	=C6-(C7*D6)				
8	=D7-(C8*C7)	=E7-(C8*E7)	=C7-(C8*D7)			
9	=D8-(C9*C8)	=E8-(C9*F8)	=F8-(C9*E8)	=C8-(C9*D8)		
10	=D9-(C10*C9)	=E9-(C10*G9)	=F9-(C10*F9)	=G9-(C10*E9)	=C9-(C10*D9)	
11	=D10-(C11*C10)	=E10-(C11*H10)	=F10-(C11*G10)	=G10-(C11*F10)	=H10-(C11*E10)	=C10-(C11*D10)
12						
13						
14	k,1	k,2	k,3	k,4	k,5	k,6
15	D	E	F	G	H	I
16						
17	=C16-(C17*C16)					
18	=D17-(C18*C17)	=C17-(C18*D17)				
19	=D18-(C19*C18)	=E18-(C19*E18)	=C18-(C19*D18)			
20	=D19-(C20*C19)	=E19-(C20*F19)	=F19-(C20*E19)	=C19-(C20*D19)		
21	=D20-(C21*C20)	=E20-(C21*G20)	=F20-(C21*F20)	=G20-(C21*E20)	=C20-(C21*D20)	
22	=D21-(C22*C21)	=E21-(C22*H21)	=F21-(C22*G21)	=G21-(C22*F21)	=H21-(C22*E21)	=C21-(C22*D21)
23						
24						
25	k,1	k,2	k,3	k,4	k,5	k,6
26	D	E	F	G	H	I
27						
28	=C27-(C28*C27)					
29	=D28-(C29*C28)	=C28-(C29*D28)				
30	=D29-(C30*C29)	=E29-(C30*E29)	=C29-(C30*D29)			
31	=D30-(C31*C30)	=E30-(C31*F30)	=F30-(C31*E30)	=C30-(C31*D30)		
32	=D31-(C32*C31)	=E31-(C32*G31)	=F31-(C32*F31)	=G31-(C32*E31)	=C31-(C32*D31)	
33	=D32-(C33*C32)	=E32-(C33*H32)	=F32-(C33*G32)	=G32-(C33*F32)	=H32-(C33*E32)	=C32-(C33*D32)

Figures 12.6, 12.7 and 12.8 Solutions *Continued*

#	A	B	C	D	E	F	G	H
1								
2	Table T12 – 4							
3								
4		PERIOD	SERIES	D=C-X'	E=D^2	F=D1*D2	G=D1*D3	H=D1*D4
5		B	C	D	E	F	G	H
6		0						
7		1	1	=C7-$C$28	=D7^2	=D7*D8	=D7*D9	=D7*D10
8		2	-2	=C8-$C$28	=D8^2	=D8*D9	=D8*D10	=D8*D11
9		3	3	=C9-$C$28	=D9^2	=D9*D10	=D9*D11	=D9*D12
10		4	0	=C10-$C$28	=D10^2	=D10*D11	=D10*D12	=D10*D13
11		5	-1	=C11-$C$28	=D11^2	=D11*D12	=D11*D13	=D11*D14
12		6	2	=C12-$C$28	=D12^2	=D12*D13	=D12*D14	=D12*D15
13		7	-2	=C13-$C$28	=D13^2	=D13*D14	=D13*D15	=D13*D16
14		8	3	=C14-$C$28	=D14^2	=D14*D15	=D14*D16	=D14*D17
15		9	1	=C15-$C$28	=D15^2	=D15*D16	=D15*D17	=D15*D18
16		10	-1	=C16-$C$28	=D16^2	=D16*D17	=D16*D18	=D16*D19
17		11	-2	=C17-$C$28	=D17^2	=D17*D18	=D17*D19	=D17*D20
18		12	1	=C18-$C$28	=D18^2	=D18*D19	=D18*D20	=D18*D21
19		13	-2	=C19-$C$28	=D19^2	=D19*D20	=D19*D21	=D19*D22
20		14	5	=C20-$C$28	=D20^2	=D20*D21	=D20*D22	=D20*D23
21		15	-1	=C21-$C$28	=D21^2	=D21*D22	=D21*D23	=D21*D24
22		16	-1	=C22-$C$28	=D22^2	=D22*D23	=D22*D24	=D22*D25
23		17	3	=C23-$C$28	=D23^2	=D23*D24	=D23*D25	
24		18	-3	=C24-$C$28	=D24^2	=D24*D25		
25		19	-1	=C25-$C$28	=D25^2			
26		20						
27	SUM		3		=SUM(E7:E25)	=SUM(F7:F24)	=SUM(G7:G24)	=SUM(H7:H24)
28	AVG		=C27/B26					

Figure 12.11 Solution

	I = D1*D5	J = D1*D6	K = D1*D7	L = D1*D8	AUTOCOR-RELATIONS	AUTOCO-VARIANCES
3						
4						
5	I	J	K	L	M	N
6						=E$27/20
7	=D7*D11	=D7*D12	=D7*D13	=D7*D14	=F27/$E$27	=F$27/20
8	=D8*D12	=D8*D13	=D8*D14	=D8*D15	=G27/$E$27	=G$27/20
9	=D9*D13	=D9*D14	=D9*D15	=D9*D16	=H27/$E$27	=H$27/20
10	=D10*D14	=D10*D15	=D10*D16	=D10*D17	=I27/$E$27	=I$27/20
11	=D11*D15	=D11*D16	=D11*D17	=D11*D18	=J27/$E$27	=J$27/20
12	=D12*D16	=D12*D17	=D12*D18	=D12*D19	=K27/$E$27	=K$27/20
13	=D13*D17	=D13*D18	=D13*D19	=D13*D20	=L27/$E$27	=L$27/20
14	=D14*D18	=D14*D19	=D14*D20	=D14*D21		
15	=D15*D19	=D15*D20	=D15*D21	=D15*D22		
16	=D16*D20	=D16*D21	=D16*D22	=D16*D23		
17	=D17*D21	=D17*D22	=D17*D23	=D17*D24		
18	=D18*D22	=D18*D23	=D18*D24	=D18*D25		
19	=D19*D23	=D19*D24	=D19*D25			
20	=D20*D24	=D20*D25				
21	=D21*D25					
22						
23						
24						
25						
26						
27	=SUM(I7:I24)	=SUM(J7:J24)	=SUM(K7:K24)	=SUM(L7:L24)		
28						

Figure 12.11 Solution *Continued*

197

	A	B	C	D	E	F
1		Autocovar-iances	Parameter	Derived series	Residual	Parameter
2			f1	autocovar. c'	variance	t1
3	A	B	C	D	E	F
4	0	4.426375		=(1+C5^2)*B4-2*C5*B5		0
5	1	-2.17475	=B6/B5	=(1+C5^2)*B5-C5*(B6+B4)	=D4/(1+F5^2)	=-(D5/E5)
6	2	0.086625				
7	3	0.7805				
8	4	-1.678125				
9	5	0.75575				
10	6	0.557125				
11	7	-0.974				
12	Final				2.86796105751021	0.696814866823897

Figure 12.12 Solution

	A	B	C	D	E	F	G	H
1		Autocovar-iances	Parameters	Parameter	Derived series autocovar. c'	Residual variance	Parameter	Parameter
2			f1	f2			t2	t1
3	A	B	C	D	E	F	G	H
4	0	4.426375			=(1+C5^2)*B4-2*C5*B5	=E4/(1+G5^2+H5^2)	0	0
5	1	-2.17475	=B6/B5	=(B7-C5*B6)/B5	=(1+C5^2)*B5-C5*(B6+B4)		=-(E6/F5)	=-((E5/F5)-G5*H5)
6	2	0.086625			=(1+C5^2)*B6-C5*(B7+B5)			
7	3	0.7805						
8	4	-1.678125						
9	5	0.75575						
10	6	0.557125						
11	7	-0.974						
12	Final					2.92234262040346	-0.0106854150523497	0.676619081095251

Figure 12.13 Solution

	A	B	C	D	E
1					
2					
3	PERIOD	TIME	SERIES	FIRST DIFFERENCES	
4					-.04w(t-1)
5		t	z(t)	w(t)	
6	A	B	C	D	E
7		-3	=C8+D8	=F7-G7	=$G$3*D7
8		-2	=C9+D9	=F8-G8	=$G$3*D8
9		-1	=C10+D10	=F9-G9	=$G$3*D9
10	1	0	12	=F10-G10	=$G$3*D10
11	2	1	13	=C11-C10	=$G$3*D11
12	3	2	11	=C12-C11	=$G$3*D12
13	4	3	14	=C13-C12	=$G$3*D13
14	5	4	14	=C14-C13	=$G$3*D14
15	6	5	13	=C15-C14	=$G$3*D15
16	7	6	15	=C16-C15	=$G$3*D16
17	8	7	13	=C17-C16	=$G$3*D17
18	9	8	16	=C18-C17	=$G$3*D18
19	10	9	17	=C19-C18	=$G$3*D19
20	11	10	16	=C20-C19	=$G$3*D20
21	12	11	14	=C21-C20	=$G$3*D21
22	13	12	15	=C22-C21	=$G$3*D22
23	14	13	13	=C23-C22	=$G$3*D23
24	15	14	18	=C24-C23	=$G$3*D24
25	16	15	17	=C25-C24	=$G$3*D25
26	17	16	16	=C26-C25	=$G$3*D26
27	18	17	19	=C27-C26	=$G$3*D27
28	19	18	16	=C28-C27	=$G$3*D28
29	20	19	15	=C29-C28	=$G$3*D29
30	21	20			

	F	G	H	I	J
1					
2					
3	f=	-0.04	t=	0.7	
4					
5	.0.04w(t+1)	0.7e(t+1)	e(t)	0.7a(t-1)	a(t)
6	F	G	H	I	J
7		0	0	0	0
8	=$G$3*D10	0	0	0	0
9	=$G$3*D11	0	0	0	0
10	=$G$3*D12	=$I$3*H11	0	0	=D10-E10+I10
11	=$G$3*D13	=$I$3*H12	=D11-E11+G11	=$I$3*J10	=D11-E11+I11
12	=$G$3*D14	=$I$3*H13	=D12-E12+G12	=$I$3*J11	=D12-E12+I12
13	=$G$3*D15	=$I$3*H14	=D13-E13+G13	=$I$3*J12	=D13-E13+I13
14	=$G$3*D16	=$I$3*H15	=D14-E14+G14	=$I$3*J13	=D14-E14+I14
15	=$G$3*D17	=$I$3*H16	=D15-E15+G15	=$I$3*J14	=D15-E15+I15
16	=$G$3*D18	=$I$3*H17	=D16-E16+G16	=$I$3*J15	=D16-E16+I16
17	=$G$3*D19	=$I$3*H18	=D17-E17+G17	=$I$3*J16	=D17-E17+I17
18	=$G$3*D20	=$I$3*H19	=D18-E18+G18	=$I$3*J17	=D18-E18+I18
19	=$G$3*D21	=$I$3*H20	=D19-E19+G19	=$I$3*J18	=D19-E19+I19
20	=$G$3*D22	=$I$3*H21	=D20-E20+G20	=$I$3*J19	=D20-E20+I20
21	=$G$3*D23	=$I$3*H22	=D21-E21+G21	=$I$3*J20	=D21-E21+I21
22	=$G$3*D24	=$I$3*H23	=D22-E22+G22	=$I$3*J21	=D22-E22+I22
23	=$G$3*D25	=$I$3*H24	=D23-E23+G23	=$I$3*J22	=D23-E23+I23
24	=$G$3*D26	=$I$3*H25	=D24-E24+G24	=$I$3*J23	=D24-E24+I24
25	=$G$3*D27	=$I$3*H26	=D25-E25+G25	=$I$3*J24	=D25-E25+I25
26	=$G$3*D28	=$I$3*H27	=D26-E26+G26	=$I$3*J25	=D26-E26+I26
27	=$G$3*D29	=$I$3*H28	=D27-E27+G27	=$I$3*J26	=D27-E27+I27
28	0	0	=D28-E28+G28	=$I$3*J27	=D28-E28+I28
29				=$I$3*J28	=D29-E29+I29
30				=$I$3*J29	
31					

Figure 13.1 Solution *Continued*

	A	B	C	D	E	F	G	H	I	J
1										
2										
3	PERIOD	TIME	SERIES	FIRST	f1 =	0.22	f2 =	0.25		
4				DIFFERENCES	t1 =	0.85	t2 =	-0.95		
5		t	z(t)	w(t)	0.22w(t-1)	0.25w(t-2)	0.22w(t+1)	0.25w(t+2)	0.85e(t+1)	.-0.95e(t+2)
6	A	B	C	D	E	F	G	H		
7		-7	=C8+D8	=G7+H7			=$F$3*D8	=$H$3*D9	0	0
8		-6	=C9+D9	=G8+H8	=$F$3*D7		=$F$3*D9	=$H$3*D10	0	0
9		-5	=C10+D10	=G9+H9	=$F$3*D8	=$H$3*D7	=$F$3*D10	=$H$3*D11	0	0
10		-4	=C11+D11	=G10+H10	=$F$3*D9	=$H$3*D8	=$F$3*D11	=$H$3*D12	0	0
11		-3	=C12+D12	=G11+H11	=$F$3*D10	=$H$3*D9	=$F$3*D12	=$H$3*D13	0	0
12		-2	=C13+D13	=G12+H12	=$F$3*D11	=$H$3*D10	=$F$3*D13	=$H$3*D14	0	0
13		-1	=C14+D14	=G13+H13-J13	=$F$3*D12	=$H$3*D11	=$F$3*D14	=$H$3*D15	0	=$H$4*K15
14	1	0	12	=G14+H14-I14-J14	=$F$3*D13	=$H$3*D12	=$F$3*D15	=$H$3*D16	=$F$4*K15	=$H$4*K16
15	2	1	13	=C15-C14	=$F$3*D14	=$H$3*D13	=$F$3*D16	=$H$3*D17	=$F$4*K16	=$H$4*K17
16	3	1	14	=C16-C15	=$F$3*D15	=$H$3*D14	=$F$3*D17	=$H$3*D18	=$F$4*K17	=$H$4*K18
17	4	2	7	=C17-C16	=$F$3*D16	=$H$3*D15	=$F$3*D18	=$H$3*D19	=$F$4*K18	=$H$4*K19
18	5	3	22	=C18-C17	=$F$3*D17	=$H$3*D16	=$F$3*D19	=$H$3*D20	=$F$4*K19	=$H$4*K20
19	6	4	15	=C19-C18	=$F$3*D18	=$H$3*D17	=$F$3*D20	=$H$3*D21	=$F$4*K20	=$H$4*K21
20	7	5	18	=C20-C19	=$F$3*D19	=$H$3*D18	=$F$3*D21	=$H$3*D22	=$F$4*K21	=$H$4*K22
21	8	6	28	=C21-C20	=$F$3*D20	=$H$3*D19	=$F$3*D22	=$H$3*D23	=$F$4*K22	=$H$4*K23
22	9	7	16	=C22-C21	=$F$3*D21	=$H$3*D20	=$F$3*D23	=$H$3*D24	=$F$4*K23	=$H$4*K24
23	10	8	28	=C23-C22	=$F$3*D22	=$H$3*D21	=$F$3*D24	=$H$3*D25	=$F$4*K24	=$H$4*K25
24	11	9	20	=C24-C23	=$F$3*D23	=$H$3*D22	=$F$3*D25	=$H$3*D26	=$F$4*K25	=$H$4*K26
25	12	10	48	=C25-C24	=$F$3*D24	=$H$3*D23	=$F$3*D26	=$H$3*D27	=$F$4*K26	=$H$4*K27
26	13	11	28	=C26-C25	=$F$3*D25	=$H$3*D24	=$F$3*D27	=$H$3*D28	=$F$4*K27	=$H$4*K28
27	14	12	40	=C27-C26	=$F$3*D26	=$H$3*D25	=$F$3*D28	=$H$3*D29	=$F$4*K28	=$H$4*K29
28	15	13	55	=C28-C27	=$F$3*D27	=$H$3*D26	=$F$3*D29	=$H$3*D30	=$F$4*K29	=$H$4*K30
29	16	14	38	=C29-C28	=$F$3*D28	=$H$3*D27	=$F$3*D30	=$H$3*D31	=$F$4*K30	=$H$4*K31
30	17	15	60	=C30-C29	=$F$3*D29	=$H$3*D28	=$F$3*D31	=$H$3*D32	=$F$4*K31	=$H$4*K32
31	18	16	75	=C31-C30	=$F$3*D30	=$H$3*D29	=$F$3*D32	=$H$3*D33	=$F$4*K32	=$H$4*K33
32	19	17	65	=C32-C31	=$F$3*D31	=$H$3*D30	=$F$3*D33			
33	20	18	90	=C33-C32	=$F$3*D32	=$H$3*D31				
34	21	19								
35	22	20								
36	23	21								
37	24	22								
38	25	23								

	e(t)	0.85a(t-1)	-0.95a(t-2)	a(t)	FORECAST Z*(t)
	I			J	K
6	0				
7	0			0	
8	0			0	
9	0		=$H$4*N7	0	
10	0	=$F$4*N9	=$H$4*N8	-4.13074596697935	
11	0	=$F$4*N10	=$H$4*N9	=D11-E12-F12+L11+M11	
12	0	=$F$4*N11	=$H$4*N10	=D12-E13-F13+L12+M12	
13	0	=$F$4*N12	=$H$4*N11	=D13-E14-F14+L13+M13	
14	0	=$F$4*N13	=$H$4*N12	=D14-E15-F15+L14+M14	
15	=D15-G15-H15+I15+J15	=$F$4*N14	=$H$4*N13	=D15-E16-F16+L15+M15	=C14+E15+F15+N15-L15-M15
16	=D16-G16-H16+I16+J16	=$F$4*N15	=$H$4*N14	=D16-E17-F17+L16+M16	=C15+E16+F16+N16-L16-M16
17	=D17-G17-H17+I17+J17	=$F$4*N16	=$H$4*N15	=D17-E18-F18+L17+M17	=C16+E17+F17+N17-L17-M17
18	=D18-G18-H18+I18+J18	=$F$4*N17	=$H$4*N16	=D18-E19-F19+L18+M18	=C17+E18+F18+N18-L18-M18
19	=D19-G19-H19+I19+J19	=$F$4*N18	=$H$4*N17	=D19-E20-F20+L19+M19	=C18+E19+F19+N19-L19-M19
20	=D20-G20-H20+I20+J20	=$F$4*N19	=$H$4*N18	=D20-E21-F21+L20+M20	=C19+E20+F20+N20-L20-M20
21	=D21-G21-H21+I21+J21	=$F$4*N20	=$H$4*N19	=D21-E22-F22+L21+M21	=C20+E21+F21+N21-L21-M21
22	=D22-G22-H22+I22+J22	=$F$4*N21	=$H$4*N20	=D22-E23-F23+L22+M22	=C21+E22+F22+N22-L22-M22
23	=D23-G23-H23+I23+J23	=$F$4*N22	=$H$4*N21	=D23-E24-F24+L23+M23	=C22+E23+F23+N23-L23-M23
24	=D24-G24-H24+I24+J24	=$F$4*N23	=$H$4*N22	=D24-E25-F25+L24+M24	=C23+E24+F24+N24-L24-M24
25	=D25-G25-H25+I25+J25	=$F$4*N24	=$H$4*N23	=D25-E26-F26+L25+M25	=C24+E25+F25+N25-L25-M25
26	=D26-G26-H26+I26+J26	=$F$4*N25	=$H$4*N24	=D26-E27-F27+L26+M26	=C25+E26+F26+N26-L26-M26
27	=D27-G27-H27+I27+J27	=$F$4*N26	=$H$4*N25	=D27-E28-F28+L27+M27	=C26+E27+F27+N27-L27-M27
28	=D28-G28-H28+I28+J28	=$F$4*N27	=$H$4*N26	=D28-E29-F29+L28+M28	=C27+E28+F28+N28-L28-M28
29	=D29-G29-H29+I29+J29	=$F$4*N28	=$H$4*N27	=D29-E30-F30+L29+M29	=C28+E29+F29+N29-L29-M29
30	=D30-G30-H30+I30+J30	=$F$4*N29	=$H$4*N28	=D30-E31-F31+L30+M30	=C29+E30+F30+N30-L30-M30
31	=D31-G31-H31+I31+J31	=$F$4*N30	=$H$4*N29	=D31-E32-F32+L31+M31	=C30+E31+F31+N31-L31-M31
32	0	=$F$4*N31	=$H$4*N30	=D32-E33-F33+L32+M32	=C31+E32+F32+N32-L32-M32
33	0	=$F$4*N32	=$H$4*N31	=D33-E34-F34+L33+M33	=C32+E33+F33+N33-L33-M33
34					=C32+$F$3*(C33-C32)+$H$3*(C33-C32)-$F$4*N33-$H$4*N32
35					=O34+$F$3*(O35-O34)+$H$3*(O34-C33)
36					=O35+$F$3*(O36-O35)+$H$3*(O35-O34)
37					=O36+$F$3*(O37-O36)+$H$3*(O36-O35)

Figure 13.8 Solution *Continued*

	A	B	C	D	E	F	G	H	I
	PERIOD	SERIES	FORECAST	MEAN ERROR ME	ABSOLUTE ERROR MAD	MEAN SQUARE ERROR MSE	ROOT MEAN SQUARE ERROR RMS	RELAT. ROOT MEAN SQUARE ERROR (RRMS)	ERROR VARIANCE S
6	A	B	C	D	E	F	G	H	I
7	1	12							
8	2	13							
9	3	14	15.26874246	=B9-C9	=ABS(D9)	=D9^2	1.60970744909	=F9/B9	=(E9-$E$28)^2
10	4	7	16.24768990	=B10-C10	=ABS(D10)	=D10^2	85.5197685538	=F10/B10	=(E10-$E$28)^2
11	5	22	14.28041962	=B11-C11	=ABS(D11)	=D11^2	59.5919212143	=F11/B11	=(E11-$E$28)^2
12	6	15	11.53471805	=B12-C12	=ABS(D12)	=D12^2	12.0081789903	=F12/B12	=(E12-$E$28)^2
13	7	18	26.27940934	=B13-C13	=ABS(D13)	=D13^2	68.5486191714	=F13/B13	=(E13-$E$28)^2
14	8	28	18.26082392	=B14-C14	=ABS(D14)	=D14^2	94.8515505411	=F14/B14	=(E14-$E$28)^2
15	9	16	25.87119524	=B15-C15	=ABS(D15)	=D15^2	97.4404955394	=F15/B15	=(E15-$E$28)^2
16	10	28	31.56934105	=B16-C16	=ABS(D16)	=D16^2	12.7401955949	=F16/B16	=(E16-$E$28)^2
17	11	20	21.25938994	=B17-C17	=ABS(D17)	=D17^2	1.58606302415	=F17/B17	=(E17-$E$28)^2
18	12	48	31.38085519	=B18-C18	=ABS(D18)	=D18^2	276.195973905	=F18/B18	=(E18-$E$28)^2
19	13	28	32.93921867	=B19-C19	=ABS(D19)	=D19^2	24.3958810904	=F19/B19	=(E19-$E$28)^2
20	14	40	57.13251018	=B20-C20	=ABS(D20)	=D20^2	293.522905128	=F20/B20	=(E20-$E$28)^2
21	15	55	35.89941338	=B21-C21	=ABS(D21)	=D21^2	364.832408999	=F21/B21	=(E21-$E$28)^2
22	16	38	56.19097334	=B22-C22	=ABS(D22)	=D22^2	330.911511140	=F22/B22	=(E22-$E$28)^2
23	17	60	64.20952862	=B23-C23	=ABS(D23)	=D23^2	17.7201312273	=F23/B23	=(E23-$E$28)^2
24	18	75	50.76013560	=B24-C24	=ABS(D24)	=D24^2	587.571025684	=F24/B24	=(E24-$E$28)^2
25	19	65	82.58232890	=B25-C25	=ABS(D25)	=D25^2	309.138289834	=F25/B25	=(E25-$E$28)^2
26	20	90	92.05054330	=B26-C26	=ABS(D26)	=D26^2	4.20472783922	=F26/B26	=(E26-$E$28)^2
27	SUM	=SUM(B7:B26)	=SUM(C9:C2)	=SUM(D9:D26)	=SUM(E9:E26)	=SUM(F9:F26)	=SUM(G9:G26)	=SUM(H9:H26)	=SUM(I9:I26)
28	AVG	=B27/20	=C27/20	=D27/18	=E27/18	=F27/18	=G27/18	=H27/18	=I27/18
29	ROOT						=SQRT(G28)	=SQRT(H28)	=SQRT(I28)
30	STATIS						=G29/B28*100	=SQRT(I28)	=(I29/E28)*100

Figure 15.2 Solution

	A	B	C	D	E	F	G
37							
38							
39	PERIOD	SERIES	FORECAST	MEAN PERCENTAGE ERROR (MPE)	MEAN ABS. PERCENTAGE ERROR (MAPE)	THEIL U1	COEFFICIENT
40							
41							
42	A	B	C	D	E	F	G
43	1	12					
44	2	13					
45	3	14	15.2687424676009	=(D9/B9)*100	=(E9/B9)*100	=B9^2	=C9^2
46	4	7	16.247689036408	=(D10/B10)*100	=(E10/B10)*100	=B10^2	=C10^2
47	5	22	14.2804196218707	=(D11/B11)*100	=(E11/B11)*100	=B11^2	=C11^2
48	6	15	11.5347180503836	=(D12/B12)*100	=(E12/B12)*100	=B12^2	=C12^2
49	7	18	26.2794093491873	=(D13/B13)*100	=(E13/B13)*100	=B13^2	=C13^2
50	8	28	18.2608239290404	=(D14/B14)*100	=(E14/B14)*100	=B14^2	=C14^2
51	9	16	25.8711952437121	=(D15/B15)*100	=(E15/B15)*100	=B15^2	=C15^2
52	10	28	31.5693410589325	=(D16/B16)*100	=(E16/B16)*100	=B16^2	=C16^2
53	11	20	21.2593899412612	=(D17/B17)*100	=(E17/B17)*100	=B17^2	=C17^2
54	12	48	31.3808551993322	=(D18/B18)*100	=(E18/B18)*100	=B18^2	=C18^2
55	13	28	32.9392186720632	=(D19/B19)*100	=(E19/B19)*100	=B19^2	=C19^2
56	14	40	57.1325101817856	=(D20/B20)*100	=(E20/B20)*100	=B20^2	=C20^2
57	15	55	35.8994133859967	=(D21/B21)*100	=(E21/B21)*100	=B21^2	=C21^2
58	16	38	56.190973342301	=(D22/B22)*100	=(E22/B22)*100	=B22^2	=C22^2
59	17	60	64.2095286229374	=(D23/B23)*100	=(E23/B23)*100	=B23^2	=C23^2
60	18	75	50.7601356091994	=(D24/B24)*100	=(E24/B24)*100	=B24^2	=C24^2
61	19	65	82.5823289081431	=(D25/B25)*100	=(E25/B25)*100	=B25^2	=C25^2
62	20	90	92.0505433034262	=(D26/B26)*100	=(E26/B26)*100	=B26^2	=C26^2
63	SUM			=SUM(D45:D62)	=SUM(E45:E62)	=SUM(F45:F62)	=SUM(G45:G62)
64	AVG			=D63/18	=E63/18	=F63/18	=G63/18
65	ROOT					=SQRT(F64)	=SQRT(G64)
66	STATIS						=G29/(F65 + G65)

Figure 15.2 Solution *Continued*

205

	H	I	J
37			
38			
39		COEFFICIENTS OF	
40	CORRELATION		DETERMINAT.
41	r		R
42	H	I	J
43			
44			
45	$=(B9-\$B\$28)*(C9-\$C\$28)$	$=(B9-\$B\$28)^2$	$=(C9-\$C\$28)^2$
46	$=(B10-\$B\$28)*(C10-\$C\$28)$	$=(B10-\$B\$28)^2$	$=(C10-\$C\$28)^2$
47	$=(B11-\$B\$28)*(C11-\$C\$28)$	$=(B11-\$B\$28)^2$	$=(C11-\$C\$28)^2$
48	$=(B12-\$B\$28)*(C12-\$C\$28)$	$=(B12-\$B\$28)^2$	$=(C12-\$C\$28)^2$
49	$=(B13-\$B\$28)*(C13-\$C\$28)$	$=(B13-\$B\$28)^2$	$=(C13-\$C\$28)^2$
50	$=(B14-\$B\$28)*(C14-\$C\$28)$	$=(B14-\$B\$28)^2$	$=(C14-\$C\$28)^2$
51	$=(B15-\$B\$28)*(C15-\$C\$28)$	$=(B15-\$B\$28)^2$	$=(C15-\$C\$28)^2$
52	$=(B16-\$B\$28)*(C16-\$C\$28)$	$=(B16-\$B\$28)^2$	$=(C16-\$C\$28)^2$
53	$=(B17-\$B\$28)*(C17-\$C\$28)$	$=(B17-\$B\$28)^2$	$=(C17-\$C\$28)^2$
54	$=(B18-\$B\$28)*(C18-\$C\$28)$	$=(B18-\$B\$28)^2$	$=(C18-\$C\$28)^2$
55	$=(B19-\$B\$28)*(C19-\$C\$28)$	$=(B19-\$B\$28)^2$	$=(C19-\$C\$28)^2$
56	$=(B20-\$B\$28)*(C20-\$C\$28)$	$=(B20-\$B\$28)^2$	$=(C20-\$C\$28)^2$
57	$=(B21-\$B\$28)*(C21-\$C\$28)$	$=(B21-\$B\$28)^2$	$=(C21-\$C\$28)^2$
58	$=(B22-\$B\$28)*(C22-\$C\$28)$	$=(B22-\$B\$28)^2$	$=(C22-\$C\$28)^2$
59	$=(B23-\$B\$28)*(C23-\$C\$28)$	$=(B23-\$B\$28)^2$	$=(C23-\$C\$28)^2$
60	$=(B24-\$B\$28)*(C24-\$C\$28)$	$=(B24-\$B\$28)^2$	$=(C24-\$C\$28)^2$
61	$=(B25-\$B\$28)*(C25-\$C\$28)$	$=(B25-\$B\$28)^2$	$=(C25-\$C\$28)^2$
62	$=(B26-\$B\$28)*(C26-\$C\$28)$	$=(B26-\$B\$28)^2$	$=(C26-\$C\$28)^2$
63	=SUM(H45:H62)	=SUM(I45:I62)	=SUM(J45:J62)
64			
65	=H63/I65	=SQRT(I63*J63)	
66			=H66^2

Appendix 2
Solutions to chapter examples

SOLUTIONS

Example 4.1 Solutions

(a) Plotting $x(t)$ against t.
(b) We can show that the above trend is second order by calculating the second differences (see spreadsheet (Table A)). From the spreadsheet we can see that the second differences are constant.

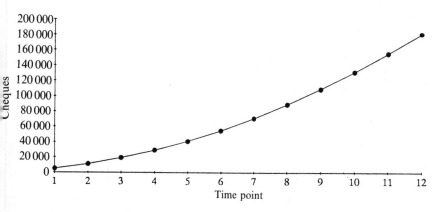

Solution 4.1(a) Cheque processing curve

Table A Quadratic trend recognition

	A	B	C	D	E	F	G
1							
2							
3	Year	Time Point	Series	Transformations		1st Diffs	2nd Diffs
4		T	X	T*	X*		
5	1982	1	5000	1	5000		
6	1983	2	11001	2	11001	6001	
7	1984	3	19001	3	19001	8000	1999
8	1085	4	29003	4	29003	10002	2002
9	1986	5	41003	5	41003	12000	1998
10	1987	6	55003	6	55003	14000	2000
11	1988	7	71005	7	71005	16002	2002
12	1989	8	89008	8	89008	18003	2001
13	1990	9	109000	9	109000	19992	1989
14	1991	10	131010	10	131010	22010	2018
15	1992	11	155006	11	155006	23996	1986
16	1993	12	181008	12	181008	26002	2006
17							

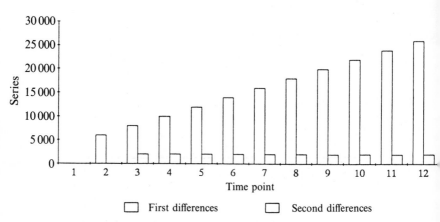

Solution 4.1(b) Quadratic curve recognition—second order differencing

Example 6.1   Solutions

(a) Using the least squares method described on page 42 we may determine the parameter values a, b and c. From the attached spreadsheet (Table B) the parameter values are calculated to be:

$$a = 62\,754.071$$
$$b = 16\,000.692$$
$$c = 999.994$$

(b) Hence the trend equation can be written as

$$x(t') = 62\,754.071 + 16\,000.692t' + 999.994t'^2$$

where $t' = t - t''$ (where $t'' = $ mean t value).

Table B Parabolic curve fitting

	A	B	C	D	E	F	G	H	I	J
1										
2										
3	Time Point	Series								
4	T	X	T*	X*	(T*)^2	T*X*	(X*)^2	(T*)^4	X*(T*)^2	XPredicted
5										
6	1	5000	-5.5000	5000	30.2500	-27500	25000000	915	151250	5000
7	2	11001	-4.5000	11001	20.2500	-49505	121022001	410	222770	11001
8	3	19001	-3.5000	19001	12.2500	-66504	361038001	150	232762	19002
9	4	29003	-2.5000	29003	6.2500	-72508	841174009	39	181269	29002
10	5	41003	-1.5000	41003	2.2500	-61505	1.681E+09	5	92257	41003
11	6	55003	-0.5000	55003	0.2500	-27502	3.025E+09	0	13751	55004
12	7	71005	0.5000	71005	0.2500	35503	5.042E+09	0	17751	71004
13	8	89008	1.5000	89008	2.2500	133512	7.922E+09	5	200268	89005
14	9	109000	2.5000	109000	6.2500	272500	1.188E+10	39	681250	109006
15	10	131010	3.5000	131010	12.2500	458535	1.716E+10	150	1604873	131006
16	11	155006	4.5000	155006	20.2500	697527	2.403E+10	410	3138872	155007
17	12	181008	5.5000	181008	30.2500	995544	3.276E+10	915	5475492	181008
18										
19										
20										
21						Regression Coefficients				
22	Column Totals									
23										
24	Sum T* =		0.00		n=	12				
25	Sum X* =		896048.00		a=	62754.071				
26	Sum (T*)^2 =		143.00		b=	16000.692				
27	Sum (T*X*) =		2288099		c=	999.9940				
28	Sum (X*)^2 =		1.049E+11							
29	Sum (T*)^4 =		3038.75							
30	Sum X*(T*)^2 =		12012564							

209

Example 7.1   Solutions

(a) **Trend line forecast fit**   Using least squares linear regression analysis we find that (see spreadsheet (Table C)):

$$b = 21.1765 \text{ to 4 dps}$$
$$a = 616.0000 \text{ to 4 dps}$$
$$T = 616.0000 + 21.1765* \text{ (time point)}$$

Table C Chapter 7 example

	A	B	C	D	E	F
1						
2						
3						
4						
5	Time	Sales				
6	Point	Data				
7	x	A	x^2	xA	Trend	
8	1	672	1	672	637.1765	
9	2	636	4	1272	658.3529	
10	3	680	9	2040	679.5294	
11	4	704	16	2816	700.7059	
12	5	744	25	3720	721.8824	
13	6	700	36	4200	743.0588	
14	7	756	49	5292	764.2353	
15	8	784	64	6272	785.4118	
16	9	828	81	7452	806.5882	
17	10	800	100	8000	827.7647	
18	11	840	121	9240	848.9412	
19	12	880	144	10560	870.1176	
20	13	936	169	12168	891.2941	
21	14	860	196	12040	912.4706	
22	15	944	225	14160	933.6471	
23	16	972	256	15552	954.8235	
24	17				976.0000	
25						
26						
27	n =	16				
28	sum x =	136				
29	sum A=	12736				
30	sum x^2 =	1496				
31	sum xA =	115456				
32						
33	b =	21.1765				
34	a =	616.0000				
35						
36	T =	616 + 21.17(X)				
37						

This enables the trend line to be fitted to the original graph (Fig. 7.6), to give the result shown in Solution 7.1(a).

A simple forecast, based upon the trend line, may now be obtained:

$$X = 17$$
$$T = 616.0000 + 21.1765*(17) = 976.0000 \text{ to 4 dps}$$

(b) **Estimation of seasonal components**   The seasonal component can now be estimated by detrending the time series (see spreadsheet (Tables D and E)).

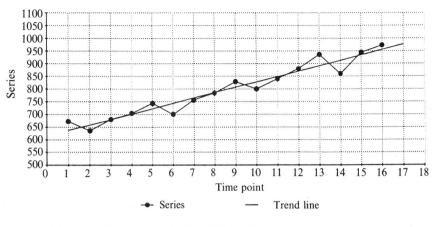

Solution 7.1(a) Sales of Doogie Co. Ltd, 1976–1979 (tons)

Table D Detrended time series: proportional solution

	A	B	C	D	E	F
38						
39						
40	Time	Sales		Detended	Seasonal	Forecast
41	Point	Data	Trend	Series	Component	Fit
42	x	A	T	(A/T)	S	A=T*S
43	1	672	637.1765	1.0547	1.0404	662.9109
44	2	636	658.3529	0.9660	0.9542	628.1691
45	3	680	679.5294	1.0007	0.9975	677.8357
46	4	704	700.7059	1.0047	1.0080	706.2777
47	5	744	721.8824	1.0306	1.0404	751.0379
48	6	700	743.0588	0.9421	0.9542	708.9915
49	7	756	764.2353	0.9892	0.9975	762.3304
50	8	784	785.4118	0.9982	1.0080	791.6572
51	9	828	806.5882	1.0265	1.0404	839.1649
52	10	800	827.7647	0.9665	0.9542	789.8138
53	11	840	848.9412	0.9895	0.9975	846.8252
54	12	880	870.1176	1.0114	1.0080	877.0366
55	13	936	891.2941	1.0502	1.0404	927.2919
56	14	860	912.4706	0.9425	0.9542	870.6361
57	15	944	933.6471	1.0111	0.9975	931.3199
58	16	972	954.8235	1.0180	1.0080	962.4160
59	17		976.0000		1.0404	1015.4189
60						
61	Detrended series in table form					
62						
63						
64						
65	Year	Q1	Q2	Q3	Q4	
66	1976	1.0547	0.9660	1.0007	1.0047	
67	1977	1.0306	0.9421	0.9892	0.9982	
68	1978	1.0265	0.9665	0.9895	1.0114	
69	1979	1.0502	0.9425	1.0111	1.0180	
70						
71	Total	4.1620	3.8171	3.9905	4.0323	
72	Average	1.0405	0.9543	0.9976	1.0081	
73						
74						
75	Total Mean	4.0004	Over est of		0.0004	
76			Over est per q			
77					0.0001	
78						
79	Seasonal components					
80						
81		Q1	Q2	Q3	Q4	
82	S	1.0404	0.9542	0.9975	1.0080	
83						

Table E Detrended time series: additive solution

	A	B	C	D	E	F
84						
85						
86						
87						
88	Time	Sales		Detrended	Seasonal	Forecast
89	Point	Data	Trend	Series	Component	Fit
90	x	A	T	(A - T)	S	A=T+S
91	1	672	637.1765	34.8235	30.7647	667.9412
92	2	636	658.3529	-22.3529	-36.4118	621.9412
93	3	680	679.5294	0.4706	-1.5882	677.9412
94	4	704	700.7059	3.2941	7.2353	707.9412
95	5	744	721.8824	22.1176	30.7647	752.6471
96	6	700	743.0588	-43.0588	-36.4118	706.6471
97	7	756	764.2353	-8.2353	-1.5882	762.6471
98	8	784	785.4118	-1.4118	7.2353	792.6471
99	9	828	806.5882	21.4118	30.7647	837.3529
100	10	800	827.7647	-27.7647	-36.4118	791.3529
101	11	840	848.9412	-8.9412	-1.5882	847.3529
102	12	880	870.1176	9.8824	7.2353	877.3529
103	13	936	891.2941	44.7059	30.7647	922.0588
104	14	860	912.4706	-52.4706	-36.4118	876.0588
105	15	944	933.6471	10.3529	-1.5882	932.0588
106	16	972	954.8235	17.1765	7.2353	962.0588
107		17	976.0000		30.7647	1006.7647
108						
109						
110	Detrended series in table form					
111						
112						
113						
114	Year	Q1	Q2	Q3	Q4	
115	1976	34.8235	-22.3529	0.4706	3.2941	
116	1977	22.1176	-43.0588	-8.2353	-1.4118	
117	1978	21.4118	-27.7647	-8.9412	9.8824	
118	1979	44.7059	-52.4706	10.3529	17.1765	
119						
120	Total	123.0588	-145.6471	-6.3529	28.9412	
121	Average	30.7647	-36.4118	-1.5882	7.2353	
122						
123						
124	Total Mean	2.84217E-14	Over-Est =		2.84217E-14	
125			Over-est per Q =		7.10543E-15	
126	Seasonal components					
127						
128		Q1	Q2	Q3	Q4	
129	S	30.7647	-36.4118	-1.5882	7.2353	
130						

Using the proportional mode we find that:

$$S = 1.0404 \text{ to 4 dps for Q1}$$
$$S = 0.9542 \text{ to 4 dps for Q2}$$
$$S = 0.9975 \text{ to 4 dps for Q3}$$
$$S = 1.0080 \text{ to 4 dps for Q4}$$

Forecast for Q1 1980 is:

$$T = 976.0000 \text{ to 4 dps}$$
$$S = 1.0404$$
$$F = T*S = 1015.4189 \text{ to 4 dps}$$

Using the additive model we find that:

$$S = 30.7647 \text{ to 4 dps for Q1}$$

$$S = -36.4118 \text{ to 4 dps for Q2}$$
$$S = -1.5882 \text{ to 4 dps for Q3}$$
$$S = 7.2353 \text{ to 4 dps for Q4}$$

Forecast for Q1 1980 is:

$$T = 976.0000 \text{ to 4 dps}$$
$$S = 30.7674$$
$$F = T + S = 1006.7647 \text{ to 4 dps}$$

The model fit at each internal and external time point is plotted on Solution 7.1(b). It can be seen, that for the problem under discussion, the two models produce comparable forecasts. If the sales amplitude were to increase over time then a discrepancy between the two methods would occur. In this case one would only use the proportional model.

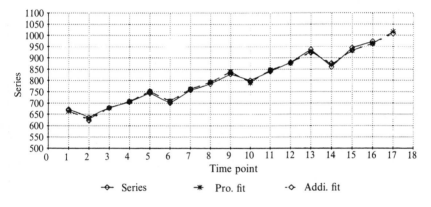

Solution 7.1(b) Sales of Doogie Co. Ltd, 1976–1979 (tons)

Example 8.1 Solutions

(a) Plotting $x(t)$ against t. From the graph in Solution 8.1(a) we can see that the trend is non-stationary.
stationary.

(b) The single and double moving average forecasts of length 3 are provided on the spreadsheet (Table F) and superimposed onto Solution 8.1(a) to give Solution 8.1(b).

(c) Using the double moving average we find that the forecast is 956 tons to the nearest ton.

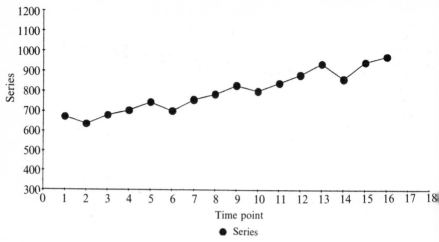

Solution 8.1(a) Sales of Doogie Co. Ltd

Table F Chapter 8 example

	A	B	C	D	E	F	G	H
1								
2								
3								
4							Forecast	Foreca
5	PERIOD	SERIES	M*	M**	at	bt	M*	M**
6								
7	1	672						
8	2	636						
9	3	680	662.6667					
10	4	704	673.3333				662.6667	
11	5	744	709.3333	681.7778	736.8889	27.5556	673.3333	
12	6	700	716.0000	699.5556	732.4444	16.4444	709.3333	764.44
13	7	756	733.3333	719.5556	747.1111	13.7778	716.0000	748.88
14	8	784	746.6667	732.0000	761.3333	14.6667	733.3333	760.88
15	9	828	789.3333	756.4444	822.2222	32.8889	746.6667	776.00
16	10	800	804.0000	780.0000	828.0000	24.0000	789.3333	855.11
17	11	840	822.6667	805.3333	840.0000	17.3333	804.0000	852.00
18	12	880	840.0000	822.2222	857.7778	17.7778	822.6667	857.33
19	13	936	885.3333	849.3333	921.3333	36.0000	840.0000	875.55
20	14	860	892.0000	872.4444	911.5556	19.5556	885.3333	957.33
21	15	944	913.3333	896.8889	929.7778	16.4444	892.0000	931.11
22	16	972	925.3333	910.2222	940.4444	15.1111	913.3333	946.22
23	17						925.3333	955.55
24								
25								
26								
27								

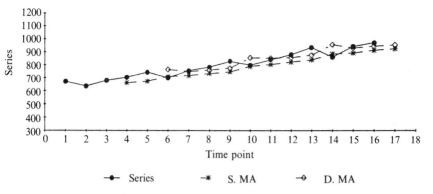

$$\begin{array}{c}
\text{--●--} \quad \text{Series} \qquad \text{--*} \quad \text{S. MA} \qquad \text{--◒} \quad \text{D. MA}
\end{array}$$

Solution 8.1(b) Sales of Doogie Co. Ltd, moving average forecast

Example 9.1   Solutions

(a) Plotting $x(t)$ against t. From Solution 9.1(a) we can see that the trend is non-stationary.

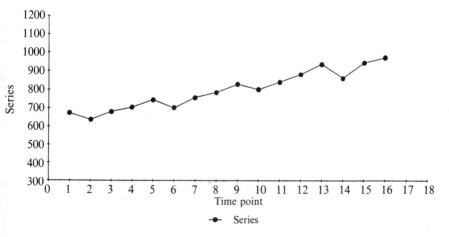

Solution 9.1(a) Sales of Doogie Co. Ltd

(b) Using Brown's exponential smoothing method provides single, double and triple forecasts (see spreadsheet (Table G)). The forecast solutions can be plotted onto the original graph to give Solution 9.1(b).

(c) The forecast for quarter 1 1980 will be:

Single exponential smoothing 909 to the nearest ton.
Double exponential smoothing 983 to the nearest ton.
Triple exponential smoothing 995 to the nearest ton.

	A	B	C	D	E	F	G	H	I	J
1										
2										
3										
4										
5	ALPHA = 0.3									
6										
7										
8										
9	TIME	SERIES	SINGLE	DOUBLE	TRIPLE		DOUBLE SMOOTHING			TRIPLE SMO
10	t	X(t)	S*	S**	S***		at	bt		at
11										
12	1	672	672.0000	672.0000	672.0000					
13	2	636	661.2000	668.7600	671.0280		653.6400	-3.2400		648.3480
14	3	680	666.8400	668.1840	670.1748		665.4960	-0.5760		666.1428
15	4	704	677.9880	671.1252	670.4599		684.8508	2.9412		691.0483
16	5	744	697.7916	679.1251	673.0595		716.4581	7.9999		729.0589
17	6	700	698.4541	684.9238	676.6188		711.9844	5.7987		717.2097
18	7	756	715.7179	694.1620	681.8818		737.2737	9.2382		746.5493
19	8	784	736.2025	706.7742	689.3495		765.6309	12.6121		777.6345
20	9	828	763.7418	723.8645	699.7040		803.6191	17.0903		819.3359
21	10	800	774.6192	739.0909	711.5201		810.1476	15.2264		818.1051
22	11	840	794.2335	755.6337	724.7541		832.8333	16.5428		840.5535
23	12	880	819.9634	774.9326	739.8077		864.9943	19.2989		874.9002
24	13	936	854.7744	798.8851	757.5309		910.6637	23.3525		925.1987
25	14	860	856.3421	816.1222	775.1083		896.5619	17.2371		895.7679
26	15	944	882.6395	836.0774	793.3990		929.2015	19.9552		933.0852
27	16	972	909.4476	858.0885	812.8059		960.8068	22.0111		966.8833
28	17									

Table G Chapter 9 example

	K	L	M	N	O	P
1						
2						
3						
4						
5						
6						
7						
8	OTHING			SINGLE	DOUBLE	TRIPLE
9	bt	ct		Ft+m	Ft+m	Ft+m
10						
11						
12						
13	-8.2620	-0.4860		672.0000		
14	0.0378	0.0594		661.2000	650.4000	639.6000
15	8.8225	0.5692		666.8400	664.9200	666.2400
16	19.9579	1.1572		677.9880	687.7920	700.4400
17	10.7574	0.4799		697.7916	724.4580	750.1740
18	18.0405	0.8518		698.4541	717.7831	728.4469
19	24.0034	1.1024		715.7179	746.5119	765.4417
20	32.0052	1.4434		736.2025	778.2430	802.7402
21	22.7779	0.7308		763.7418	820.7093	852.7845
22	23.8692	0.7090		774.6192	825.3740	841.6138
23	28.6994	0.9097		794.2335	849.3760	865.1317
24	37.7460	1.3349		819.9634	884.2932	904.5093
25	16.4835	-0.0729		854.7744	934.6162	964.2796
26	23.6407	0.3567		856.3421	913.7990	912.1785
27	27.7776	0.5581		882.6395	949.1567	957.0826
28				909.4476	982.8178	995.2190

Table G *Continued*

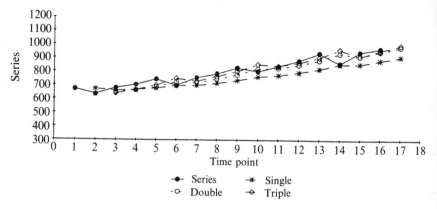

Solution 9.1(b) Sales of Doogie Co. Ltd, smoothed forecast

Example 10.1   Solutions

(a) Plotting $x(t)$ against t. From Solution 10.1(a) we see that the trend is non-stationary.
(b) Using Winters' method to fit a forecast (see spreadsheet solution (Table H)) to the original data we have Solution 10.1(b).
(c) The forecast for quarter 1 1980 using Winters' method is 1053 to the nearest ton.

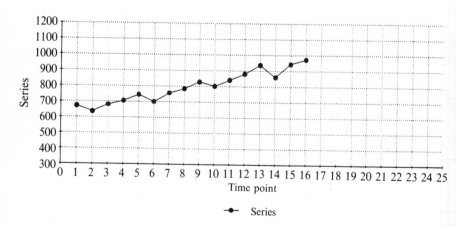

Solution 10.1(a) Sales of Doogie, Winters' forecasting

Table H Chapter 10 example

Time Point t	Series X(t)	t^2	t X(t)	INDEX	T	at	bt	St	Ft+1
1	672	1	672	1.0547	637.1765			1.0405	
2	636	4	1272	0.9660	658.3529			0.9543	
3	680	9	2040	1.0007	679.5294			0.9976	
4	704	16	2816	1.0047	700.7059			1.0081	
5	744	25	3720	1.0306	721.8824	721.8824	21.1765	1.0375	709.0738
6	700	36	4200	0.9421	743.0588	742.1080	21.0814	0.9510	761.3717
7	756	49	5292	0.9892	764.2353	762.6509	21.0275	0.9957	789.9969
8	784	64	6272	0.9982	785.4118	783.0835	20.9680	1.0060	834.2365
9	828	81	7452	1.0265	806.5882	803.4505	20.9079	1.0354	783.9336
10	800	100	8000	0.9665	827.7647	826.0479	21.0769	0.9562	843.4962
11	840	121	9240	0.9895	848.9412	846.7737	21.0418	0.9946	873.0179
12	880	144	10560	1.0114	870.1176	868.5095	21.1112	1.0082	921.1535
13	936	169	12168	1.0502	891.2941	891.0545	21.2446	1.0399	872.3622
14	860	196	12040	0.9425	912.4706	911.0163	21.1253	0.9525	927.1096
15	944	225	14160	1.0111	933.6471	933.8397	21.2951	0.9995	962.9340
16	972	256	15552	1.0180	954.8235	956.0341	21.3850	1.0107	1016.461
17					976.0000				951.4106
18					997.1765				1019.664
19					1018.3529				1052.746
20					1039.5294				1127.657
21					1060.7059				1053.262
22					1081.8824				

Regression Coefficient Calculations:

Column Totals:

- n = 16
- sum t = 136
- sum X(t) = 12736
- sum t^2 = 1496
- sum t X(t) = 115456

- b = 21.1765
- a = 616.0000

Smoothing Constants:

ALPHA	GAMMA	BETA
0.1	0.1	0.3

SEASONAL MOMENT

	PERIOD 1	PERIOD 2	PERIOD 3	PERIOD 4	MEAN
1	1.0547	1.0306	1.0265	1.0502	1.0405
2	0.9660	0.9421	0.9665	0.9425	0.9543
3	1.0007	0.9892	0.9895	1.0111	0.9976
4	1.0047	0.9982	1.0114	1.0180	1.0081

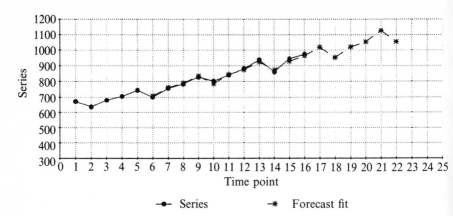

Solution 10.1(b) Sales of Doogie, Winters' forecasting

Example 11.1 Solutions

(a) Plotting $x(t)$ against t. From Solution 11.1(a) we see that the trend is non-stationary.
(b) Using the adaptive filtering method (see Table I) to provide a forecast fit to the above data gives Solution 11.1(b).
(c) The forecast for quarter 1 1980 using the adaptive filtering method is 1001 to the nearest ton.

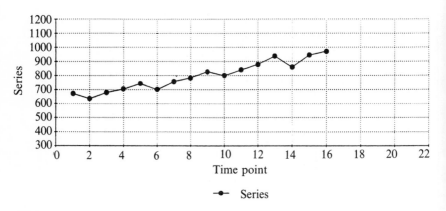

Solution 11.1(a) Sales of Doogie Co. Ltd

	A	B	C	D	E	F	G	H	I
1									
2									
3									
4	PERIOD	SERIES	FORECAST	FORECAST ERROR	WEIGHT 1	WEIGHT 2	SQUARED SERIES	SUMMED SQUARED SERIES	SQUARE ROOTS
5							SERIES	SERIES	ROOTS
6			K=0.1		W=0.05	W=0.05	B^2	SERIES	SQRT(h)
7									
8	1	672					451584		
9	2	636					404496	856080	925.246
10	3	680	685.8704	-5.8704	0.4737	0.5724	462400	866896	931.072
11	4	704	684.9238	19.0762	0.4728	0.5714	495616	958016	978.783
12	5	744	725.4240	18.5760	0.4758	0.5742	553536	1049152	1024.281
13	6	700	762.1233	-62.1233	0.4785	0.5769	490000	1043536	1021.536
14	7	756	751.7729	4.2271	0.4697	0.5685	571536	1061536	1030.309
15	8	784	753.9096	30.0904	0.4703	0.5691	614656	1186192	1089.124
16	9	828	805.3079	22.6921	0.4745	0.5731	685584	1300240	1140.281
17	10	800	846.9851	-46.9851	0.4775	0.5760	640000	1325584	1151.340
18	11	840	849.4784	-9.4784	0.4716	0.5703	705600	1345600	1160.000
19	12	880	850.4620	29.5380	0.4704	0.5692	774400	1480000	1216.553
20	13	936	898.2391	37.7609	0.4741	0.5727	876096	1650496	1284.716
21	14	860	955.6691	-95.6691	0.4786	0.5769	739600	1615696	1271.100
22	15	944	932.7379	11.2621	0.4677	0.5667	891136	1630736	1277.003
23	16	972	931.1965	40.8035	0.4689	0.5681	944784		
24	17		1000.7002		0.4737	0.5724			
25	18		1030.3203						
26	19		1060.7769						
27	20		1092.1561						
28									
29									

Table I Chapter 11 example

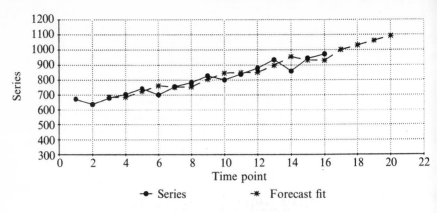

Solution 11.1(b) Sales of Doogie Co. Ltd

Suggested readings

Anderson, O. D., *Time Series Analysis and Forecasting*, Butterworths, London, 1976.

Armstrong, J. S., *Long Range Forecasting*, John Wiley and Sons, New York, 1978.

Benton, K. William, *Forecasting for Management*, Addison-Wesley Publishing Co., Reading, Massachusetts, 1972.

Box, E. P. George and Gwilym M. Jenkins, *Time Series Analysis: Forecasting and Control*, Holden Day, San Francisco, 1976.

Bowerman, L. Bruce and Richard T. O'Connell, *Time Series Forecasting*, Duxbury Press, Boston, 1989.

Brown, Robert, *Statistical Forecasting for Inventory Control*, McGraw-Hill Book Co., New York, 1958.

Chatfield, C., *The Analysis of Time Series: An Introduction*, Chapman and Hall, London, 1980.

Cooper-Jones, Dennis, *Business Planning and Forecasting*, Business Books, London, 1974.

Coutie, G. A., O. L. Davies, C. H. Hossell, D. W. G. P. Millar and A. J. H. Morrell, *Short Term Forecasting*, Oliver and Boyd, Edinburgh, 1967.

Cuthbert, Daniel, Fred S. Wood and John W. Gorman, *Fitting Equations to Data*, John Wiley and Sons, New York, 1971.

Dodd, T. F., *Sales Forecasting*, Gower Press, Essex, 1974.

Eby, H. Frank and William O'Neill, *The Management of Sales Forecasting*, Lexington Books, Lexington, 1977.

Ehrenberg, A. S. C., *Data Reduction*, John Wiley and Sons, New York, 1975.

Farnum, R. Nicholas and LaVerne W. Stanton, *Quantitative Forecasting Methods*, PWS–Kent Publishing Co., Boston, 1989.

Firth, Michael, *Forecasting Methods in Business and Management*, Edward Arnold, London, 1977.

Fuller, A. Wayne, *Introduction to Statistical Time Series*, John Wiley and Sons, New York, 1976.

Gilchrist, Warren, *Statistical Forecasting*, John Wiley and Sons, New York, 1976.

Granger, C. W. J. and Paul Newbold, *Forecasting Economic Time Series*, Academic Press, New York, 1977.

Gregg, J. V., C. H. Hossell and J. T. Rischardson, *Mathematical Trend Curves: An Aid to Forecasting*, Oliver and Boyd, Edinburgh, 1967.

Hannan, E. J., *Time Series Analysis*, Chapman and Hall, London, 1977.

Harvey, C. Andrew, *Forecasting, Structural Time Series Models and the Kalman Filter*, Cambridge University Press, Cambridge, 1989.

Hoff, C. John, *A Practical Guide to Box–Jenkins Forecasting*, Lifetime Learning Publications, Belmont, California, 1983.

Jarrett, Jeffrey, *Business Forecasting Methods*, Basil Blackwell, Oxford, 1991.

Jenkins, Gwilym M., *Practical Experiences with Modeling and Forecasting Time Series*, A GJP Publication, Channel Islands, 1979.

Jones, Harey and Brian C. Twiss, *Forecasting Technology for Planning Decisions*, The Macmillan Press, London, 1978.

Keay, Frederick, *Marketing and Sales Forecasting*, Pergamon Press, Oxford, 1972.

Kendall, Sir Maurice, *Time Series*, Charles Griffin and Co., London, 1976.

Makridakis, Spyros and Steven C. Wheelwright, *Interactive Forecasting*, Holden Day, San Francisco, 1978.

Makridakis, Spyros and Steven C. Wheelwright, *The Handbook of Forecasting*, John Wiley and Sons, New York, 1982.

McLaughlin, R. L., 'Time series forecasting', *Marketing Research Technique Series No. 6*, AMA, 1962.

Michael, C. George, 'Sales forecasting', *Monograph Series No. 10*, AMA, Chicago, 1979.

Montgomery, C. Douglas and Lynwood A. Johnson, *Forecasting and Time Series Analysis*, McGraw-Hill Book Co., New York, 1976.

Nelson, R. Charles, *Applied Time Series Analysis*, Holden Day, San Francisco, 1973.

Pearce, Colin, *Prediction Techniques for Marketing Planners*, Associated Business Programmes, London, 1971.

Sullivan, G. William and W. Wayne Claycombe, *Fundamentals of Forecasting*, Reston Publishing Co., Reston, Virginia, 1977.

Theil, Henry, *Applied Economic Forecasting*, North Holland Publishing Co., Amsterdam, 1971.

Thomopoulos, T. Nick, *Applied Forecasting Methods*, Prentice-Hall, Englewood Cliffs, New Jersey, 1980.

Winters, R. Peter, 'Forecasting sales by exponentially weighted moving averages', *Management Science*, April 1960.

Wood, Doug and Robert Fildes, *Forecasting for Business: Methods and Applications*, Longman, London, 1976.

Glossary

accuracy Deviation from the actual series of the series generated by the model. Various statistics are used to measure accuracy; the one most commonly used is MSE.

actual series Another expression used for empirical variable, i.e. a series that is the subject of the forecasting exercise.

adaptive filtering One of the stochastic methods which uses iterative techniques and the so-called learning constant to find the optimum weights.

AIC Akaike Information Criterion, a measure of selecting the forecasts. The smaller the value of AIC, the better.

algebraic curves A set of curves defined by algebraic equations, such as straight lines (linear) and parabolas, whose origins are in a normal coordinate system.

ARIMA(p,d,q) Autoregressive integrated moving average model. A stochastic model with an autoregressive and moving average component where the non-stationary empirical series was created through integration (summation) of the white noise process and the passage through a linear filter. Order d is greater than zero, signifying the number of differencing needed to make the series stationary again.

ARMA(p,d,q) A stochastic model with an autoregressive component of order p, moving average component of order q and order d equal to zero, i.e. non-differenced series.

autocorrelations A series of correlations between the original and lagged observations of the empirical variable. This is a very important measure of stationarity and seasonality. When plotted as a series, autocorrelation coefficients constitute the autocorrelations function. The maximum practical number of autocorrelation coefficients that should be calculated should not exceed one third of the length of the original series.

autocorrelated residuals If residuals show autocorrelation, this is a sign that either the method applied has not been adequate, or the model does not describe the actual series. Residuals should be randomly distributed around zero.

autocovariance A covariance between the series and its lagged values (at a particular lag).

autoregressive component (AR) A component used by a few methods (predominantly by the Box–Jenkins method) to determine how much every observation is dependent on the previous observation in the series.

AR(p) model A stochastic model of order p with the autoregressive component only.

backward difference operator When using the Box–Jenkins method, a simpler way of writing the difference between the two consecutive observations.

backward shift operator When using the Box–Jenkins method, a simpler way of writing the previous observation in the series.

black box A figurative expression used for a model (or a formula), which transforms a theoretical time series with known statistical properties into an empirical variable.

Box–Pierce statistic A statistic that determines at what level of significance a certain model is adequate.

causal methods Another expression used for regression methods.

Census II A more advanced version of the classical decomposition method.

conditional sum of squares All unknown shock or error terms are conditionally assigned zeros, and their total sum should be minimum in order to select the model as optimal in the Box–Jenkins method.

confidence limit An area on both sides of the forecast (or residuals or any other series) which has a certain probability that the majority of data will be within specified boundaries.

constant A value that is the same for every case. Also a term present in some stochastic (and other) models.

correlation Statistical measure of association between two or more phenomena.

correlation coefficient A coefficient measuring the strength of correlation. The closer to 1, the higher the correlation. The closer to -1, the higher negative the correlation. If close to 0, there is no correlation.

covariance A joint variation between two variables.

curve fitting A simple approach to forecasting in which there is an attempt to fit a curve to the actual series.

cyclical series A series that follows a regular pattern of oscillations, either around the fixed or moving mean value. The convention is that observations should represent data expressed in at least annual period values.

decomposition methods In its original form, called the classical decomposition method. A method which splits the pattern into constituent components, and, after extrapolating these components, produces forecasts by recomposing them. The components involved are the trend, cyclical, seasonal and irregular components.

determination coefficient A statistic explaining the proportion of described variance.

diagnostic checking A stage in applying the Box–Jenkins method, during which the initially selected model is checked for its adequacy.

differencing A simple technique in which previous observation in the series is subtracted from the current observation. This technique has, among other things, an effect of making the series stationary.

differencing, second If we apply differencing to already differenced values, this newly obtained series is called second differences.

dummy variable A variable with a binary value of zero or one. It is used as an arbitrary variable in the model and its purpose is to quantify existence of some qualitative phenomenon (zero = non-existent, one = existent).

Durbin–Watson test A test that tests the hypothesis that residuals are not autocorrelated.

econometric methods A set of methods, mainly of regression type, in which outputs are measured through a relationship with relevant inputs.

empirical variable A phenomenon that one wants to forecast and whose observations are used to build the model to generate the forecasts. See also actual series.

equidistance A principle that requires that every observation, or data, in a variable or the time series should, on the time scale, be equally apart from the one before and the one after.

error In the forecasting context, error is the difference between the actual and the forecasted observation. See also residual.

ex-ante forecasting Forecasting ahead from the forecasting origin. A normal and conventional forecasting.

exponential smoothing One of the forecasting methods in which previous values of the variable are smoothed by one or more smoothing constants. The effects of these constants decrease exponentially with previous observations of the series.

ex-post forecasting Forecasting backwards from the forecasting origin. The forecasts obtained simulate the series, using the assumptions from the method applied. This process is also called fitting and, as such, is used as a basis for evaluating the method and forecasts.

fitting See ex-post forecasting.

forecasting A process of predicting the future values of the phenomena, based on the knowledge of their past performance.

forecasting horizon The distance in the future to which we are interested in forecasting. Usually understood to be the short term if we forecast one to three values, the medium term if three to five future observations are forecasted, or the long term if more than five observations are forecasted. A horizon is not determined by the length of actual time (weeks, months or years), but by the number of periods.

forecasting interval A set of periods within which certain tendencies (like periodicity) are shown.

forecasting, long-term A set of methods used to predict the long-term tendency of the variable. The data used do not have to represent annual values (they could be weekly, monthly or quarterly values) but the method should aim to provide at least a five-period forecast.

forecasting, medium-term   A set of methods used to predict three to five periods ahead.

forecasting origin   A period used as the starting point for forecasting. Usually it corresponds with the last value in the series, although sometimes it could be shifted backwards. In this case, forecasts from the origin until the end of the series overlap with the actual observations, and they are called validation forecasts.

forecasting period   A unit of time that defines the variable. If the values represent weekly data, a period is a week.

forecasting, qualitative   A forecasting approach that uses methods not formally structured as mathematical. However, the results obtained by qualitative forecasting could be subject to numerical analysis.

forecasting, quantitative   A forecasting approach that uses numerical methods whose origins are in mathematics and statistics. However, the final result could be subject to non-numerical interpretation.

forecasting, short-term   A set of methods used to predict only the following one to three future values of the variable. The data used could be either the annual values or any other time-period values.

forward shift operator   When using the Box–Jenkins method, a simpler way of writing the following observation in the series.

generalized adaptive forecasting   A more advanced version of the ordinary adaptive filtering method developed to become a typical stochastic approach.

Gompertz curve   One of the transcendent curves with the typical S-shape form.

heteroscedasticity   A condition that implies that the variance changes as the variable changes.

homoscedasticity   A condition describing a constant variance of the series across time.

integrating   The opposite process to differencing. By differencing the empirical variable, we get the stationary series. By integrating the stationary series, we get the empirical non-stationary variable.

invertibility   A condition in the Box–Jenkins method which implies that the values of all MA parameters (weights), should be within a certain region. Every value in the series could be described as a result of every past value multiplied by a certain weight, plus a certain error. In order to prevent the weights from increasing the further we go into the past, we have to restrict them to a certain region. If we do this, the series is invertible.

irregulars   A component in the decomposition method which represents the difference between the actual observations and the sum (or the product) of the predictable components, such as trend, cycle and seasonals.

lagging   By dropping the first observation in the series, we get first lags. Lagged series of various degrees (first, second, etc.) are important for calculating autocorrelations.

learning constant   A constant used in the adaptive filtering method which changes the values of weights as the pattern and, consequently the errors, change.

least squares method   A statistical principle that states that the sum of the squares of all residuals in the model should be minimum. If we compare various models then the best one describing the empirical variable is the one that has the smallest values of squared differences between the model data and the observations in empirical variable.

linear filter   A model (or a formula) that has a set of weights (or parameters) that are in linear relationship with the model data. After multiplying the weights with the white noise process, the model generates the empirical variable. In other words, our empirical variable is only one version of the white noise process, after being passed through the linear filter.

log differences   Differencing the logarithmic values of the series instead of the original observations.

logistic curve   One of the transcendent curves with the typical S-shape form.

MAD   Mean absolute deviation, also called mean absolute error (MAE).

MAPE   Mean absolute percentage error.

management, scientific   A business decision-making process based on scientific methods.

MA(q) model   A stochastic model of order q with the moving average component only.

ME   Mean error.

method   A set of formal procedures based on certain assumptions which involves specific techniques to achieve an aim.

model   A formula, or a method, that tries to simulate the original variable. The simulation is achieved by feeding the variable's observations into the model (see ex-post forecasting). Its syntax includes variables and parameters.

model estimation   A stage in applying the Box–Jenkins method during which the model parameters are estimated.

model identification   A stage in applying the Box–Jenkins method during which one decides which tentative model one should use.

moving average component (MA)   A component used by few methods (predominantly by the Box–Jenkins method) to determine how much every observation is dependent on the residuals (errors) in the model.

moving averages   The mean values that are calculated from the limited number of periods in one interval. Every subsequent interval excludes the first observation from the previous interval, and adds the following observation not included in the previous interval.

moving averages, single, double and triple   If calculated from the original observations of the variable, sometimes they are called single moving averages. If the basis for calculation is an already-formed series of moving averages, then the newly calculated series is called double moving averages. The same analogy applies to the triple.

MPE Mean percentage error.

MSE Mean square error.

multivariate time series analysis A time series analysis in which one variable is analysed as dependent on both the time and other variables, and, on the basis of this relationship, is forecasted.

noise Random appearance of the series. See white noise.

non-stationary series A series that oscillates around the moving mean value.

observations A set of values representing a variable. In the time series analysis they should, by default, always be equidistant.

outlier An observation in the variable (a data in the series) which is unusually high or low. Some forecasting methods require outliers to be removed from the series before building the model. The simplest way of removing it is by substituting an average value of the two neighbouring observations.

parameter In different contexts it could imply a weight, a constant or a coefficient. It is a constitutive element of the model syntax.

parsimony A principle that requires that the minimum number of parameters is used to describe (or approximate) the empirical variable. As a concession for using the smallest possible number of parameters, we are prepared to tolerate a certain amount of error.

partial autocorrelation A correlation between the series of original observations and one of the lagged observations of the empirical variable, where influences of all other lagged observations are kept constant (no sub-influence). The series of partial autocorrelation coefficients constitute the partial autocorrelation function.

pattern A shape that the variable follows when presented in a graphical form. The shapes could correspond to various mathematical curves, although the clues should be based on mathematical and not visual inspections.

periodicity Regular repetition of the pattern within the fixed interval of forecasting periods.

R Determination coefficient.

r Correlation coefficient.

random shocks See shock term.

random walk A series of data that is random and oscillates around the fixed mean value equal to zero. Its autocorrelations are zero at all lags. If the model has a constant term then the series is called random walk with a drift.

regression A family of methods, or statistical approach, which predicts the values of one variable by relating it to a set of other variables or itself, dependent on time.

reliability A property that implies that a method, or the results, could be accepted with considerable certainty.

residuals Differences (or errors) between the actual series and the series fitted by the model (ex-post forecasts). In the decomposition context it applies to the difference between the actual series and the sum (or product) of the other three components (trend, cycle and seasonal).

residual variance   A variance of the residuals.

RMS   Root mean square error or standard error.

RRMS   Relative root mean square error.

SBC   Schwartz Bayesian Criterion, a measure of selecting the forecasts. The smaller the better.

SE   Standard error (sometimes equivalent to RMS).

seasonal series   A series that follows a regular pattern of oscillations either around the fixed or moving mean value. The convention is that observations should represent data expressed in periods smaller than annual values.

SER   Relative standard error.

shock term   A constituting element of every stochastic model. In practice it is equal to the series of errors.

smoothing   A generic group of methods that use constants in order to smooth the oscillations, primarily eliminating the irregular variations in the series.

standard deviation   A measure of the dispersion of all values around the mean.

standard error of estimate   An interval within which a certain number of estimates has to fall (usually 95 per cent).

stationary series   A (horizontal) series that oscillates around the fixed mean value.

stochastics   An area of mathematics and statistics in which the results are in accordance with a probability distribution.

system   A collection of individual elements interacting in order to achieve a common goal.

Theil's statistic   A measure of accuracy of forecasts.

time series   A series of equidistant observations representing a variable or a phenomenon.

time series analysis   An approach to forecasting in which the history of observations is analysed with certain statistical methods in order to predict the future of these observations, using the same logic applied in the past.

tracking signal   A way of indicating the change in the basic pattern of the series.

transcendent curves   Non-algebraic curves such as exponential, logistic, Gompertz or any trigonometric function.

transformations   Ways of transforming observations of the variable in order to achieve certain properties. Most of the time this applies either to making the residuals homogeneous or to achieving the independence from the series movements. More frequently used transformations are taking logarithms, calculating moving averages, taking differences from the mean value, etc.

trend   A tendency shown by the variable through time. Some forecasters refer to it only as an upward or downward tendency in the series, and never as horizontal. In the decomposition context, this is the underlying component upon which other components were built.

trend parameter   Another expression for a constant present in some stochastic models.

U_1 Theil's statistic.

unconditional sum of squares Unknown shock, or error terms, are calculated recursively, and their total sum should be minimum in order to select the model as optimal in the Box–Jenkins method.

univariate time series analysis A time series analysis in which only one variable, dependent on time, is analysed and forecasted.

V Variation coefficient.

validation forecasts Forecasts from the forecasting origin until the end of the actual values of the series. If a medium or long-term method is used, validation forecasts will not simulate the observation, as ex-post forecasts do, but they will predominantly simulate the method's principles.

validation period If the forecasting origin is moved backwards, then the period from the forecasting origin until the end of the variable (the last actual observation), is called the validation period. Validation forecasts correspond with the actual values of the variable in the same way as the ex-post forecasts do, if a short-term method, with only one period ahead, is used.

variable In the forecasting context, usually understood as a set of values (observations) describing a phenomenon. It is a constitutive element of a model syntax.

variance A sum of total deviations from either the mean or some other value (deviations of forecasts from the actual series).

weight A parameter that gives the relative importance of a particular variable.

white noise A linear combination (a series) of random and independent observations. Another expression for random series.

Winters' method A method that uses the exponential smoothing principle with several smoothing constants, and is suitable for handling a seasonal series.

Index